The European Folktale: form and nature

The European
Folktale: form and nature

Max Lüthi
John D. Niles, translator

INDIANA UNIVERSITY PRESS
Bloomington & Indianapolis

This book is a publication of

Indiana University Press
601 North Morton Street
Bloomington, IN 47404-3797 USA

http://iupress.indiana.edu

Telephone orders 800-842-6796
Fax orders 812-855-7931
Orders by e-mail iuporder@indiana.edu

© 1982 by ISHI,
Institute for the Study of Human Issues, Inc.
Reprinted by arrangement with Institute for the Study of Human Issues
First Midland edition 1986

The paper used in this publication meets the minimum requirements of American
National Standard for Information Sciences—Permanence of Paper for Printed
Library Materials, ANSI Z39.48-1984.

Manufactured in the United States of America

Library of Congress Cataloging-in-Publication Data

Lüthi, Max, 1909–
    The European folktale.

    (Folklore studies in translation)
    Translation of : Das europäische Volksmärchen.
    Includes bibliographies and indexes.
    1. Tales—Europe—History and criticism. I. Title. II. Series.
GR135.L8313   1986   398.2'094   85-45990
ISBN 0-253-20393-7 (pbk.)

ISBN-13 978-0-253-20393-9 (pbk.)

3   4   5   6   7   14   13   12   11   10   09

Contents

folk narrative. The folktale as wish-fulfillment, as a depiction of what should be, as a depiction of what is. Symbolism. Meaningfulness. Tendency toward the comic. The folktale as a late form. Period of origin. Possible means of origin, possible means of continuing vitality (folktale authors and tellers). The true style and the false style. Significance for the future.

Foreword

DAN BEN-AMOS

Since its appearance thirty-five years ago, Max Lüthi's *Das europäische Volksmärchen* has been regarded by readers of German as a classic, a definitive statement about the nature, style, and form of the folktale genre in its European variety. Lüthi's exposition is authoritative: his familiarity with these European narratives is evident in every observation and every example. The numerous textual illustrations he includes in his analysis fully represent the nature of the European folktale and do not merely affirm the validity of his own interpretation.

Lüthi's primary goal is clear: his study is an attempt "to identify what makes the folktale a folktale" (page 3). More specifically, he offers "a sort of phenomenology of folk narrative as we find it in Europe . . . a literary interpretation of the folktale whose goal [is] to establish the essential laws of the genre" (page 107). Yet his examination is not confined to form alone. Instead Lüthi finds evidence of these laws in the "formal traits" or "stylistic features" of the folktale. The abstract concepts he sets forth as defining the folktale—one-dimensionality, depthlessness, and abstraction, and their application to the categories of time and space, society and reality, emotion and thought—are manifested in the narrative style of the genre. Language and style, then, serve as the keys for the discovery of the folktale's essential laws.

The attempt to define the laws of folk narrative goes back in folklore studies to the turn of the century, when the Norwegian folklorist Moltke Moe debated the issue with his friend the Danish folklorist Axel Olrik. As the latter mentions in his reminiscence of their friendship, Moe had been occupied with the subject since 1889. In the 1890s he treated such laws in his lectures on ballads and tales, and they were frequently a topic of conversation between the two friends.[1] Moe's paper "Episke Grundlove" ("Epic Fundamental Laws"),[2] published posthumously in 1914–1917, presents in fact a system of laws that Moe had developed two decades earlier.

The basic idea that set both Moe and Olrik in search of such laws is rooted in the romantic conception of folk literature. If the prose and poetry of the rural folk are natural poetry, then it should be possible, even necessary, to discover the natural laws that affect their formation, transformation, and persistence in tradition. Revealing, in that regard, is Olrik's suggestion that Moe's formulation was "meant to be a complete representation of the 'epic instinct,' 'the great laws of nature for folk poetry,' 'the epic fundamental laws.' "[3] Of course, this attitude drew not only on romantic ideas of natural poetry, but also on the recurrence, evident to any folklorist, of themes, forms, and structures in folk literature the world over. If repetition, rather than originality and uniqueness, is dominant in traditional literature, then the discovery of the laws that govern this literature is both possible and essential.

In his search for regularities in folklore, Moe attempted to delineate common factors that affect its formation. His "laws," however, are only explanatory postulates. He assumes the existence of distinct psychological and historical factors that influence the shape of folkloric forms and texts. Among the psychological factors he distinguishes two groups: the universal and the individual. The former are what he thought to be fundamental human instincts, including continuity, plastic representation, synthesis, analogy, combination, and separation. The latter are personal associations and metaphors used by individual narrators and singers. These universal and personal factors, which are at times conflicting, at times complementary, affect the emergence and development of folk narratives and songs.[4]

Narrative transformation was a central issue in the historic-geographic school of folklore research. While the ultimate goal of this school was to identify the primary forms of the folktale, it also attempted to describe and explain the impulses that govern thematic change and stability in oral tradition. Antti Aarne termed "laws" *(Gesetze)* the factors that, in his opinion, contributed to variation and continuity in oral transmission. Among them he counted such actions as forgetting secondary details, adding details (particularly at the beginning or end of a tale), combining tales, substituting characters, and changing the narrative point of view from third to first person.[5] Clearly these also are not laws, since they are not indispensable to narrative transmission. Rather they are possible explanations for omissions and variations in folktales. However, it is understandable that in their constant search for the essential principles that govern oral narrative transmission, folklorists conceived of these factors and explanations as laws.

Similarly, when Walter Anderson formulated his hypothetical explanation of narrative stability he called it a "law": the Law of Self-Correction. According to Anderson's theory, thematic stability is possible in oral transmission, even in the absence of support from written texts, because each narrator draws on several sources and reconciles in his own narration any contradictions and conflicts that might exist in the tradition. In turn his version becomes one of the sources for a subsequent telling of the same story, and thus at every point of oral transmission narrators create composite versions of their tales. In this manner the tales eventually achieve a high degree of standardization.[6]

While Moe, Aarne, and Anderson sought for regularities in the formation and transmission of oral narratives, Axel Olrik formulated his "epic laws" on the basis of literary observations. His "laws" are neither postulates nor hypotheses; rather they are inductive observations identifying literary regularities in oral narratives. Drawing his generalizations from the examination of narrative texts, Olrik focused on the unfolding of the story and the relations of characters to objects and actions. His formulations underscore the fact that narratives neither begin nor end abruptly (the Law of Opening and the Law of Closing), and they point to the essential nature of repetition (the Law of Repetition), particularly in threes, which itself becomes a law (the Law of Threes). By examining the numerical aspect of narration, Olrik also developed the Law of Two to a Scene, which points to the rather limited descriptive capacity of oral narration.[7] These and similar laws are empirical formulations; they are subject to confirmation or falsification and are available for repeated scrutiny. They are literary equivalents to scientific "experimental laws," as Ernest Nagel defined them,[8] which are subject to observation, verification, and manipulation. Furthermore, they constitute specific narrative traits that can be employed in comparative cross-cultural studies of verbal art.

Lüthi's work is closest to that of Olrik, among all these earlier attempts to identify narrative laws. Like Olrik, Lüthi deals with the folktale primarily on the literary level, and like him he attempts to ground his laws in the texts themselves. These two scholars differ, however, in two major respects. First, they interpret their discovered laws differently. Olrik believes that his "epic laws" are universal; they are the natural laws of oral poetry. In contrast, Lüthi's laws are culturally specific in that they are limited to Europe before the modern era; any extension to cross-cultural analysis would require further study. Second, and more fundamentally, the laws they formulated differ in kind. While Olrik approaches the folktale "experimentally," Lüthi defines abstract qualities of the folktale which he then applies to style, thus establishing a set of correlations between each of the two genres of folktale and legend and specific describable relations between space, time, and character in the narratives. Each genre has its own set of features that dominate the actions and characters of the story.

Lüthi's system ingeniously transforms critical terms of evaluation into analytical concepts for description. The negative connotation that the term "one-dimensionality" might have in the vocabulary of literary criticism, for example, disappears in Lüthi's system. Instead the term gains descriptive specificity relating to space, emotion, and social relations. The multi-dimensionality of the legend allows the plot to move between heaven, hell, and human reality and leads to the expression of emotions and the recognition of social class differences. In the folktale, in contrast, one and the same dimension embraces the real and the enchanted world.

In spite of the closeness in meaning between the concepts of one-dimensionality and depthlessness, to Lüthi they are not synonymous. Depthlessness applies primarily to the psychological dimension, to the inner life, or rather lack thereof, of the folktale character. Lüthi finds in the folktale hero the absence of biography; as a result he is a figure without ties to space, time, or kin. Heroes, who are usually nameless, appear in a single event; they remain eternally young or eternally old. The depthless world of the folktale is a rigid environment that denies its figures the flexibility and change that are, as Henri Bergson suggests, essential to the reality of life.

Psychological considerations are also implicit in the concept of "abstract style," despite its strictly literary connotations. Lüthi has borrowed the notion of "abstract style" from Wilhelm Worringer, who, in his book *Abstraction and Empathy: A Contribution to the Psychology of Style*,[9] explains that the abstract nature of primitive art derives not from a technical inability to imitate objects naturalistically but from a distinct psychological attitude toward the external world. According to this view, primitive man, like children of all eras, sees external reality as menacing and dangerous. The representation of this reality in abstract forms enables man to instill order, to control this external world, and to gain, through art, confidence and security. Abstract artistic expression is thus a psychological mechanism that offers man tranquility in the face of menace. It is a reassuring mechanism that responds to specific needs of primitive man and of children. The infusion of nineteenth-century evolutionary theories notwithstanding, by choosing the term "abstract style," Lüthi implies that the style of the folktale, like the final resolution of its plot, provides psychological relief and reassurance. Furthermore, through his reference to Worringer's formulation, Lüthi implies that the European folktale offers its participants the same qualities of order and reassurance that are provided by traditional art.

The concept of abstract style becomes the dominant idea in Lüthi's discussion; the other properties he identifies—isolation and universal interconnection, the truncated motif, and sublimation and all-inclusiveness—all result from this abstractness. "Abstract stylization," Lüthi writes, "permeates all elements of the folktale" (page 36).

Like all major works of scholarship, Lüthi's *The European Folktale* raises many questions. The perennial problem of universals in folklore immediately comes to mind. Could Lüthi's description be a solution to the problem of universal laws of folklore that Olrik first suggested? Are the literary properties he describes found only in the European folktale, or are they the customary qualities of the genre of the fantastic[10] in its oral variety? Do the peoples of Africa, Asia, Australia, and North and South America narrate about their fantastic worlds in an abstract style while formulating their accounts of actual experiences in realistic terms? Whatever the case might be, Lüthi has provided us with an analytical base that can be extended to other genres and other cultures.

The opposite pole of folklore studies, the ethnographic research of narrative performance in particular cultures and specific situations, provides new testing grounds for Lüthi's ideas as well. In fact, the examination of narratives in performance is a crucial application of Lüthi's formulations. Could it be that in performance narrators add a certain degree of dimension and depth to the verbal form? Could it be that the abstractness Lüthi finds in folk narratives results, to some extent, from the transformation of narrative performance into literary narration?

Whatever the answers to these and other questions will be, whether they will confirm or challenge Lüthi's original insights, we are indebted to him for developing descriptive concepts of analysis that enable us to continue our explorations into the essential laws of the folktale.

NOTES

1. Axel Olrik, *Personal Impressions of Moltke Moe*, FFC No. 17 (Hamina: Suomalaisen Tiedeakatemian Kustantama, 1915), pp. 50–51.

2. Moltke Moe, "Episke Grundlove," *Edda*, 2 (1914), 1–16, 233–248; 4 (1915), 85–127; 7 (1917), 72–88.

3. Olrik, *Personal Impressions*, p. 51.

4. Moe, "Episke Grundlove." See also Walter A. Berendsohn, "Epische Gesetze der Volksdichtung," in *Handwörterbuch des deutschen Marchens*, ed. Lutz Mackensen, I (Berlin: de Gruyter, 1930), 566; Lauritz Bødker, *Folk Literature (Germanic)*, International Dictionary of Regional European Ethnology and Folklore, Vol. II (Copenhagen: Rosenkilde and Bagger, 1965), pp. 84–85.

5. Antti Aarne, *Leitfaden der vergleichenden Märchenforschung*, FFC No. 13 (Hamina: Suomalaisen Tiedeakatemian Kustantama, 1913), pp.

23-56. See also Stith Thompson, *The Folktale*, 2nd ed. (New York: Holt, 1951), pp. 435-436.

6. Walter Anderson, *Kaiser und Abt: Die Geschichte eines Schwanks*, FFC No. 42 (Helsinki: Suomalainen Tiedeakatemia, 1923), pp. 397-403. See also Thompson, *The Folktale*, p. 437.

7. Axel Olrik, "Epische Gesetze der Volksdichtung" (see page 139 note 5 below).

8. Ernest Nagel, *The Structure of Science: Problems in the Logic of Scientific Explanation* (New York: Harcourt, Brace and World, 1961), pp. 79-105.

9. Originally published as *Abstraktion und Einfühlung* (1908), this work was translated into English by Michael Bullock in 1953. The current reprint edition is published by International Universities Press, New York, 1967.

10. Tzvetan Todorov, *The Fantastic: A Structural Approach to a Literary Genre*, trans. Richard Howard (Cleveland: The Press of Case Western Reserve University, 1973).

Author's Preface

My purpose in this short preface is to express my delight that *Das europäische Volksmärchen* has finally been translated into English, thirty-four years after its first publication. It has thereby broken a famous record: Vladimir Propp's *Morfológija skázki (The Morphology of the Folktale)*, published in 1928, had to wait only thirty years for its English translation. In an overly dynamic century like ours—a century that is so fond of change and innovation—it is noteworthy and, for the author, comforting that a scholarly work can still be of interest after several decades.

Although in many ways, like everything human, the folktale is to be interpreted historically, I have preferred to search for its lasting truths. Today more than ever I am convinced that, despite increased interest in the function of tales and in what has been called folktale biology, the tales themselves merit the greatest attention, just as always. Even though much is clarified by their context, the texts themselves take on an ever new life with the passage of time. They speak to all kinds of people and to widely separated generations; they speak in terms that sometimes differ and yet in many ways remain the same. Only a small part of the secret and the fascination of folktales can be grasped by research into the present-day context of their performance or by reconstruction of the context of their performance in days past. This secret of the folktale resides essentially in its message, structure, and style.

I am especially glad that the English translation has been undertaken and introduced by a North American scholar. For me, John Niles represents the many North American folktale scholars to whom I owe thanks. I shall not speak of the numerous ways in which I have been stimulated by the work of North Americans who are still active today, but rather of the friendship of those who are no longer with us. In 1948, long before he came to know me personally, Archer Taylor wrote a complimentary review of the present book that included one sentence in particular I now recall with fond remembrance: "His book gives a first impression of simplicity, but any effort to restate his ideas will demonstrate that appearances are deceptive." In 1961 Stith Thompson took the trouble to send me a weighty and expensive parcel in time for me to make use of it in one of my publications: it enclosed the proofs of his still unpublished second revision of *The Types of the Folktale*.

The names of Niles, Taylor, and Thompson stand symbolically for the many persons who live or lived in North America whom I should like to thank for their scholarly achievement and their friendship.

Max Lüthi
Zürich, Spring 1981

Translator's Preface

Few studies in the field of folk narrative have won such general and unreserved praise as *Das europäische Volksmärchen: Form und Wesen*, by Max Lüthi, recently retired Professor of European Folk Literature at the University of Zürich. Since its initial publication in 1947, this book has gone through seven German editions, has been translated into Japanese and Italian, and has earned its author an international reputation for the skill with which he probes the style, form, and meaning of the European folktale. Publication of an English edition of Lüthi's study should be of interest not only to professional folklorists, most of whom already know (or know of) the work in the original, but to all persons of humanistic background and concerns who have an interest in those simple yet deep tales that have been told and retold in the Occident for generations, to the point that some of them seem embedded in our consciousness almost as second nature.

Two aspects of Lüthi's work stand out: the discrimination with which he analyses the style of the folktale as a genre, and the seriousness with which he views the folktale as a record of a certain kind of human consciousness. The first of these aspects is self-evident. The second perhaps deserves brief comment.

In the British Isles and North America, folktales have enjoyed a certain vogue for the past several hundred years as a charming and harmless type of literature that, suitably edited and decorated, can serve for the entertainment of most children and many adults. Such a view was first promoted by Charles Perrault and other aristocratic French writers of fairy tales and by those who translated these tales into English, chiefly for the benefit of a growing middle-class reading public. It was advanced by such authors as Andrew Lang, with his *Blue Fairy Book, Red Fairy Book, Pink Fairy Book,* and the like, and Joseph Jacobs, whose collection *English Fairy Tales* has enjoyed popularity and influence up to the present day. Even the genuine oral folktales that Jacob and Wilhelm Grimm collected in Germany at the beginning of the nineteenth century—tales that are not always charming and that hint of a spirit alien to bourgeois mentality—were generally retold in a pleasanter mode for an English-speaking audience. Eventually several of the Grimm favorites were changed into attractive caricatures of their original selves at the hands of Walt Disney, whose animated film versions have established the canonical form of these tales in present-day North America.

The early history of the fairy tale in English has been charted in Iona and Peter Opie's book *The Classic Fairy Tales* (London: Oxford Univ. Press, 1974), which reproduces, with an informed commentary, two dozen favorite fairy tales as they were first published in Britain. Here one can see at a glance how simple European tales were dressed in an artificial language and imbued with a set of conventional ethics that sometimes worked directly against their true narrative message.[1] It is essential to keep in mind the distinction between the commercial English fairy tale and the true oral folktale of Europe if one is to understand Lüthi's earnestness in addressing the folktale as a form of literature that not only is meant to amuse but also embodies the collective wisdom and vision of unknown generations of tellers.[2]

Lüthi's book stands in a tradition of folktale scholarship that in Germany and other European countries reaches back to the time of Jacob and Wilhelm Grimm. In the view of the Grimms, oral folktales were highly conservative narratives that "encoded" messages from the Germanic and Indo-European past. The peasant culture they reflected had been bypassed by industrial and urban culture and by organized religion, but it still remained strong as unconsciously preserved by the common people of the countryside. Although the Grimms' specific views are largely discredited today, their veneration for *das Volk* exerted an enormous influence on subsequent European scholarship. Insofar as German Romanticism gave birth to a new religion of *das Volk*, the Grimms' anthology of folktales became its vernacular Bible. Subsequent European scholarship has gone far beyond the Grimms in its ability to trace the historical evolution of various folktale types and in its understanding of the art of individual narrators and the mechanism of oral transmission. What has remained firm is a belief that folktales *are* important, in a way that is not evident from their innocuous cousins, the French and English fairy tales.

In our own century, C. G. Jung and his followers have done much to promote the serious study of myths and folktales as a symbolic language that, once deciphered, can provide a key to unlocking the secrets of the collective unconscious. In his recent book *The Uses of Enchantment*, Bruno Bettelheim has stressed the healing force that folktales can exert on a child's development through the ability to achieve symbolic resolutions of psychological crises.[3] While Lüthi does not accept the simplistic interpretations of tales that psychoanalysis sometimes has to offer, he emphatically affirms that the folktale deserves to be studied not only because it is a popular literary form, but because it expresses the spiritual concerns of the people who cultivate it. He parts company from many scholars by refusing to identify these concerns solely through the study of individual motifs and plots, which can recur in a wholly different ambience in myth, romance, legendry, hagiography, and any of a number of other types of narrative. Instead, he tries to reveal the inner meaning of the folktale through a study of its characteristics as a genre. To Lüthi (p. 3), "the secret power of the folktale lies not in the motifs it employs, but in the manner in which it uses them—that is, in its form." In his view, the form remains constant while its constituent motifs change.

Lüthi thus attempts to do for the style of the folktale what the Russian formalist critic Vladimir Propp tried to do for its structure in the classic study discussed on pp. 126–133. He keeps to what is constant, while ignoring everything inessential, in an effort to see what makes a folktale a folktale. His method is more eclectic than Propp's in that he cites examples from a number of different collections of folktales rather than relying on a single national or regional corpus. His conclusions are thus more ambitious, for they admit no restrictions of time or place. Thematically as well, his book goes beyond Propp's in that he is not content to ask how the folktale is put together, but also asks why it has been composed as it is and not in some other way. He does so not only to demonstrate the existence of a system of order in the midst of apparent chaos but to persuade us that this system can be read as a unified view of the world. Because he finds this view healthy, he wishes to share it with others. The book reflects concerns that, while valid at any time, may have been felt more acutely in postwar German-speaking areas than elsewhere. In Lüthi's view, the folktale does not regard human beings as isolated parts of a disinterested material universe or as passive respondents to certain social stimuli. It sees them as free and potentially heroic individuals who at any moment are capable of standing in beneficent contact with the mighty powers of the universe. The most important formal characteristics of the folktale follow self-consistently from this vision. Lüthi writes with a detached, scientific eye, but also with a passionate awareness that some readers may not understand the self-consistent logic of the folktale and may mistake its abstract style for something naive or primitive.

While the eclecticism of Lüthi's methods permits him to come to significant conclusions, it leads to certain potential problems as well. One may ask to what extent he is describing the ideal folktale rather than what folktales actually prove themselves to be in their innumerable European variants. Lüthi discusses this problem on pp. 101–104 and 108–109 and grants that any one tale may diverge from the type that he has described. He also acknowledges that some of the most popular published folktales, including those of the Grimms, reflect the style of literate editors as well as the style of oral storytellers. Although he claims that his description of the European folktale is more valid for the genuine oral folktale than the literary folktale of the kind popularized by Wilhelm Grimm, he is unwilling to accept twentieth-century tape-recorded folktales as accurate indications of what the folktale was like when it flourished in former centuries. His examples are often drawn from either the Grimms' *Kinder- und Hausmärchen* or the extensive German series *Märchen der Weltliteratur*, a collection that includes edited texts. Most folklorists are not so willing to favor the stylistic evidence derived from such published sources over what is provided by verbatim recordings of the performances of skilled storytellers. Some readers may thus regard Lüthi's concept of the genuine folktale as an abstraction that has never in fact existed. Methodological quibbles of these kinds should not obscure the greatness of Lüthi's achievement, but they should encourage one to view this achievement with an open eye and with attention to counter-examples that could be cited to certain of the author's points.

Lüthi's book also should not be criticized for failing to accomplish what it never sets out to do. It never aims, for example, to provide an ethnographic account of the kind that Linda Dégh offers in her exemplary study *Folktales and Society: Storytelling in a Hungarian Peasant Community*.[4] While Lüthi accepts the validity of contextual approaches to storytelling as a living art, his own approach is textual and literary. He is concerned with the image of man in the folktale, not with the actual men and women who tell the tales. The sorts of questions that Lüthi asks should be supplemented by the sorts of questions that are being posed by folklorists who see the materials they study not just as texts, but as communicative events shared among members of a community.[5] Lüthi's stylistic analysis, Propp's structural analysis, and Dégh's ethnographic study can be taken as three points from which the nature of the folktale can be plotted fairly accurately by a process of triangulation. None of the three provides this full perspective by itself.

British and North American tales fall largely outside the scope of the book. Until recently, in fact, it has been possible to claim that the oral folktale died out in English-speaking areas sometime before the nineteenth century and the advent of modern collecting methods. While Ireland and the Scottish Highlands have been known to possess a treasure house of Gaelic tales, England, Lowland Scotland, and North America were thought to be practically devoid of the true folktale—a curious anomaly, as the tradition of ballad singing has remained vigorous in English-speaking areas and other forms of folklore are well represented.

By now it has become clear that this view needs to be modified. Traditional European oral folktales have been preserved in English-speaking areas, but only in relatively remote regions or among the socially isolated. In North America, a fairly rich tradition of "Jack" tales has been documented in the Beech Mountain area of North Carolina, and other traditional folktales have been collected in the Ozarks.[6] In Scotland, many long, involved folktales have been recorded from the traveling folk or "tinkers," social outcasts whom some scholars believe to have inherited elements of what was once an aristocratic Highland culture.[7] As more of such tales are published and evaluated, readers will be in a better position to see to what extent Lüthi's conclusions hold true for English-speaking areas as well as for the Continent.

An awareness of the existence of certain English-language sources for the study of folktales will help the reader who is unable to pursue Lüthi's many references to German collections. The two most important English collections are Katharine M. Briggs' *Dictionary of British Folk-Tales*,[8] a four-volume compendium of tales and tale-abstracts from a variety of written sources, and the series of *Folktales of the World* that has been undertaken by the University of Chicago Press under the general editorship of Richard M. Dorson. As of 1981, thirteen national collections have been published in this series, each volume edited by a distinguished folklorist from the country in question.[9] Unlike many tales in Briggs' *Dictionary*, most of the tales in this series are drawn directly from oral tradition. Readers who wish to gain a more complete knowledge of the range of European folktale plots may consult Stith Thompson's *One Hundred Favorite Folktales* (Bloomington: Indiana Univ. Press, 1968). This collection includes representative tales from many lands in an order that corresponds to Thompson's invaluable *Type-Index* (discussed by Lüthi on pp. 120–121). Richard M. Dorson also edited *Folktales Told Around the World* (Chicago: Univ. of Chicago Press, 1975), a volume that includes only genuine oral narratives and arranges them by geographical area. Folktales in the narrow sense are supplemented by legends, saints' legends, jokes, personal anecdotes, and a variety of other narrative forms, just as in the series *Folktales of the World*. Readers who wish a basic introduction to the forms of oral prose narrative may consult Linda Dégh's essay "Folk Narrative" in *Folklore and Folklife: An Introduction*, edited by Dorson (Chicago: Univ. of Chicago Press, 1972), pp. 53–83.

Although Lüthi regards the present book as his most important single achievement, it is only one of a number of studies of the folktale and related narrative forms that have occupied his scholarly life. Most useful for general and bibliographical purposes is his booklet *Märchen*, first published in 1962 as Volume 16 of the Metzler Sammlung and now in its seventh edition (Stuttgart, 1979). This volume has been updated from edition to edition to take account of the most recent research in the field. The two books *Volksmärchen und Volkssage: Zwei Grundformen erzählender Dichtung* (Bern: Francke, 1961; 3rd. ed. 1975) and *Volksliteratur und Hochliteratur: Menschenbild, Thematik, Formstreben* (Bern: Francke, 1970) contain between them thirty related studies that first appeared in the form of independent articles. These cover a wide range of subjects in the realm of folk literature and art literature, including such topics as *Rapunzel*, the image of humanity in folk literature, freedom and restriction in the folktale, Shakespeare and the folktale, and the relation between folkloristics and literary scholarship. Lüthi's most recent book, *Das Volksmärchen als Dichtung: Ästhetik und Anthropologie* (Düsseldorf: Diderichs, 1975), is in many ways his crowning achievement. It addresses such topics as the folktale's depiction of the beautiful, its style, structure, and artistic effects, its use of particular motifs and themes, and its image of humanity.

More popular in their orientation are Lüthi's two pocketbooks *Es war einmal: Vom Wesen des Volksmärchens* (1962; 5th ed., 1970) and *So leben sie noch heute: Betrachtungen zum Volksmärchen* (1969; 2nd ed. 1976), both published by Vandenhoeck and Ruprecht, Göttingen. These preserve much of their original character as radio broadcasts and offer a number of interpretations of particular folktales and folktale types. The first of these has been published in English as *Once Upon a Time: On the Nature of Fairy Tales*, translated by Lee Chadeayne and Paul Gottwald with an introduction by Francis Lee Utley (1970; rpt. Bloomington: Indiana Univ. Press, 1976). Also available in English are three of Lüthi's essays: "Aspects of the *Märchen* and the Legend," *Genre*, 2 (1969), 162–178, rpt. in *Folklore Genres*, ed. Dan Ben-Amos (Austin: Univ. of Texas Press, 1976), pp. 17–33; "Goal Orientation in Storytelling," in *Folklore Today: A Festschrift for Richard M. Dorson*, ed. Linda Dégh and Henry Glassie (Bloomington: Indiana Univ. Research Center for Language and Semiotic Studies, 1976), pp. 357–368; and "Imitations and Anticipations in Folktales," in *Folklore on Two Continents: Essays in Honor of Linda Dégh* (Bloomington: Trickster Press, 1980).[10]

The present translation of *Das europäische Volksmärchen* is based on the seventh (1981) German edition, which includes a supplementary chapter on structural folktale research that first appeared in the fourth edition (1974). In its original form the book concluded with Chapter 6 ("Function and Significance of the Folktale"). Tale-type numbers from the Aarne-Thompson *Type Index* (AT) and tale numbers from the Grimms' *Kinder- und Hausmärchen* (KHM) have been added at appropriate points for easy reference. Also new to the English edition is an Index of Tale Types (pp. 164–166). Some cross references have been omitted, additional bibliographical information has occasionally been provided, and some references have been given to English translations of German editions.

A few key German terms have presented special problems. I am not speaking of compounds such as *Flächenhaftigkeit* and *Allverbundenheit*, which are a translator's nightmare, but of such basic terms as *Märchen*, *Sage*, and *Legende*. A *Märchen* is not so vague a thing as a "folktale"; on the other hand, it is not a "fairy tale," which in English suggests something pretty and tongue-in-cheek. Lüthi usually uses the term to refer to tales numbered 300–749 in the Aarne-Thompson *Type-Index*, the so-called "tales of magic." The term "wondertale" is not a bad equivalent. As a rule I have translated the term *Märchen* or *Volksmärchen* simply as "folktale," hoping that the reader will not interpret the English word too broadly. The term *Sage* I have rendered as "legend" or "migratory legend." The term usually refers to short belief tales involving a supernatural encounter. These legends are often called "migratory" because they have a way of traveling from place to place and attaching themselves now to one locale and set of persons and circumstances, now to another. Although the term *Legende* is often rendered as "saint's life," I have used the designation "saint's legend" throughout, for these stories more often relate a single miraculous incident than an entire biography. Other German terms are explained in the text. Where an explanation in the body of the text would be cumbersome, notes have been added at the foot of the page.[11]

In preparing the translation I have benefitted from the help of two native German speakers, Ms. Elke Dettmer and, particularly, Mr. Egon Selge. Professor Don Yoder of the University of Pennsylvania and Professor Lüthi kindly read the completed typescript and offered a number of suggestions for its improvement. Both the author and the translator wish to express their indebtedness to Alan Dundes, Donald Ward, Dan Ben-Amos, and the late Richard M. Dorson for supporting the project, and the National Endowment for the Humanities for helping to finance it.

J. Niles
University of California, Berkeley

Introduction

The European folktale has a very special power. Not only the children of each new generation feel its attraction, but adults experience its magic again and again as well. Since Charles Perrault first made the folktale an object of serious literary attention in 1696-97, writers, readers, and scholars have never ceased to feel the attraction of this new form. Elegant, moralistic French writers of the eighteenth century seized upon it at once and began to compose folktales in their own style. Authors of the German Rococo were quick to respond to the stimulus: Musäus published his *Volksmärchen*, while Wieland wrote fairy-tale epics. In the Classical period, Goethe delighted in composing dreamlike folktale pieces. For the Romantics, the folktale became the poetical canon. "Everything poetic must be like a fairy tale," writes Novalis. "In the fairy tale I feel that I am best able to find my own voice. *Alles ist ein Märchen:* everything is a fairy tale."[1]

The Romantics' deep love for the folktale stems largely from the *Kinder- und Hausmärchen* of Wilhelm and Jacob Grimm, first published in 1812 and 1815. Since then the collecting of folktales has continued ever more widely and has brought to light an enormous number of tales in Europe and the rest of the world. The penetrating research of many scholars has sought to account for the structure and history of folktales and the ways in which tales are transmitted and diffused. The question of folktale origins has been perennially raised. Central problems are still unresolved; hypothesis opposes hypothesis. Still, today the Grimms' collection of folktales is on every shelf, while their collection of German legends has remained in relative obscurity.[2]

Like folksongs, folktales are popular and anonymous. Despite many questions that remain unanswered, however, scholarly research has established a far clearer picture of the evolution and nature of folksongs than it has of folktales. Students of the folktale have not been able to agree whether the tales still current today are many thousands of years old in their basic form or only a few hundred. Moreover, the content of folktales is more mysterious than that of folksongs. Some scholars have seen the otherworld motifs of folktales as their "true" content.[3] C. W. von Sydow refers to the Indo-European folktale as the "chimera tale" or "chimerate" *(Schimärenmärchen)*.[4] Mackensen, Peuckert, Löwis of Menar, and others speak of the "tale of magic" or "wondertale" *(Zaubermärchen)* as "the most complete and pure form of the folktale."[5] It is "the folktale in its truest sense."[6] According to Löwis of Menar, "what most distinguishes the content of folktales is their interweaving with the miraculous."[7] And yet the strange spell that is cast by folktales does not derive simply from their otherworld motifs. Legends *(Sagen)* as well as saints' legends *(Legenden)* also tell of miracles, enchantments, and otherworld beings. Indeed, these narrative genres concern themselves with such things far more exclusively than does the folktale. Miracles are the heart of the saint's legend, which strives with undivided effort to relate them. The term *miraculum* is allied inseparably with the saint's legend. As for the migratory legend, its preferred subject is the Wholly Other *(das Ganz Andere)*. "The legend is grounded upon man's relationship with the supernatural."[8] "The legend wishes to call attention to the daemonic basis of life, to warn of unknown enemies and powers, and to disclose the 'other' world to the listener in any way possible."[9] And yet saints' legends and migratory legends do not have half so mysterious an effect as folktales. So transparent is the intent of legends to depict the miraculous and the Wholly Other that the resulting stories are stripped of their mystery. Folktales strike us as enigmatic because they mix the miraculous with the natural, the near with the far, and the ordinary with the incomprehensible in a completely effortless way. The saint's legend is an attempt to make converts or to confirm a faith. Migratory legends draw attention to events that are extraordinary or remarkable; they are intended to shock or to teach a lesson. But what is the aim of the folktale? Simply to entertain, as has been claimed for too long? Even if this were so, why then should human beings find this particular type of narrative so entertaining?

The secret power of the folktale lies not in the motifs it employs, but in the manner in which it uses them—that is, in its form. The form of a legend or a saint's legend stands in a one-to-one relationship to what is told. An event, an experience, or a deed (whether real or imaginary) is turned into speech. The subject determines the mood, and the two together, the subject and the mood, determine the form that the narrative takes. For this reason André Jolles was correct in designating the legend and the saint's legend as "primary forms" (*einfache Formen*).[10] Folktales are different. The form of folktales does not derive from their content but has a life of its own. Jolles' designation of the folktale as a primary form immediately met with opposition.[11] Compared with the legend and the saint's legend, the folktale has the appearance of a work of art. Its form cries out for an exact and searching study, a study that may lead to the resolution of a number of basic questions.

The present book is an attempt to delineate the principal formal traits of the European folktale. No comprehensive attempt will be made to compare the folktales of different lands; instead, I shall seek to identify the basic form that all folktales have in common. My interest does not lie in the individual differences that can be observed from narrator to narrator and from people to people; rather, I shall seek to identify what makes the folktale a folktale. The type never occurs in its pure form, but it may be derived from a comparison of many individual tales. I shall hold fast to what remains constant while disregarding the superficial differences that vary from one tale to another.

The present investigation is based primarily on folktales from Germany, France, Italy, the Rhaeto-Romanic area, Ireland, Scandinavia, Finland, Russia, Latvia, Estonia, Hungary, Bulgaria, Albania, Yugoslavia, and Greece. Non-European forms lie beyond the scope of this book. The narratives of Oriental and so-called primitive peoples that are known by the name of folktales are creations of a very different sort and require separate investigation.

1

One=Dimensionality

In migratory legends, as in the saint's legend, side by side with the world of everyday reality there exists an "other" world whose spirit is clearly distinct. To all outward appearances this otherworld is not so far away. At any moment it can affect the everyday world, and its inhabitants often dwell among humankind. But the otherworldly is experienced as something wholly different from anything in ordinary life. Contact with the otherworld awakens a peculiar shiver in man. It attracts him and at the same time repels him; it arouses both fear and longing. However alien he may find this world, he senses that he is bound to it by ties of compelling necessity. *It* is real, this strange dimension, and its claims are more important and irresistible than any claims of this world.

In the saint's legend everything depends on the ability of the narrative to reveal the existence and effects of this transcendent world and to proclaim its demands. Migratory legends, too, darker than the saint's legend and not so purposeful, gaze toward this other world as if with enchanted eyes. They tell of human beings' hairraising and bewildering encounters with otherworld creatures of every kind: the dead, underworld beings, creatures of the forest and waters, field daemons, house kobolds,* mountain spirits, giants, and dwarves.

---

*The household spirit or familiar of German folklore, the equivalent of the English brownie or boggart; by extension, the name of creatures who live in the wild. They can take the form of animals, objects, or fire, as well as human form, and sometimes they manage to stay entirely out of sight. The kobold can be friendly, but he is seldom wholly benevolent. He likes a daily

Migratory legends explore this strange world in short, self-contained accounts, and no scrap of information that they can discover about it seems unimportant. Fear, curiosity, or a sense of transgressing limits grips the person who comes across the trace of an otherworld being. In horror he hears the thundering hooves of the wild host, he sees the specters on their nightly ride. His senses are numbed when he feels himself suddenly lifted up and transported to a strange land. In the distorted features of many otherworld beings—in the fiery eyes and contorted heads and feet of dwarves, elves, and spirits of the night, in the kobold's hunchback, in the abnormal size of dwarves and giants—we see reflected the fright of the person who encounters them. The same is true of the injuries, deformities, and diseases that are believed to result from such encounters. In the arrogance of village boys who tease the *Nickelmann** or who try to trick the *wild Mannli,*† as well as in the harmless curiosity of housewives who scatter ashes, flour, or peas for the brownies, we see mirrored the anxiety that grips human beings in the face of the Wholly Other.

Even when people tell legends of significant personages or events from history, they do so for the sake of what is strange or marvelous in the events described. Outstandingly good or outstandingly evil human beings are thought to be basically strange and un-

---

platter of milk or other food or he will raise a great fuss. See Hans Bächtold-Stäubli, ed., *Handwörterbuch des deutschen Aberglaubens*, 10 vols. (Berlin: de Gruyter, 1927–1942), s.v. *kobold.—Trans.*

*Throughout central Germany the term *Nickelmann* is used interchangeably with the terms *Nickert* and *Nix* to designate mermen or spirits of the springs, streams, and lakes. See Oswald A. Erich and Richard Beitl, *Wörterbuch der deutschen Volkskunde*, 3rd ed. (Stuttgart: Kröner, 1974), s.v. *Wässergeister.—Trans.*

†In south German and Swiss folk belief, the wild man (*wild Mann*, diminutive *wild Mannli*, feminine *wilde Frau*, plural *wilde Leute*) lives outside the village in the forest or mountains. He may be either fearsome or benevolent; meeting him forebodes either sickness or good luck. He is known to take part in the *wilde Jagd*, or annual ride of the wild host. A wild man often takes part in south German Fasnacht (Carnival) parades. He is clothed in moss, bark, or skins, has a long beard, and carries an uprooted sapling in his hand. See the *Handwörterbuch des deutschen Aberglaubens*, s.v. *wild Mann*, and the *Wörterbuch der deutschen Volkskunde*, s.v. *wilde Leute.—Trans.*

fathomable, and for this reason they are the subject of story after story. The numinous, the supernatural—these are the preferred subjects of legends, and these features are associated with great men and women as well, for according to legend, the special abilities of a great human being are often due to a pact with the devil or with another creature of the otherworld.

Folktales too tell of many beings who could be called otherworldly: witches, fairies, clairvoyant women, the grateful dead, trolls, giants, dwarves, good and evil sorcerers, dragons, and mythical animals. Creatures that may at first appear perfectly ordinary—ants, birds, fish, bears, or foxes—suddenly begin to speak and reveal supernatural capabilities. The stars and the wind speak and act. Old men and women the hero has never before met give him magical gifts or for no reason offer him exactly the advice he needs. And yet an actor in a folktale, whether a hero or an ordinary person, a man or a woman, deals with these otherworld beings as though he perceived no difference between them and him. With complete equanimity he accepts their gifts or casts these gifts aside, he lets himself be helped by them or offers them a fight, and then he goes on his way. He seems unaware of any gulf separating him from these other beings. They are important to him as helpers or adversaries, but in themselves they have no interest.

In legends, if a person sees a white woman* sitting in a meadow or hears of a farmer at the plough who is given an inexhaustible supply of bread by underworld beings, he broods over these strange events. He is more concerned with their mystery than their practical effects. But the folktale hero sees and experiences things far more fantastic than these and never bats an eye. As an actor, not a spectator, he approaches the twelve-headed dragon who, when pressed, turns into a rabbit and then a dove. He is able to overcome the creature because a lion once gave him a single hair and said: " 'If you are ever in trouble, bend this hair and you will turn into a lion three times stronger than I.' The hunter said, 'Thank you,' and went on his way"—this is all the tale says.[1] The hero shows neither astonishment

---

*A spirit or apparition who is seen in lonely places and is associated with the living dead. See the *Handwörterbuch des deutschen Aberglaubens*, s.v. *weiß*, and the *Wörterbuch der deutschen Volkskunde*, s.v. *weiße Frau.*—*Trans.*

nor doubt. He does not try out the magic objects but uses them only when he has need, and in most folktales this happens only once. Afterward the magic object is neither needed nor mentioned; it has no more interest. If a folktale hero journeys to a glass mountain, he does so not out of any desire to explore the fabulous peak, but because a princess there needs to be rescued. Neither curiosity nor a thirst for knowledge spurs him on to hell, the great griffin, the land at the world's end, or the land of the water of life and golden apples. He goes because a task is set by a cruel king, or because he wants to bring a remedy to his sick father, or because of a princess's whim, or in order to win back his lost bride. The folktale hero *acts*, and he has neither the time nor the temperament to be puzzled with mysteries.

In folktales the numinous excites neither fear nor curiosity. If curiosity exists then it is of an everyday kind. It is directed toward events, not underlying essentials. A cottage in the forest is shaken by a mighty knocking and banging, and the folktale hero is naturally struck with "great wonder" about what is happening, for it may involve him in an adventure, in some course of action.[2] But if he comes upon a mysterious little chest in the underworld, he leaves it unopened until he finds himself in tight straits. Only then does he look into it to see what it contains, not because it interests him but in hope of some kind of aid.[3] Similarly, if the folktale hero is afraid, his fear is of an everyday kind. He is afraid of dangers, not of the uncanny. Witches, dragons, and giants frighten him no more than do human rogues and robbers. He avoids such creatures because they have power to kill or injure, not because of their supernatural character. All fear of the numinous is absent. In a legend, people are horrified if an animal begins to speak.[4] The folktale hero who meets with speaking animals, winds, or stars evinces neither astonishment nor fear. His equanimity cannot be traced to familiarity with speaking animals or stars, for these things have no place in his domestic world, and there is no indication that he has ever heard of the existence of animals who talk.[5] But he is not astonished, and he is not afraid. He lacks all sense of the extraordinary. To him, everything belongs to the same dimension. He is even calmed when a wild beast begins to speak,[6] for a wild beast frightens him—it could tear him apart—while he finds nothing uncanny about an animal who speaks.

In legends otherworld beings are physically close to human beings. They dwell in his house, in his field, or in the nearby woods, stream, mountain, or lake. Often they do work for him and he gives them food. But spiritually these house kobolds, nickelmen, *Fänggen,** alpine spirits, and wild men inhabit a world of their own, and human beings encounter them as the Wholly Other. In folktales exactly the opposite is true. Otherworld beings do not dwell side by side with the inhabitants of this world. Rarely does the hero meet them in his house or village. He comes across them only when he wanders far and wide. Then they come to meet him—little dwarves, old men and women, beggars, hermits, animals and stars that speak and have magical powers, devils, dragons, and trolls, along with their friendly and helpful spouses and daughters. The folktale hero calmly accepts their advice, receives their help, or suffers their injuries. Through it all he is no more aroused than when dealing with ordinary beings. The strange nature of creatures of the otherworld is of no concern to him; only their actions are important. He knows neither whence they come nor whither they disappear. He has no idea who granted them their knowledge and their magical power, and he does not ask. If the story happens to deal with persons under a spell, for him all that is important is that the persons are enchanted and must be disenchanted. Who cursed them and why—these matters are beside the point and often are not reported at all. The question of the hidden laws by which enchantment comes about is never raised. The marvelous events of the folktale require no more explanation than do the events of daily life. In legends otherworld beings are phys-

---

*In Bavaria, the Tyrol, and other southern German-speaking areas, the *Fängge* (plural *Fänggen;* feminine *Fänggin;* feminine plural *Fängginnen*) is a giant-like or dwarf-like creature believed to live in the wild. Such creatures are also known as *wilde Leute* (see note, p. 5) and are sometimes associated with the devil. In the Tyrol they are usually female; their whole body is hairy, their mouth stretches from ear to ear, and their voice is deep like a man's. They may be cannibalistic, or they may mate with giants and give their children to human households. In summer they go naked; in winter they clothe themselves in animal skins. They can be benevolent as well as threatening, and they sometimes do work for people or look after children who have lost their way. See the *Handwörterbuch des deutschen Aberglaubens,* s.v. *Fängge,* and the *Wörterbuch der deutschen Volkskunde,* s.v. *Fenken.—Trans.*

ically near human beings but spiritually far. In folktales they are far away geographically but near in spirit and in the realm of experience. Apparently the only way that folktales can express spiritual otherness is through geographical separation. The folktale hero encounters otherworld beings not in familiar woods, as in the legend, but in an unknown forest. In his own village the peasant of legends discovers poor souls who are awaiting release from a spell; the folktale hero has to travel to the world's end to reach the enchanted princess. But this world's end is really distant only geographically, not spiritually. Any otherworld kingdom can be reached by walking or flying. "You still have a long way to go," says a wolf to the hero after the hero has been walking for three days; and three days later a bear says to him, "You still have a long way to go." But after three more days a lion is able to tell him, "You don't have much farther to go at all; a good hour from here the princess is sitting in the hunter's lodge."[7] The bottom of the sea, the clouds, and the different otherworld kingdoms that can be reached by flying, by climbing a tree, or in some magical way—for the folktale hero these are distant only outwardly, not spiritually. Legends do not need to separate the everyday world from the otherworld geographically, for the two realms are represented as two sharply distinct spiritual dimensions. Only folktales, in which spiritual "otherness" is not perceived, tend to put spatial barriers between our world and the other world. The folktale projects spiritual differences onto a straight line; it expresses inner distance through visible separation.

The folktale hero does not hesitate to marry an otherworld bride, whether a fairy, a swan maiden, or a witch's daughter who is endowed with magical skills. He notices nothing disturbing about her. In the tale of *Beauty and the Beast* (AT 425C and related types) the bride does not fear or abhor the demon she has married. She fears the beast. She breathes a sigh of relief as soon as she discovers that her husband is not an animal but an otherworld being. When an otherworld bride is forfeited by some mistake, usually the violation of some interdiction or condition, she is simply removed—she is shifted in space. The hero's attempt to regain her succeeds every time. All he must do is cross the distance that separates them, and she is his forever. In legends marriages with *Fängginnen*, witches, and water nymphs are inherently cause for alarm and usually end unhappily. Such unions are always represented as something extra-ordinary. In legends people do not marry disenchanted spirits. In folktales it is taken for granted that the hero will marry the enchanted princess whom he has rescued. He sees nothing unusual in such a match.

This lack of a sense of the numinous in folktales is especially noteworthy since folktales do differentiate between this-worldly and otherworldly figures. Not all folktale personages are endowed with magical powers or otherworldly traits. Occasionally, to be sure, the hero's father, mother, or master has magical skills. Usually no reason for this ability is given because of the folktale's isolating style (see pp. 37–65 below). Often evil stepmothers and mothers-in-law are skilled in the black arts. But as a rule, the hero (along with his brothers, sisters, and often parents and subordinate human characters as well) belongs squarely in the world of everyday life. The folktale is no wild magical tale in which anyone can do anything.[8] Usually the human hero acquires supernatural powers only as the result of an encounter with a being whose otherworldly nature is explicit. The false hero—the older brother, for example—never manages to acquire magical capabilities. Everyday characters and otherworld characters are thus distinguished in the folktale, as in the legend; but in the folktale these actors stand side by side and freely interact with one another. Everyday folktale characters do not feel that an encounter with an otherworld being is an encounter with an alien dimension. It is in this sense that we may speak of the "one-dimensionality" *(Eindimensionalität)* of the folktale.

2
Depthlessness

Not only does the folktale lack a sense of any gap separating the everyday world from the world of the supernatural. In its essence and in every sense, it lacks the dimension of depth. Its characters are figures without substance, without inner life, without an environment; they lack any relation to past and future, to time altogether. The depthlessness *(Flächenhaftigkeit)* of the folktale becomes especially clear when we again compare the characteristics of legends.

The legend realistically portrays actual persons and objects that have a variety of different relations to the everyday world and the other world. A person who hears a legend recounted immediately becomes aware of the physical dimensions of the objects of which it speaks. They are utensils of daily life: kettles, pans, jugs, mugs, coulters, finely crafted shoes, garments, balls of yarn, cow bells, skittle balls, loaves of bread—all objects of pronounced spatial depth. But the folktale most often shows us staffs, rings, keys, swords, rifles, animal hairs, feathers—figures without depth, that even have a tendency toward linearity. In legends one becomes even more aware of the three-dimensionality of objects because of their propensity to grow great or small. The ball of yarn, the loaf, or the peas that a person receives from an underworld being are made use of, melt away, and then grow back again in secret. But the flat or linear objects of the folktale remain as rigid and unchanging as metal. If they do change into something quite different (for example, during a hero's magical flight from danger), then this sudden and mechanical change, unlike the slow growth of the objects of legendry, still has nothing to do with our perception of three-dimensional space.

Even in a metaphorical sense, the objects of legendry are endowed with greater three-dimensionality than are the objects of the folktale. They are displayed to us in living, constantly repeated use. They exist in the midst of the three-dimensional world of everyday life, and the atmosphere of their environment clings to them. But the objects depicted in folktales are usually tailored to a very special situation in a sequence of adventures and used only once: the golden spinning wheel, to regain the lost husband; the dress of stars, to dance with the prince; the staff, ring, feather, or hair, to summon an otherworld helper. They do not bear the signs of active daily use; they are not embedded in the living space of their owner but remain isolated in themselves.[1]

The persons and animals depicted in folktales, similarly, lack physical and psychological depth. Legends make us conscious of human bodies chiefly by showing how they are transformed by disease. We see how the finger, leg, cheek, or breasts of a person who has been touched or struck by an otherworld being swell hideously. Red spots, disgusting sores, or toads appear on his cheeks. He is left with a deep wound or stiff, lame, or crippled limbs. Plague or murrain disfigures and wastes his body; years of fever lead to its debilitation. In the folktale we find nothing of the kind. Folktales depict many an ailing princess but never name the type of malady. They tell us nothing of the effect of the disease on her body and thus do not place the body before our eyes. If nevertheless we do visualize it, then involuntarily we see it intact, not eaten away by illness, ripped open by wounds, or disfigured by tumors; that is, we do not see its depth and spatiality, only its surface.

Even when actual mutilations occur in folktales we are not allowed to visualize the physical body of the victim. If the heroine's hands or forearms are hacked off, if she herself cuts off one of her fingers, or if the leg of a little horse is torn off by wolves, we do not see blood flowing or a real wound developing. Either the change appears to be purely ornamental—the symmetrically shortened arms are as perfect formally as before—or it has no effect at all, and the little three-legged horse does not limp and runs just as fast as if it had four legs. The Latvian folktale hero Kurbads, who has to "cut off his own left calf with his sword to feed the griffin," not only does so in a calm and collected way, without loss of blood or strength, but in the next moment he is already walking about again without any noticeable ill effects.[2] It is as if the persons of the folktale were paper figures from which anything at all could be cut off without causing a substantial change. As a rule such mutilations call forth no expressions of physical or psychological suffering. Tears are shed only if this is important for the development of the plot.[3] Otherwise, people cut off their limbs without batting an eye.

In the Grimms' folktale of *The Seven Ravens* (KHM No. 25), we are told of the little sister who arrives at the glass mountain: "What was she to do now? She wanted to save her brothers and had no key to the glass mountain. The good little sister took a knife, cut off one of her little fingers, put it into the gate, and thus managed to open it. Once she had made her way in, a little dwarf came to meet her"—and so on, without the slightest indication of physical or psychological distress. Much the same thing happens in another German tale: "In this predicament the boy wanted to slip the ring off his finger at once, but he could no longer do so. Then he quickly took his knife and cut off the ring and finger both together and threw them into a big lake that was nearby. Then he ran all around the lake shouting, 'Here I am! Here I am!' "[4] Similarly, we hear no cry of pain from villains who are punished by being forced to dance in red-hot shoes or by being thrown down a mountain in a spiked barrel.

Only rarely does the folktale mention sentiments and attributes for their own sake or to create a certain atmosphere. It mentions them when they influence the plot. Even then it does not like to mention them by name. It does not speak of the hero's compassion, credulity, or magnanimity, but rather shows him as he pays ransom for a mistreated corpse, as he trusts his brothers instead of regarding them with suspicion, or as he helps them instead of punishing them. Attributes and sentiments are expressed in actions:[5] that is, they are projected onto the same plane on which everything else takes place. The whole realm of sentiment is absent from folktale characters, and as a result they lack all psychological depth. Individual narrators, of course, may interject a word about the hero's sorrow or joy. But we clearly sense that this is incidental embellishment and does not pertain essentially to the folktale as a form. The bride and bridegroom who find one another after many wild adventures celebrate their wedding simply and without emotional outburst, just as the many people who are disenchanted experience no transport of joy. Turns of phrase like, "Almost fainting for joy, the princess sank to the feet of her savior"⁶ are rare exceptions whose false style can be recognized at once. If a folktale hero sits down crying on a stone because he is at a loss over how to help himself, we are not told this so as to be shown the state of his soul, but because in such a situation it is just this kind of reaction on the part of the hero that leads to contact with an otherworld helper.

No one inquires after the feelings or rights of the second husband of the wife or bride who has been lost and is then recovered. In order for the woman to be free of him, he only has to be asked whether, when an old lost key is found again, the new key or the old one should be used. The answer is always "The old," and with these words the unsuspecting husband pronounces judgment on himself. The marriage is dissolved by a simple interplay of question and answer, without excitement, without any consideration of the internal emotional state of the second husband (see pp. 70–71 below). Nowhere is this internal emotional state expressed, for the folktale shows us flat figures rather than human beings with active inner lives. A heroine succeeds in observing a command to keep silent for seven years, but of the psychological distress and conflicts that must arise within her as a result, the true folktale tells us nothing. It only relates how her evil mother-in-law takes away her children and slanders her to her husband, without adding a word about the heroine's psychological reaction.⁷

In legends the most disparate feelings battle with one another within a person's breast—utter fearlessness and faintheartedness, anxiety and hope, greed and disgust. But the folktale, which knows nothing of such exaggerated feelings as these, even distributes the various possible courses of action among various figures that can be placed side by side on a single plane. It shows correct conduct in the hero and unsuccessful conduct in his brothers. In legends a person who rescues another person does so with excitement and trembling, for he is conscious of the possibility of failure. Unsure of himself, he vacillates between different possible courses and makes the wrong choice more often than the right. But the folktale hero hits upon the right course of action as unerringly as the antihero (*der Unheld*) hits upon the wrong. Without hesitation or vacillation the youngest brother shares his bread with the seemingly contemptible beggar, while without hesitation the two older brothers turn the beggar away. For each brother there exists only one kind of action, and all three react with mechanical precision.

Folktales break down the rich complexity of human beings. Instead of different possible modes of behavior being combined in a single person, we see them sharply separated from one another and divided among persons who stand side by side. One cannot even speak of the characters of folktale as being intelligent. The tasks of cleverness that occur in the folktale are not truly tests of intelligence, as Charlotte Bühler has observed, because "they are derived from such a specific situation that no cunning could ever hit upon it. . . . The solution depends on very specific aids that do not depend on the sagacity of the person but are offered to him by lucky chance."⁸ The same author confuses terms, however, when she claims that as a rule, it is an internal emotional state that leads the way to decisive action. Not internal emotions but external impulses propel the characters of the folktale onward. They are impelled and guided by gifts, discoveries, tasks, suggestions, prohibitions, miraculous aids, challenges, difficulties, and lucky happenstances, not by the promptings of their hearts. When it is important to stay awake the antiheroes can be counted upon to fall asleep as mechanically as puppets. No mention is made of their having struggled to stay awake. If the hero wishes to stay awake, however, he sits down on an ant heap⁹ or in a thicket of thorns.¹⁰ Here again he relies not on the strength and persistence of his own will but on a form of external "help." Wherever possible, the folktale expresses internal feelings through external events, psychological motivations through external impulses.

In essence, folktale characters* always act with composure. Even when rage, anger, jealousy, possessiveness, love, and longing are mentioned,¹¹ there can be no question of real surges of emotion, greed, or passion. The folktale tells of cruel punishments, but it

---

*The author wishes to stress that by the term "characters" he means simply those figures who carry forward the plot (*Handlungsträger*), without any suggestion that these figures have an actual character or inner life.—*Trans.*

knows no vindictiveness. The hero himself almost never punishes the villain; that is the task of subordinate figures or otherworld beings. The folktale knows of engagement and marriage but not erotic sensations. It knows of otherworld beings but has no sense of the numinous. In general it avoids portraying feelings. It translates feelings into actions by transposing the internal world onto the level of external events. In legends, fear of the supernatural and internal emotional tension often drive a person mad. The characters of folktales never go mad. There is nothing in them that could become deranged, for they have no depth, only surface.

The characters of folktales not only possess no internal reality, they also lack an environment. The protagonists of legends live and work in their native village. They do not leave it, but rather live and experience, act and dream at home. Here they have their most important relationships, with their village companions and with a wholly other world. The scenes where the events of the legend take place are familiar to them from childhood, whether these are the fields, meadows, and streams of their village, or its houses and its church, or the neighboring woods and alpine pastures. When the people of legendry do leave home, they are gripped by a feeling of homesickness that drives them irresistibly homeward until they begin to feel themselves grow well again.

Folktales tell us nothing about the town or village where the hero has grown up. On the contrary, they prefer to show him at the very moment when he leaves home and sets out into the world. If he ever returns to his point of departure, he does so only because the plot calls for it, not because he is bound to this place by psychological or physical necessity. The folktale finds a thousand reasons to have its hero set forth from home—his parents' need, his own poverty, his stepmother's malice, a task set by the king, his love of adventure, any kind of errand, or a contest. Any motive is suitable that will isolate the hero and turn him into a wanderer. In one and the same tale, the father sends his two elder sons out into the world to punish them, yet sends the younger son out as a reward![12] People depicted in legends do not need to leave home to have a significant experience, for they have their own spiritual depths and know no lack of rich, suspenseful relationships in their immediate environment. The folktale hero must set forth from home in order to meet with what is essential. Whatever the legend portrays as a multilayered inner life and environment, the folktale sets side by side on a single plane.

In like manner, the folktale hero is not embedded in a family structure. He separates himself from his parents except insofar as they remain instigators of the plot, and his brothers (or sisters, if there is a heroine) are mere foils. Mothers-in-law are only significant as adversaries. The heroine's children are only introduced if they influence the development of the plot, while the hero's children are scarcely ever mentioned. The hero has no inner or outwardly visible relationship to his family or even to an ethnic community. His bride or spouse is only of interest as the instigator or goal of the plot. With the hero's marriage the folktale comes to an end, unless a second separation occasions new tasks, dangers, and adventures. His union with the bride is postponed as long as possible, not only by the multiplication, tiering, and variation of obstacles but often by the hero's simply deciding that he will first look at the world for a year. In effect, marriage is not the hero's long-awaited goal but rather just the endpoint of the series of adventures that constitute the plot.

Among the various characters of the folktale there exist no firm, lasting relations. Parents, brothers and sisters, and subordinate figures who have been rescued all disappear from sight as soon as they have no more bearing on the action. Otherworld helpers are not the domestic companions or fellow-workers of ordinary people, but rather they flash from the void whenever the plot requires them. Each new situation generally calls forth a new helper, but even if the same otherworld beings appear more than once, they disappear from sight in the meantime—not to any particular place, or into an abyss existing behind things, but rather just by not being mentioned any more. They materialize only when they enter into the level of the action, and when they do so it is with outlines just as sharp and colors just as strong as those that set off the people of this world. None of the misty outlines or barely tangible bodies of the otherworld beings of legendry pertain to them. They are portrayed with the same lucidity and in the same manner as are the people of this world, and they stand side by side with them on the same plane.

Furthermore, relationships themselves do not remain intangible. There exist no invisible internal bonds knitting persons together, but rather relationships generally become visible in the form of a gift. The relationship between the hero and a helpful animal is made manifest in the hair, feather, or scale that the animal gives him. Not by his spiritual powers or by an effort of will does the hero draw the helper to him, but he invokes him effortlessly by simply making use of the gift that embodies the relationship. When the hero takes leave of the princess he has rescued, he is bound to her not by inner sentiment but by a visible token of recognition. A mere bobbin brings about the kind sister's contact with the realm of Frau Holle (KHM No. 24). The relations between characters thus do not create an inner bond but are externalized and thereby stand on the same plane as the characters. Instead of building depth, they contribute to the flat appearance of the whole. Not even physically, as material possessions, do they lend three-dimensionality to the hero, for he uses them only once in his life, or at most three times, whenever he is confronted with his crucial task. Before and after, he never thinks of using them. The wonderful keys, rings, and garments, the flying shoes, carpets, and horses, the miraculous salves and fruits of the folktale do not serve to give the hero amenity and comfort or to help him in his calling (for he usually does not practice a calling, even when one is named; even in this respect he is portrayed without depth). Such magical gifts have no other purpose than to help the hero overcome certain tasks and dangers or to provide the occasion for certain adventures. They do not belong to the hero's real environment any more than anything else does, for he *has* no environment but is an isolated figure.

Even the otherworld is structured no more three-dimensionally than the world of everyday reality. It is of interest to the folktale only insofar as it encroaches on the plot. Its own life is revealed neither to the folktale hero nor to us. Otherworld beings appear at the moment when they are needed. For the most part they appear singly. With the greatest precision and certainty they fulfill their function in the plot, and then they disappear again. How they have come to possess their knowledge, whence their power derives, whether they themselves make use of the magical objects that they place at the disposal of ordinary mortals, and to what end, in what way—all this we are not told. Of their characteristics, their station in life, or their relations between themselves, we see only what the plot reveals to us.[13] With them, too, we have no glimpse into psychological depths, whereas in legends we are deeply affected when witnessing the torment and longing of otherworld beings. In legends the world of supernatural beings can just barely be discerned and vanishes gradually in the dark. In the folktale both otherworld beings and ordinary beings are no more than figures in the plot. Both are presented as equally clear and flat, without their outlines being blurred by real depth, nuances, and entanglements. Both are isolated internally and externally. The fundamental distance between them is therefore slight. They can meet one another without surprise to themselves or to the listening audience—but only meet, not enter into an intimate relationship. In spite of the encounter, they continue to exist side by side. Standing between them is the gift that the otherworld being gives to the human being and that nevertheless is not specifically tied to either of them. It simultaneously unites and divides them.

Finally, the depthless world of the folktale also lacks the dimension of time. There do exist young and old people, of course: princes and kings, daughters and mothers, younger and older brothers and sisters, and young and old dwarves, witches, and otherworld animals. But there are no aging persons, and no aging otherworld beings either. Kings, princes, and servants may be changed into animals, plants, or stones for any length of time, and when they are released from their spell they are just as old or young as at the moment when they were bewitched.

This indifference to the passage of time on the part of the folktale is most familiar to us from *Sleeping Beauty* (KHM No. 50), in which the heroine, along with all that surrounds her, awakes after a hundred-year sleep just as young and beautiful as she was before. Here the Grimms could not resist the temptation to call attention to this phenomenon through far-fetched details: "The flies started crawling up the walls again, the fire in the kitchen sprang up, flickered, and cooked the food, the roast began to sputter again, the cook gave the boy such a box on the ear that he cried out aloud, and the maid finished plucking the chicken." What Jacob Grimm originally wrote down was simply: "And everything awoke from sleep."[14] The long, playful description violates the concise style of the true folktale, which only notes the incidents of the plot (see pp. 24–26 below). At the same time, however, it gives us a striking impression of that other essential characteristic of the folktale, the insignificance of the passage of time. In the Grimm version it never occurs to the rescuing prince to notice something antiquated in the costumes and the style of architecture, and neither does the audience of the tale pause to think that fashions could have changed in the course of a hundred years. It is different with Perrault:[15]

The prince helped the princess rise. She was fully dressed, and in splendid style; but he took good care not to mention to her that she was dressed like my grandmother and that she wore a high collar. She was no less beautiful on this account. They went into a room that was lined with mirrors and dined there, waited on by the princess's servants. The violins and oboes played pieces that were beautiful, for all their age, even though no one had played them for nearly a hundred years.

With this charming and witty realism, the French author destroys the timelessness that is an essential characteristic of the folktale.

German folktales like to have the otherworld being who crosses the path of the hero take the form of an "old man" or "old woman." Inflexibly it repeats the exact same wording: *alt* ("old"). The close variation *uralt* ("very old") is almost never used, for it would too strongly suggest the process of aging. More frequently one finds *steinalt* ("old as a stone") and *meeralt* ("old as the sea"). By calling to mind inanimate, inorganic substances, such terms work hand in hand with the tendency of the folktale to rigidity of form and in no way suggest the processes of life. But the simple word *alt* is most common, as it is clear, short, and neutral, without any hidden possibilities of change.

The heroes of the folktale possess eternal youth. Nothing can break this youth down—no span of time and no sorrow, not the longest wandering from home, and not the worst blows of fate. Just as enchanted persons can be transformed into a strange shape and forced into harsh servitude for years without showing the slightest trace of their suffering after they are rescued, in much the same way the hero, the actor, remains unmarked by the dangers and difficulties he has overcome. No matter how horrifying his experiences have been, his beauty and youth remain untouched. No furrows are engraved on his brow; his hair does not turn white. If the folktale hero loses one or more of his limbs in the course of an adventure, then they grow back again later—not gradually, but with mechanical abruptness as soon as a certain point in the development of the plot is reached, or else their loss remains a truncated motif that is disregarded in the subsequent course of the narrative. Here it becomes evident that lack of temporal depth complements the folktale's lack of psychological depth. Since the blows of fate that afflict the folktale hero—all his battles, dangers, losses, or privations—propel him forward physically but have no effect on his psychic depths, they have no power to change him. After the battle he is the same man that he was before; he does not age. Time is a function of psychological experience. Since the characters of the folktale are only figures who carry forward the plot and have no inner life, folktales must also lack the experience of time.

A glance at legends demonstrates with great clarity what is unique about the style of the folktale. In legends, where fear, wonder, suspense, shock, and spiritual malaise play a central role in the narration, the substantiality of time also unfolds in all its depth-creating reality. Even physically the dwarves of legendry often bear the signs of aging in the form of shriveled skin, bent posture, and gray hair. When we hear them talk of how the village forest has been cut down and has grown back three times since they were born, then we almost seem able to reach out our hands and touch the slow passage of time. A similar effect is produced when the Wandering Jew relates that every time he returns, the landscape has completely changed. If a legend tells of a person who falls asleep or dwells in an underground realm for a hundred or more years, then at his return to humankind he crumbles into dust and ashes or shrinks into an ancient little man or woman. As soon as someone makes him aware of the years that have passed since he vanished, he becomes conscious at once of the whole temporal lapse and experiences in one instant, psychologically and physically, all that he could not experience in that wholly different state of being that was governed by other-than-human rules: the power of time. This power is so completely dependent on personal experience that it has no force as long as people are not aware of it, but as soon as the time that has lapsed enters into consciousness, the body makes up in a single moment for what had been delayed for years. It shrivels up and decays. Legends thereby make physically visible a process of aging that otherwise comes about gradually and imperceptibly. In folktales, the young are unalterably young and the old are unalterably old. Old kings only die so that heroes can inherit their kingdoms and the plot can come to its end; no lapse of time is thereby perceptible.[16]

Legends often tell how a person who has been touched by the otherworld slowly wastes away. They describe how gifts presented by otherworld beings change their form, as occurs with the magic piece of cheese or magic ball of yarn that grows small and then returns to its former size. In the folktale all changes of form come about with mechanical abruptness. They do not give rise to a sense of development, of a process of becoming, growing, or vanishing, a sense of any passage of time.[17] In legendry a curse affects whole generations; it takes effect for centuries and burdens all progeny. Once-flowering alps are glaciated and their former state is gone forever. Valuable talismans and secrets are likewise inherited from generation to generation. In folktales the hero's children, parents, and brothers and sisters are mentioned only when they are important to the plot. Only the hero himself makes use of magic objects, and even he uses them only once or three times, in a very specific situation when he must carry out an important task or overcome a danger. Then the magic object bursts upon our attention; thereafter it becomes insignificant and is never mentioned again. It is never an heirloom connecting earlier with later times. The folktale curse affects only figures who exist side by side; it never extends from early ancestors to later descendants. After a curse is lifted, even people who have been bewitched for centuries do not hesitate to marry their young saviors, for savior and saved exist on the same level. In legends a marriage between the savior and the redeemed soul is almost unthinkable, for Death and Time stand between them. Once people have entered the otherworld they never become human again. The otherworld of the folktale is not only not a different dimension, but in it the past stands at ease side by side with the present.

The folktale abjures deep spatial, temporal, spiritual, and psychological relationships. It metamorphoses interlayered reality (*das Ineinander*) and sequential reality (*das Nacheinander*) into juxtaposed reality (*das Nebeneinander*). With admirable consistency it projects the materials of the most varied spheres onto one and the same plane. It renders bodies and objects as flat figures, characteristics as actions, and relationships between individuals as physically visible material gifts; it assigns different possible modes of conduct to different figures (the hero and the antihero); it represents spiritual or psychological distance in terms of physical separation. If we see the hero set forth resolutely across wide expanses in quest of adventures, magic objects, or a lost bride, or if the wonderful gifts of otherworld beings draw him effortlessly into far realms, then we sense that the whole depthless presentation rises not from ineptitude but from a very definite and sure striving toward form on the part of the folktale. The primitive short form of the legend is familiar with three-dimensional reality in every sense and lets it stand before us realistically. The folktale siphons off all three-dimensionality from objects and phenomena and shows them to us as flat figures and figured events on a brightly lit plane.

3

Abstract Style

The clear-cut way in which the folktale achieves its depthlessness lends it a lack of realism. From the outset, the folktale does not seek empathetically to recreate the concrete world with its many dimensions. The folktale transforms the world; it puts a spell on its elements and gives them a different form, and thus it creates a world with a distinct character of its own.

Within the depthless world of the folktale, individual figures are physically set off from each other by sharp outlines and pure colors. By its nature, a flat surface calls for outlines and colors. A painter's picture needs frame and coloring, whereas a sculptor's image can dispense with both. The contours of a three-dimensional form blur in the depths of space; they fade into the indefinite. On a flat surface, however, lines are sharp and unequivocal. The exterior of a body constantly informs us of a hidden interior, whereas a flat surface is isolated in and of itself. A painting can either obscure or intensify the unrealistic character of the pure plane. It can simulate curves, three-dimensionality, and reality, and it can make the flat surface appear to have depth. But a painting can also permit the flat quality to stand by itself and can emphasize it by means of geometric lines and stark colors. The folktale follows this latter approach.

The sharp contours of the folktale are evident at once in the way that it does not describe particular objects but only names them. Action-oriented as it is, it leads its figures on from point to point without pausing to describe anything at length. The legend gazes spellbound at certain buildings, trees, caves, paths, and apparitions and constantly tries to discover new aspects of them. The stories of *The Arabian Nights* likewise tend to lose themselves in descriptions of the fabulous palaces and the towns made of stone into which the hero makes his way, and thus they attain a fullness that bewilders. Detailed descriptions do not convey distinct images, rather they make us lose all perspective. The European folktale is not addicted to description. When it has its hero set off in search of his brother and sister and come upon a town made of iron, it does not waste a single word describing the iron buildings. Looking neither left nor right, and without the slightest trace of astonishment, the hero pursues his goal:[1]

Now the new king decided to search for his brother and sister. He wandered through many towns but found nothing. At last he arrived at a town that was made all of iron. He entered, but there was not a living soul there; all the houses were locked and there was no one in the street. He found only one big house standing open. As soon as he entered it, he saw a big dragon roasting a lamb on a spit. He went up to it and gave it a respectful greeting. The dragon made no reply. The young king became angry and struck the dragon a blow, and a bloody struggle broke out between them.

Only what is essential to the plot is mentioned; nothing is stated for its own sake, and nothing is amplified. As a rule only one attribute goes with each noun: a town made all of iron, a big house, a big dragon, the young king, a bloody struggle. Thanks to this true epic technique of merely naming things, everything that is named appears as a definitively understood unit. Any attempt at detailed description gives rise to the feeling that only a fraction of all that could be said has in fact been told. A detailed description lures us into the infinite and shows us the elusive depth of things. Mere naming, on the other hand, automatically transforms things into simple, motionless images. The world is captured in the word; there is no tentative amplification that would make us feel that something has been left out. The brief labels isolate things by giving them sharp outlines. Not only human beings and otherworld beings, but also all the objects and places of the folktale are designated in this way. The forest in which the folktale hero loses his way is always simply named, never described. The Grimm brothers lose touch with the style of the genuine folktale when they speak of the red eyes and wagging head of the witch and of her long bespectacled nose (KHM Nos. 15, 69, 193). Genuine folktales only speak of an "ugly old hag," an "old witch," an

"evil witch," or simply an "old woman." Gerhart Hauptmann has re-
marked that "Whatever one adds to the plot is at the expense of the
characters."[2] This rule applies to the folktale as well, for the folktale
consistently foregoes any individualizing characterization. This is no
loss to its construction, but gain. The brief labels impart to all of the
elements of the tale that definitive form to which the folktale style
aspires by its very nature.

Among the most frequently named things in folktales are objects that are distinguished by sharp contours and that consist of
solid material. Rings, staffs, swords, hair, nuts, eggs, coffers, purses,
and apples pass as gifts from otherworld beings to the inhabitants of
this world. Unlike the subterranean creatures of legendry, these
otherworld beings rarely live in the impenetrable thickets of the
forest or in caves; the folktale gives them solid houses or castles or
splendid underground lodgings. The forest witch in *Hansel and
Gretel* lives in a small house that is sharply set off from its surroundings, just as both Frau Holle and the underworld devil of the Latvian
folktale about Kurbads live in "a little house" in a luminous subterranean realm. The Nordic troll can be the lord of a castle;[3] even the
gnome Rumpelstiltskin lives in his own little house. Again and again,
the hero enters towns, castles, or rooms within whose four walls the
action takes its course. "The brave youth left the chambers of white
stone, walked out of the town, and went on and on, whether it was
near or far, low or high—and there stood a huge barn." It is this barn
that provides the setting for the following adventure.[4] How often the
folktale calls up the scene in which the protagonist stays behind
alone in an otherworld palace and then enters all of its rooms, one by
one, even the forbidden twelfth! With what readiness it locks up the
hero or the heroine in a tower, palace, trunk or chest! The human beings and the otherworld creatures of the folktale are self-contained
figures with nothing indefinite about them. Even people who are
sentenced to death and are torn apart by horses are not bloodily
dismembered and torn to pieces, but are split neatly in two; they fall
"into pieces." "At once the prince ordered his servants to tie each of
the sisters to a pair of horses, one leg to each horse, and to whip the
horses and drive them apart. This was done, and the sisters of the
princess were thus torn into two pieces."[5] John the Bear "split the
giant in two."[6] Sick princesses are cured by means of a purely

mechanical treatment: they are cut into pieces and then flawlessly reassembled. Rumpelstiltskin tears himself "right in two." We see the symmetrically and sharply sundered halves, from which no blood flows and which lose none of their precision of form.

In much the same way, the folktale tends to render things and animate beings in metallic or mineral terms. Not only are towns, bridges, and shoes made of stone, iron, or glass, and houses and castles made of gold or diamonds, but forests, horses, ducks, or people can be made of gold, silver, iron, or copper, or they can suddenly turn to stone. Gems and pearls, or metal rings, keys, or bells, or golden gowns, hair, or feathers occur in almost every folktale. Golden apples are especially favored. Golden and silver pears, nuts, or flowers, tools of glass, or golden spinning wheels are some of the folktale's regular accessories. Hands, fingers, feet, or hairs are turned to silver or copper. Certain folktale heroes have a golden star on their forehead or knee. The daughter of the South Slavic emperor has a star on her forehead, a sun on her bosom, and a moon on her knee.[7] A downpour of golden rain gilds the heroine of the tale of Frau Holle: "Here comes our golden girl!"[8] But the antiheroine, as well, is showered with pitch or enclosed in a wooden dress that is then coated with pitch.[9] Instead of the supple human figure, we see a rigid, black hull. Garments made of stone, or a waistcoat[10] or trousers[11] made of marble also occur. This predilection of the folktale for anything metallic or mineral, for inflexible materials in general, contributes in large measure to giving it a fixed form and well-defined shape. This becomes especially apparent when the folktale renders living organisms in metallic or mineral terms.

Among the metals, the folktale prefers the precious and rare: gold, silver, copper. The flying ship is made "all of gold, the masts of silver, but the sails of silk."[12] The rare, precious object is set off against its environment and stands alone. In addition, there is the great radiance of precious metals and the stars. A golden or copper horse not only seems unrealistic because it cannot occur in the real world, but the sheer brilliance of its color alone strongly contrasts with any horse in real life.

The real world shows us a richness of different hues and shadings. Blended colors are far more frequent than pure tones. By contrast, the folktale prefers clear, ultrapure colors: gold, silver, red, white, black, and sometimes blue as well. Gold and silver have a metallic luster, black and white are nonspecific contrasts, and red is the least subtle of all colors and the first to attract the attention of infants. The only blended color to appear is gray, but in the folktale gray, too, is of a metallic character. Instead of telling of a "little gray man" *(Graumännchen)*, the folktale sometimes speaks of a "little iron man" *(eisernes Männchen)*. Green, the color of living nature, is strikingly rare. The folktale forest is a "large forest," sometimes a "dark forest," practically never a "green forest." The more subtle shadings such as brown and yellowish are not found at all. Snow White is as white as snow, as red as blood, and as black as ebony. The sun, the moon, and the stars color and adorn the clothes and even the bodies of princesses. The horses of folktales are black, white, or red;[13] there are also red sheep,[14] black men[15]—in Bulgarian folktales, as in *The Arabian Nights*, the Negro is a figure much favored[16]—and black and white wolves, billy goats, and roosters. All the same, the folktale does not overvalue colors. A rich profusion of bright colors would interfere with its strict linearity. Only a few things and persons are distinguished by a color term, and so they contrast all the more strongly with those that are colorless.

The story line of the folktale is just as sharply defined and distinct as are the outlines, substance, and color of its characters. The action of the folktale, unlike that of the legend, does not take place in a circumscribed domestic environment among an indefinite number of participants. It reaches out resolutely toward the distance and leads its few protagonists over great expanses to faraway realms—realms that stand before us as brightly illuminated and sharply outlined as does everything else. After long wanderings, a Norwegian folktale hero finally comes "in the winter to a country where all of the streets were straight and had no turnings whatsoever"[17]—a true fairy-tale landscape of wintry clarity and geometrical linearity!

Among the gifts given by otherworld helpers to folktale heroes, means of transportation are especially frequent. Fabulous horses, carriages, shoes, or overcoats carry the hero to faraway places, or a ring conveys him wherever he wishes to go. All sorts of motives are found to enable the hero or antihero to wander abroad.[18] The folktale hero is essentially a wanderer. The line of the plot unfolds before us untrammeled and clear. It is sustained by individual characters, and in the true folktale each individual character is significant to the story line. The hero is almost always alone when he sets out, even though he may be a prince or a king. He may be accompanied by a single servant, but this servant too has a function of his own,[19] and as a separate figure he is set off from his surroundings as visibly as is the hero.

A complete perspective is afforded by the juxtaposition and succession of narrative events rather than by their interlacement. Whatever in the real world forms an unfathomable whole or unfolds in slow, hidden development takes place in the folktale in sharply divided stages. The hero must accomplish three tasks in order to win the princess, but after that she is his once and for all: "And they lived happily ever after." "From that day forth the prince and princess lived without danger or harm."[20] Alternatively, the hero may lose his bride again, but not through her gradually turning away from him. Thanks to a certain infraction of form, usually the violation of a prohibition, she is stolen from him out of the blue, and then he takes to the road to find her again. Just as he lost her through a single mistake, he wins her back through a stroke of luck, usually at the third attempt after failing twice. No hesitation, vacillation, or half measures impede his progress or the folktale's sharp delineation of form. Right reactions or wrong reactions result in determined advances or equally determined evasions and retreats. Everything psychological is externalized onto the level of actions or objects (for example, as gifts that objectify a relationship) and thus is made distinctly and impressively manifest. Nothing remains vague or enigmatic.

Internally as well, this clear and purposeful conduct of the folktale, with its strongly colored, sharply outlined characters and its clean, ever-progressing story line, is distinguished by the most pointed effects. Its protagonists are assigned very specific tasks: they are to cure sick princesses, guard magic cows, build a golden bridge or a magnificent garden overnight, or spin a roomful of straw into gold; or they must fetch faraway magic objects, win fights against dragons and giants,.defeat an enemy army, ride up a glass mountain, or ride through the air to take a golden apple from the hand of the king's daughter. Whereas the antiheroes regularly fail and often pay with their lives—for the task is usually bound up with extreme forms of reward and punishment, such as the princess and the kingdom or death—the hero succeeds in doing the impossible. He always meets precisely those otherworld beings who know or are able to do just what is necessary to accomplish the task at hand. And while, with improbable certainty, his brothers treat the otherworld beings wrongly (not always evilly!), the hero, with equal certainty and without any vacillation, treats them correctly (not always benevolently!),[21] whereupon they give him the gifts that most precisely fit the special tasks with which he is confronted. If he later must fill up one or three bowls with seeds or lentils that have been scattered, he first meets some ants who now come to his assistance, or he knows—nobody tells us why—a charm that has the power to summon pigeons, as in the Grimms' version of *Cinderella* (KHM No. 21). If he has to fetch a little ring out of the sea, the one who is indebted to him is a fish; if he has to tend colts that run away in all directions, he previously—long before he knew the difficulties that he would encounter—made friends with a fox, a wolf, and a bear whose powers are just sufficient to round up the herd.[22] If he sets out to search for a magic horse or for his lost sisters and brothers, along the way he meets a hermit or some old women who are able to give him the exact advice he needs. For all that, these advisers are by no means omniscient, but they always know whatever needs to be known at the given stage of the plot.[23]

If the hero must accomplish several tasks, the folktale frequently gives him a special helper or special charm for each. All-encompassing magic objects that can conjure up practically anything desired are rare. The hero comes in possession of a table that sets itself with food, a donkey that drops gold, or a cudgel that leaps from the sack when summoned—without exception, things endowed with a single, specific faculty. If he does happen to receive an all-encompassing magic object, he never makes full use of it.[24] The magic objects of the folktale are not meant to be used playfully, to amuse the hero or provide him with amenities or riches; rather, they are to help him get through certain very specific situations that arise in the course of the plot. Often they are made available to the hero only when he is in urgent need of them. Often he gets them long before, but even then he uses them just once or three times, at the moment when an otherwise unsolvable task calls for it. Before and after, the magic object remains unused. Sometimes the hero completely forgets what he possesses, and only in the face of the urgent task does he remember it. Once he has accomplished the task, the magic device is usually no longer mentioned; it disappears from the story. It was merely an expedient without any intrinsic value and without interest for its own sake. For the characters of the folktale not only lack a geographical and personal frame of reference; they also lack a material environment. The gifts they receive are not everyday possessions but merely flash upon the scene when the plot calls for them. Whenever the story requires, at specific turning points, they show up without fail.

In the folktale everything "clicks." The antihero falls asleep at the very moment when the crucial reconnaissance has to be made, whereas the hero wakes up just in time—not a moment too early nor a moment too late.[25] He arrives in the royal city on the very day on which his bride, after long refusals, is to be married to another man. Not until the flames of the pyre are licking about their sister do the twelve brothers rush up to save her, for at that very moment the seven years of enchantment have elapsed and the brothers are free.[26] Every time limit tends to be either exactly used up or exceeded by a narrow margin.[27] At the risk of having his head cut off and impaled on a stake—extreme and starkly graphic punishments are in accord with the folktale style, sharply defined and averse to all nuances— the boy who has to watch over the herd of foals and bring them back in time delays so long each night that he does not get back to the witch's courtyard until the stroke of the bell. "When the bell struck eight he was in at the gateway, and as the old woman slammed shut the portals of the gate they all but cut off his heels. 'That was just in time,' the boy breathlessly exclaimed as he entered the house. . . ."[28] Expressions such as "no sooner had he . . ." (*kaum hatte er*) or "no sooner were they . . ." (*kaum waren sie*) are idiomatic expressions that continually recur in the folktale. In French tales a favorite phrasing is, "The giant was before him in a trice" (*Le géant ne tarda pas à paraître devant lui*) or "His wife was about to . . ." (*Sa femme venait de . . .*).[29] In Rhaeto-Romanic, it is "*Bagn tgi . . .*" (see p. 50 below). The marvelous runner who goes to fetch the hero the water of life falls asleep on the way back, and it is only shortly before the expiration of the allotted time that the hero's other helper, the marksman, spots the runner and awakens him, so that he arrives in the very nick of time.[30]

Not only moments of time are marked out with the utmost precision. The hero, the antihero, subordinate characters, and props also precisely accomplish or fail to accomplish the specific narrative task that is assigned to them. Objects and situations fit together to a T. "Everything fit her as if it had been tailor-made"—the marble trousers, the shirt of dew, and the shoes of pure gold, which actually were not woven or forged for the princess at all.[31] The youngest son sets out: "He wandered on and on without asking the way, until he came and stopped at the very spot where his brothers had rested years before."[32] The coffer that is destined to fall into the hands of the hero is offered to him for 500 piasters—exactly the amount he has saved. When he later throws his wife into the river, fishermen have just cast their nets and pull the woman out of the water instead of fish. Instantly a Turk appears, the heroine tricks him out of his horse, and she rides "hour after hour, from mountain to mountain," until at nightfall she comes "unawares" to—of all places—the distant kingdom of her royal father. Her father has just died, and since he has left no legitimate heir but the lost daughter, the officers of the kingdom decide that "in this night of such severe snow and cold that anyone lying outdoors would perish, the first person to be found outside the gates of the city should be made king." The princess has just arrived there in her fisherman's clothes, and still unrecognized, she is crowned king.

There is nothing truly magical in this Albanian folktale,[33] but the abstract stylization by which the different situations dovetail is just as miraculous as any physical magic; in fact, it is far more unrealistic. Attempts at magic and a belief in magic are part of the real life of human beings. In contrast, the folktale favors abstract composition in drawing its lines.

Rounding out the abstract style[34] of the folktale are a number of other characteristics. Since most of these are familiar and have been studied for a long time, they will merely be touched on here.

The folktale works with fixed formulas. It favors the numerals one, two, three, seven, and twelve—numbers of firm definition and originally of magic significance and power. The hero or heroine either is alone or is the last member of a triad (the youngest of three children); less frequently, heroes or heroines appear as a pair, as in the tale of *The Twins or Blood-Brothers* (AT 303). This-worldly as well as otherworldly helpers and opponents appear on the scene singly (sometimes in the form of prominent leaders of a people, such as the king or prince) or in groups of three, seven, or twelve—but the latter only if their number does not at the same time serve to form episodes, for the triad rules the development of episodes. A succession of seven or twelve episodes would destroy the overall clarity of design and stability of form. The numbers seven, twelve, and one hundred are no more than stylistic formulas that embody the principle of plurality in formula-like rigidity. By contrast, pairs and triads have a structural function as well.[35] Some folktales are bipartite, with the recovery of the lost spouse forming the second part. But it is above all the triad that is predominant: three tasks are accomplished in succession; three times a helper intervenes; three times an adversary appears. Since each gift that is presented to the hero is usually intended to resolve a single episode, the folktale prefers to mention three gifts, not seven, let alone twelve.

To a high degree, this preference for formulaic round numbers imparts a rigid quality to the folktale. Unlike the real world, the folktale knows nothing of numerical diversity and randomness; it aspires to abstract certainty. This aspiration is also evident in the verbatim repetition of entire sentences and long paragraphs. If the same event is repeated, it makes sense to state it in identical terms. Many storytellers avoid variation, not out of incompetence but because of stylistic demands. Strict word-for-word repetition, when it occurs, is an element of the folktale's abstract style. Such rigidity corresponds to that of the metals and minerals that abound in the folktale. Sentences repeated verbatim at certain intervals also have an articulating role. Like a rhythmically recurring ornament, they ring out in the corresponding parts of the story at certain specified points.[36] A similar result is produced by the recurrence of an individual expression within a sentence. When the word "bellissimo" is repeated four times in the course of eleven lines (*un bellissimo cavallo, un bellissimo prato, un bellissimo giardino,* and once again *un bellissimo prato*),[37] we perceive an articulating effect that would not be produced if different adjectives were employed in each instance. Thus, the folktale almost spontaneously achieves a consistency of style of the sort that modern aesthetics requires of true works of art: the special character of the overall composition is reflected in its constituent parts, right down to the individual verbal expression.

The fixed metrical and rhyming tags and the opening and closing formulas of the folktale likewise serve to stabilize its form. The clear single-strandedness (*Einsträngigkeit*) of its plot signifies an emphatic refusal to portray directly anything that is many-layered or inter-penetrating. Only a single sharply defined plot line is evident. A necessary correlative of the folktale's single-stranded plot is the division of this plot into more than one episode (*Mehrgliedrickeit*). Legends, which are nonepisodic, give us space, depth, stratification, atmosphere. The narrow line of the folktale plot is sustained by a plurality of episodes. Things that normally interpenetrate and co-exist are detached and isolated, and their projection onto the story line makes them successive.[38] Thus, single-strandedness and episodic structure are the foundation and the preconditions of the abstract style.

When every year the queen gives birth to a child, or even to two boys, each with golden curls and of ideal beauty, this is as much part of the abstract style of the folktale as when a gold coin or a golden ring falls out of the heroine's mouth with her every (!) word, or when the dragon must receive a human sacrifice every day or every month, or when a dwarf appears with each note of a magic flute. All of the tsar's daughter's husbands die on the very first night.[39] The folktale king is prepared to kill all of his twelve sons if he is given just one daughter; or he seeks and finds in his kingdom "eleven girls, each the perfect likeness of his daughter in countenance, figure, and size" (KHM No. 67). The sister who is to rescue her brothers keeps absolute silence unfailingly and steadfastly for seven years. Ninety-nine suitors are beheaded, but the hundredth accomplishes the task and wins the princess. A house in the forest is made entirely of gingerbread or of human bones. All this is abstract representation that is far removed from any concrete reality.

The folktale has a liking for all extremes, extreme contrasts in particular. Its characters are completely beautiful and good or com-pletely ugly and bad; they are either poor or rich, spoiled or cast out, very industrious or completely lazy. The hero is either a king's son or a peasant's son; he is either a scurfhead or a golden boy (frequently first one and then the other, by an abrupt change); the princess mar-ries the country bumpkin; the horse is either golden or mangy; and the gift that the hero receives either shines like gold or looks com-pletely undistinguished. Whereas the antiheroes are magnificently provided with clothes and horses and cake, the hero must get by with crusts of bread and lame nags (or he asks for no more than these).[40] The contrasting figures of the folktale are coated with either pitch or gold; cruel punishments and the highest rewards are set off against one another. The hero or heroine is usually an only child or is the youngest of three; frequently he or she appears as a simpleton or ashmaid. The folktale often tells of childless couples, or then again of couples with a superabundance of children. Parents die and leave their children all alone. The hero and heroine are young, but their advisers are old men and women. Hermits, beggars, and one-eyed persons come on the scene. Shabby garments or stark nakedness appear side by side with precious furs. The hero may be as strong as a bear, but the helpless heroine is surrendered to a monster. Otherworld beings take the forms of giants or dwarves. Heinous crimes, fratricide, infanticide, and malicious slander are everyday features of the folktale, as are gruesome methods of punishment. The folktale's many prohibitions and strict conditions contribute in no small way to the elaboration of its precise style.

Miracles are the quintessence of all extremes and bring the abstract style to its most pointed expression. When the peasant woman, the maid, and the mare all eat part of the talking fish, each gives birth to a son the very next night.[41] The magic ointment immediately restores the blind man's sight and brings the dead back to life.[42] Sick people are cured by being dismembered and put back together again.[43] Abrupt metamorphoses dazzle the eye. "While he was asleep, the rose leaped down from his hat and turned into a beautiful girl who sat down at the table and ate up everything served."[44] The animal bridegroom no sooner casts off his hedgehog hide than he is revealed as a handsome young man.[45] "As the princess lay there they stuck a needle into her right ear, and immediately she turned into a bird and flew away."[46] The two states of being need not be internally related. The evil queen turns her three stepsons first into three brass candlesticks, then into three clods of earth, and finally into three wolves.[47] A fox is transformed into a beautiful shop;[48] a dragon turns into a boar, the boar into a hare, and the hare into a pigeon;[49] a witch changes into a bed or a fountain;[50] a princess turns into a lemon or a fish, then into a lump of silver, and finally into a beautiful linden tree.[51] A reed turns into a silver dress or into a dun horse.[52] A large castle can be changed into an egg and back again at will.[53] In a

Lithuanian folktale, the wolf says to the simpleton: "Slaughter me! Then my body will turn into a boat, my tongue into a rudder, and my entrails into three dresses, three pairs of shoes, and three rings." Subsequently, after the simpleton has made use of all these things, the wolf comes back to life and carries him and his princess to their destination.[54] Nothing is too drastic or too remote for the folktale. The more mechanical and extreme the metamorphosis, the more clearly and precisely it unfolds before us.

The abstract stylization of the folktale gives it luminosity and firm definition. Such stylization is not the product of incapacity or incompetence, but of a high degree of formative power. With marvelous consistency it permeates all elements of the folktale and lends them fixed contours and a sublime weightlessness. It is far removed from lifeless rigidity, for the rapid and emphatic advance of the plot is an integral part of it. The hero is a wanderer who effortlessly moves across vast expanses, often carried at the speed of the wind by flying horses, carriages, coats, or magic shoes. His progress is not arbitrary, however, for its form, direction, and laws are precisely determined. The diagrammatic style of the folktale gives it stability and shape; the epic-like forward progression of the plot gives it quickness and life. Firm form and effortless elegance combine to form a unified whole. Pure and clear, with joyous, weightless mobility, the folktale observes the most stringent laws.

4

Isolation and
Universal Interconnection

The one-dimensionality of the folktale—its astonishing insensitivity to the distance between the everyday world and the "other" world—accords with the depthlessness of its representation of reality in general. This depthlessness itself makes up only one aspect of the folktale's abstract, diagrammatic style. The dominant characteristic of this abstract style is the element of *isolation*.

The disconnection of folktale characters is evident at once in their lack of surprise when face to face with the numinous and their lack of curiosity, longing, and fear in encounters with otherworld beings. Isolated human beings and isolated otherworld beings meet, associate, and part; there is no sustained relationship between them. They only interact as participants in the plot and are not linked by any real and thereby lasting interest.

A depthless depiction of reality implies a need to isolate the figures portrayed. Whereas sculpture presents a combination of elements that cannot be taken in at a glance, a flat surface is detached and isolated in itself. The characters depicted in folktales have no inner life, no environment, no relationship to past or future generations, no relationship to time.

People and things are set off by sharp outlines that are never indistinct or blurred. Bright colors and a metallic luster make individual objects, animals, or persons stand out. The metallic or mineral quality of things lends them an immutable stability. The characters of the folktale are not made of flesh and blood, of some soft, adaptable, contact-seeking substance, but of a substance that is solid, rigid, and isolating.

The prevalence of isolation in the folktale becomes fully apparent when one considers the various characteristics of the abstract style. Folktales love all that is rare, precious, or extreme—that is, anything isolated. Gold and silver, diamonds and pearls, velvet and silk are expressions of the principle of isolation, as are the only child, the youngest son, the stepdaughter, or the orphan. It is the same with the king, the poor man, the simpleton; the old witch and the beautiful princess; the scurfhead and the golden boy; Cinderella, Allerleirauh,* the naked outcast girl, the girl who dances in the radiant dress. The protagonists of the folktale are not linked by a vital relationship to any family, people, or other kind of community. The only links between children, brothers and sisters, and parents are those that are established by the plot or by the principle of contrast. Folktale characters tend to become isolated in regard to external circumstances as well: their parents die and leave them all alone, or the parents are poor and abandon the children or let them go to the devil, or three brothers set off independently for foreign lands, or two brothers part and go their different ways. The characters of the folktale are thus separated from familiar people and familiar places and go out into the wide world as isolated individuals.

The folktale's representation of the plot is equally isolating. The folktale presents only pure action and foregoes any amplifying description. It provides a story line but does not let us experience its setting. Forests, springs, castles, cottages, parents, children, and brothers and sisters are mentioned only if the plot is dependent upon them; they do not serve to establish a setting.

This bare-bones story line, in turn, is divided into separate segments that are sharply divided from one another. Each episode stands alone. Individual elements need not relate to each other. The characters of the folktale do not learn anything, nor do they gain any experience. Heedless of the similarity of the situations in which they find themselves, they act again and again from their state of isolation. To the modern reader, this is one of the most striking and objection-

---

*The heroine of KHM No. 65. The name means "All-Kinds-of-Fur"; the equivalent heroine in English tradition is "Cap o' Rushes" or "Catskin."

able peculiarities of the folktale. If we succeed in comprehending this trait clearly and interpreting it correctly we shall come a good deal closer to the solution of the riddle called folktale.

In the Swiss folktale *The Griffin*,[1] the oldest of three brothers sets out to bring the apples of healing to the sick princess. On the way, "a little iron man" (*es chlis isigs Mannli*) asks him what he is carrying in his basket. "Frogs' legs," he replies, whereupon the dwarf says: "Well, that's what it shall be and remain." And the young man finds that there really are frogs' legs instead of apples in his basket. He makes this discovery, however, only when he is standing before the king and lifts the cover. Until then he did not look into the basket or check anything, and here we see another expression of the folktale's isolating technique. The young man then goes home and tells how he fared. The second son, however, takes no warning from this. He likewise sets out, meets the very same dwarf, and gives him false information, just as his brother did—not to pay him back, but simply because he does not relate his situation to that of his brother. When the youngest son, stupid Hans, subsequently reacts differently and gives a truthful reply, this is not because he has taken a lesson from the fate of his older brothers, but only because he has to react differently in keeping with his role.

Not only do folktale characters fail to learn anything from one another. They take no lesson from their own experience, either. Later in the same folktale about the Griffin, all three brothers set out again to accomplish a further task. When the "little iron man" reappears and asks about their business, the two older brothers carelessly and thoughtlessly lie to his face again. They are acting in isolation and take no heed of the previous situation. In the second part of the tale the protagonist meets another sick girl, but it never occurs to him to try out his apples of healing again; rather, he does as he is told and asks the Griffin for the remedy. Nor does the folktale itself have any need to remind us of the first cure. We have entered a new episode, and the events of the previous one have no continuing influence. The dwarf has no role in the second part of the tale and the protagonist never thinks of obtaining his assistance, nor does the storyteller pause to explain the dwarf's disappearance in any way.

Only nontraditional storytellers who lack a sense of the logical consistency and inner necessity of the isolating folktale style feel that they owe their listeners or readers an explanation in such cases.[2]

So Kurbads remained in the underworld. There was no help for it; he had to take up his club, buckle on his sword, and think of a way out. If he had only remembered the little flute that the gnomes had given him, perhaps they would have helped him. But that's how it is: when you are in most need of your wits, your mind is a blank.

This kind of storyteller disregards what to the true folktale is a matter of course: that there is no need for a folktale character to call to mind a former helper or a charm previously received or even used, for the hero, the helper, and the magic object are all isolated. While at any time they certainly *can* link up to each other, they *need* not do so.

From the magic mountain to which he has gained entry, the simpleton fetches everything that will help him to overcome dangers and accomplish tasks: sword, horses, and precious garments.[3] But once he passes the last test and wins the princess, the magic mountain is never mentioned again. The bride herself must now see to it that her shabbily dressed peasant bridegroom is outfitted with all he needs, for at this point the magic mountain, from which the hero himself could easily have fetched the most magnificent golden and silver garments, has dropped out of the folktale. The function of the mountain was to help the hero get through his adventure. As soon as he overcomes his difficulties, the mountain loses this function and the folktale does not assign it another one. To the folktale, it is a matter of course that the mountain is no longer mentioned. In the folktale of *The Griffin*, the swift ship that travels by land as well as by sea has accomplished its task as soon as it is built and delivered to the king who ordered it. It was the object of a difficult task, and this was its sole function; the tale has no charge to tell us what the king does with it and how and to what end he uses it. The folktale's isolating style forbids such elaboration.

In the Grimm brothers' version of *Cinderella*, the stepmother cannot understand how the girl was able to pick the lentils from the ashes so quickly the first time. Nevertheless, she does not think of watching the girl the second time. Nor does she ask any questions, not even when Cinderella succeeds in picking twice as many lentils from the ashes.[4] The kind sister faithfully reports what has happened to her in Frau Holle's realm, but the unkind sister takes note of the "model" only to establish a connection: she too must drop her bobbin in the well and then jump in. She realizes that she must imitate prior forms exactly, and so she jumps into the well only after she has dropped in the bobbin. In all subsequent situations, however, she behaves unlike her sister, as though she knew nothing of what had happened to her. The two brothers who go in turn to observe the golden apple tree "that has been blossoming and bearing ripe fruit every night" fall asleep at the crucial moment, "when the apples were just about to ripen," and thus they fail to see who is picking the fruit. On their return home they, too, report what has happened. But the youngest brother, whose turn it is the third night, takes no precautions to keep from falling asleep. On the contrary:

He got ready, carried his bed under the tree, and lay down to sleep. Toward the middle of the night he woke up and glanced at the tree. The apples were just about to ripen and the entire palace reflected their radiance. At that moment nine golden peahens drew near. . . .[5]

It is as though an invisible touch had roused the hero at precisely the moment when his brothers had fallen asleep on the preceding nights. He awakens not because those brothers are bad and this brother is good, for the tale gives no evidence of any kind bearing on their morality, but solely because he is the hero, the youngest, the isolated one, while his brothers are the antiheroes.

When the princess or her royal father wants to get rid of a suitor, they either set him a task that seems impossible to solve, or they send him to hell or to a battle in which he is meant to perish. When the hero accomplishes the task and avoids destruction, the taskmaster simply demands something new of him without explaining why the first accomplishment is now no longer sufficient. A young witch says to the prince: "I will clear away the dishes and the leftovers, and then we will go get wedding shoes. We will each go our own way to look for the shoes. If my shoes are prettier you must stay and live in my country. If yours are prettier I will follow you to your country." Thanks to a helper's advice, the prince is victorious. Nothing is settled, however. After dinner the next day the bride says, as though nothing has happened: "I will clear away the meal and the dishes, and then we will go get wedding clothes. We will each go our own way. If my gown turns out to be more beautiful you must stay and live in my country. If your garments are more beautiful I will follow you to your country." Again the prince finds the most beautiful clothes. This does not prevent the witch from beginning anew the next day after dinner, without the slightest explanation: "I will clear away the dishes and the leftovers, and then we will go get silver hair for the wedding. We will each go our own way. Should I have more silver hair than you, you must stay and live in my country. If you have more I will follow you to your country."⁶ There is no need for the speaker to modify the form or content of her speech to refer back to preceding events. She does not say, "This is not yet sufficient," but sets another task without a word of transition. In a realistic story with psychological depth this would be a shortcoming. Within the framework of the folktale it is a perfectly logical consequence of the abstract and isolating style.

When the folktale hero receives a gift from an animal he does not conclude that other animals could give him gifts as well. Rather, each time, in spite of all experience to the contrary, he stereotypically repeats the same incredulous question: "You are an ant, how can you help me?" "You are a bird, how can you help me?" "You are a fish, how can you help me?"⁷ The scurfhead who to all appearances never left home nevertheless presents his oldest brother with the apple of the tsar's daughter. In the next scene, however, when he asks the second brother as well, "Brother, would you like me to give you something I found?" this brother answers just like the first: "You scurfhead, what could you possibly have found here in the ashes?"⁸ The simpleton who is off to court the tsar's daughter is joined on the way by precisely those helpers who are capable of accomplishing the task set by the tsar—a marvelous eater, a marvelous drinker, and a man who sows soldiers in the field like grain. Even though the hero is aware of the attributes of these comrades, he bursts into tears whenever he is confronted with a new task: "What shall I do now? I cannot eat up a single loaf!" or: "What in the world shall I do now? How can I muster the soldiers!"⁹ Even though the witch gives the boy a drink to take along while he tends some foals and the drink puts him to sleep and almost prevents him from accomplishing the task, the hero nonchalantly drains the bottle the second and third times, not greedily, but enjoying it, for despite the similarity of circumstances, he does not establish any connection with the previous episode.[10]

The emperor's daughter who will marry only the man who can guess her three birthmarks—the star on her forehead, the sun on her bosom, and the moon on her knee—has her terms made known "all over the world." But when she wants three piglets from a swineherd and he asks her to unveil her face in return for the first piglet, to show him her bosom in return for the second one, and to lift her dress "so that he could see her knee" in return for the third one, she "immediately" complies each time and then is "overjoyed" to receive the piglet.[11] To maintain that her craving for the piglet made her lose her composure and all circumspection would be a misinterpretation. There is no more trace here of psychological agitation than in any other true folktale. Rather, within each episode the princess acts quite consistently and composed—but only within the individual episode, to be sure. When the business at hand is concerned with obtaining a piglet, the story highlights only this event; everything else remains in the dark. Other matters *may* but *need not* come to light. The swineherd, who is concerned not with selling the piglets but with winning the princess, thinks only of the terms that have been set. But she on her part does not see that the swineherd's blunt and specific requests are aimed precisely at the three points of her courtship test.

To the folktale, her conduct is by no means strange. The folktale has no need to justify or explain her lack of understanding, for there is no question here of psychological blindness, but of a screening that is a matter of course in the folktale. It is a question of the isolation of situations and conduct. For this reason the boy does not try to conceal his intentions by finding some vague, harmless, or distracting way of phrasing his requests. He can safely comply with the laws of the folktale; he can call a spade a spade without having to fear that the princess will make the obvious connections. He does not even consider such a possibility; rather, he too pursues his objective in isolation, without considering the possibility of failure or danger —that is, without being aware of the abundance of different possibilities that would be self-evident to any real person or any figure of a realistic story. The folktale isolates people, objects, and episodes, and each character is as unfamiliar to himself as the individual characters are to one another. What the princess did or wanted at another time, in another context, need not play the slightest part in her present activities and plans. The different actions or fortunes of a single individual are sharply delineated from each other. Just as the folktale can physically cut its characters to pieces (a sick princess, for example) and then precisely and flawlessly put them back together, it can cut them apart and put them back together again mentally as well. The unity of the protagonist is split: only a single one of his components may be evident and may take effect in any one scene, and yet in the end all these components form one integral whole.

In the same way it is typical of the isolating style that immediately after a person has lost a limb, the folktale no longer pays any attention to its loss. In several Russian variants of the Brunhilda folktale, the feet of the suitor's helper are cut off, even his legs may be cut off up to the knee, but he gathers them up and sets off on his way.¹² The griffin is "omniscient" and knows the answer to any question, but it does not notice when an eavesdropper under its bed plucks three of its feathers, one by one (KHM No. 165). The bride endowed with magic powers helps the hero, but in situations in which she herself needs those powers she suddenly appears to have forgotten all about them (KHM No. 113). In a different version of the same folktale the water of life is used in one instance, but on another occasion when it is as urgently needed, it is no longer mentioned.¹³ The husband or brother whose wife or sister is slandered does not consider asking her to answer these reproaches herself. Without questioning her, he condemns her to death or exile.¹⁴ The prankish Norwegian tale of *The Marble Goose Egg* portrays the "changeling" who is hatched from the goose egg as a person of immense strength but quite normal appearance, yet he lifts stones "that were so big many horses would not have been able to drag them, and he put all of them, whether big or small, in his pocket."¹⁵ At birth, the Bear's Son in a folktale from Lorraine is "half bear and half man," but in the subsequent course of the narrative this peculiar dual nature is never again recalled.¹⁶

To overcome one obstacle, the hero is given a gift; the next obstacle he overcomes without any gift at all, as though this were a matter of course (KHM No. 127). Otherworld donors impart certain faculties to folktale protagonists by elaborate procedures, while the same protagonists possess other faculties that are just as astonishing, and no explanation is offered. They are given certain information by unknown advisers, while they themselves know other things that are just as secret, and we never learn how they came by their knowledge. But even in regard to otherworld helpers, we are not told how it is that they know or can do precisely what is required by the hero. They are not integrated into any system; their power is not derived from higher beings, such as God or the devil. They emerge in isolation and act in isolation, and the basis and nature of their existence is never unveiled. Usually they appear separately and have only a single task—either to help the hero, or to pose difficulties for him. After this they disappear into the void. As for the bewitched individuals with whom the hero has dealings, we are seldom told why or by whom they have been enchanted. All that is important is that they are now under a spell, so that they can help or harm the hero and he can rescue them. The backward-leading lines of the folktale need not be illuminated. Often the shape into which people are enchanted has nothing to do with their nature: a prince can be turned into an iron oven (KHM No. 127). The gifts presented by otherworld beings need have no specific relation to their donors: a star can give bacon, or an eagle can give clogs.[17] Each element is isolated in itself.

Side by side with all-encompassing magic objects that would seem to render all others superfluous, the folktale nonchalantly introduces special ones that are used only in certain situations. One of the hero's two companions knows "all that happens in the world," but when the hero dies, this faculty goes unmentioned. It is a bleeding hair that informs his two companions of this misfortune, and they also have to make inquiries as to the manner of his death.[18] The folktale hero who finds himself in a difficult situation much like one he has encountered before does not think of his former helpers; he is just as helpless and troubled (or untroubled) as he was the first time. And indeed, sometimes he is assisted by the same helper and sometimes by an entirely different one.

The isolating tendency of the folktale is especially evident in the questions that are posed to villains who have been unmasked. In the Grimm brothers' folktale of *The Goose-Girl* (KHM No. 89), the unfaithful maidservant who has made her mistress change places with her and who has married the prince herself is asked by the old king what should be done with a woman who had done such and such— and he recounts the exact circumstances of her particular offense.

She replies without thinking twice: " 'She deserves nothing better than to be stripped naked and put in a barrel that is studded with sharp nails, and two white horses should be harnessed to it to drag her up and down the street to her death.' That woman is you,' said the old king, 'and you have pronounced your own punishment.' "

The stepmother in the folktale *The Three Little Men in the Wood* (KHM No. 13) is asked: "What should be done to a person who drags another person from bed and throws him into the water?" She, too, passes a cruel sentence on herself without being curious about the fact that the question describes her own crime in specific terms. In any other kind of narrative the person being questioned would be bound to see the connection at once and would take evasive action, but not in the folktale.

Some people believe that the folktale poses such specific questions out of incompetence. "The simple people who cultivate the folktale are not very experienced in describing the same event in different terms or in subordinating a particular situation to a comprehensive scheme"; for this reason—so the argument goes—they are incapable of any more general formulations such as: "What does a person deserve who has killed someone else?"[19] This type of explanation fails to acknowledge that, to the folktale, more general formulations would not be an advantage but a deficiency. After all, the appeal of the situation consists of the fact that the evil woman must pass judgment on precisely her own case. Only the folktale can take the liberty of asking the question in a way that exactly corresponds to events; for to the folktale it is a matter of course that the person who is being interrogated will comprehend the question in isolation, without connecting it to the preceding episodes. Only the folktale's comprehensive structure and its all-pervasively isolating style make this possible. It is not awkwardness and clumsiness, but a highly developed sense of form that permits the folktale this effect.

Requirements of form come into play in the folktale's repetitions as well. All orally transmitted literature is fond of repetition, as it provides a point of rest for both the speaker and the listener. The verbatim repetition of certain formulas in Homer's works not only serves the convenience of the rhapsodist; it is also a sign of what remains constant in the midst of all fluctuations of external phenomena. Homer does not nod. The recurrence of identical elements intensifies the impression of solidity and reliability that is produced by the epic style. Behind what is transitory, the listener senses what is permanent. In the folktale, too, there occurs verbatim repetition, even of longer passages. In a version of the tale of *The Monster (Animal) as Bridegroom* (AT 425A) recorded toward the end of the 1920's in Schleswig-Holstein, the prince who has been searching for his three sisters comes to a castle, and a lady sitting in front of the door asks him who he is.[20]

He is de Prinz von Sizilien, seggt he. Un se is de Prinzessin von Sizilien, seggt se, se hett awer keen' Broder hadd. Do wiest he er den Truring, un do nimmt se em mit rin na't Sloß un snackt mit em. As de Klock twölf is, seggt se, nu mutt he na de anner Stuv rin. "Min Mann is 'n Löv," seggt se, "de kunn di wat don." Dunn kümmt de Löv ok al an. "Wenn min Broder hier so weer," seggt se, "schußt du den wul wat don?" "Ne, wo is he?" "In de anner Stuv." "Denn lat em mal herkamen." Un de Prinz kümmt rin, un se snackt tosamen. Klock een seggt de Löv: "Prinz von Sizilien, Sie müssen weichen oder ich zerreiße Sie!" He vill je weg, do seggt de Löv; "O, warten Sie noch ein wenig," und he gifft em dree Haar ut sin' Nacken un seggt to em, wenn he mal in Not kümmt, denn schall he de Haar nehmen un schall segg'n: "Löwe über alle Löwen und König über alle Könige, komm und steh mir bei!" Denn is he bi em un helpt em. Denn mutt he je weg na de anner Stuv hen.

(He is the Prince of Sicily, says he. And she is the Princess of Sicily, says she, but she has never had a brother. Then he shows her the wedding ring, and she invites him into the castle and talks with him. When it is twelve o'clock, she says that he must now go into the other room. "My husband is a lion," she says, "he can harm you." And sure enough, the lion arrives. "If my brother were here," she says, "would you harm him?" "No, where is he?" "In the other room." "Then tell him to come here." And the prince comes in and they talk together. At one o'clock the lion says: "Prince of Sicily, leave now or else I will tear you to pieces!" He wants to leave, but the lion says: "Oh, wait a minute," and he gives him three hairs from his neck and tells him that if he should ever be in distress, he is to take the hairs and say: "Lion over all lions and king over all kings, come and help me!" He will then stand by him and help him. Now the Prince of Sicily has to go away into the other room.)

Everything is the same when the hero meets the second sister:

He is de Prinz von Sizilien, seggt he. Un se is de Prinzessin von Sizilien, seggt se, se hett awer keen' Broder hadd. Do weist he er den Truring, un do nimmt se em mit rin na'n Sloß un snackt mit em. As de Klock twölf is, seggt se, nu mutt he na de anner Stuv rin. "Min Mann is de Vagel Greif," *seggt se, "de kunn di wat don." Dunn kümmt he ok je an. "Wenn min Broder hier weer," seggt se, "schuß de den' wul wat don?" "Ne, wo is he?" "In de anner Stuv." "Denn lat em man kerkamen." Un de Prinz kümmt rin, un se snackt tosam. Klock een seggt de* Vagel Greif: "Prinz von Sizilien, Sie müssen weichen, oder ich zerreiß Sie!" He will je weg, do seggt de* Vagel Greif: "O, warten Sie noch ein wenig," un he gifft em dree* Fellern *ut sin' Nacken un seggt to em, wenn he mal in Not is, denn schall he de dree* Fellern *dehmen un schall segg'n: "Vogel Greif über alle Vögel Greife und König über alle Könige, komm und steh mir bei!" Denn is he bi em un helpt em. Denn mutt he je weg na de anner Stuv hen.*

(He is the Prince of Sicily, says he. And she is the Princess of Sicily, says she, but she has never had a brother. So he shows her the wedding ring, and she invites him into the castle and talks with him. When it is twelve o'clock, she says that he must now go into the other room. "My husband is the Griffin," she says, "he can harm you." And sure enough, he appears. "If my brother were here," she says, "would you harm him?" "No, where is he?" "In the other room." "Then tell him to come here." And the prince comes in and they talk together. At one o'clock the Griffin says: "Prince of Sicily, leave now or else I'll tear you to pieces!" He wants to leave, but the Griffin says: "Oh, wait a minute," and he gives him three feathers from his neck and tells him that if he is ever in distress, he is to take the three feathers and say: "Griffin over all griffins and king over all kings, come and help me!" He will then stand by him and help him. Now the Prince of Sicily has to go away into the other room.)

The few changes in the two passages (here indicated by Roman type in the Low German text) are in part necessitated by the subject matter and in part so insignificant that they only accentuate the over- whelming drive toward verbatim repetition, which is at odds with a spontaneous tendency for variation. The same situation is repeated in the third episode, the encounter with the brother-in-law who is a whale. Three times the identical situation is repeated—an unrealistic construction in itself. Three times we find the same words. Not only the direct discourse is characterized by formula-like rigidity; the nar- rative links, which could be expected to be conducive to a less rigid formulation, likewise strictly adhere to the words that were used before. This is all the more noteworthy since the literary versions of the same folktale do not proceed in this manner at all. Basile (IV, 3) relates only the first encounter in detail and shortly dismisses the two others by referring back to the first. Musäus reports everything at some length but indulges in much variation in regard to subject matter and phrasing.[21]

Of course, some popular storytellers, too, show a natural delight in variation and reformulation. Just as a tendency toward repetition and a tendency toward variation vie with one another in the subject matter of the folktale—the dragon fight is repeated three times, but the first dragon has one head, the second dragon three, the third dragon six, for example—contrary tendencies appear on the verbal level as well. Charms, the magic effect of which depends on their wording, always tend to recur in the same form. That there is something magical about the folktale as such, so that strict stylization is therefore appropriate to it, is hardly an article of belief among many present-day narrators. The delight in telling tales and in varying the wording may be predominant. Wilhelmine Schröder, from Majenfelde and Brackrade (of the district of Eutin), who in 1928—at the age of 73—told the tale of *The Monster (Animal) as Bridegroom* in the version just cited, may be an exception in regard to the extreme repetitiveness of her phrasing. But the feeling has remained alive that each episode should be self-contained and should not be abridged through mere reference to a preceding one. This is expressed in a particularly delightful way when the storyteller—*per farvela più breve, capite* ("to shorten the tale, you see")—refers back to the preceding account, but nevertheless tells everything once again, albeit in modified form.[22] In folk narratives based on Musäus, one can perceive that the folk version tends to revert spontaneously to a uniform stylization. In 1937, at the age of 66, Plasch Spinas—a cobbler and sexton by trade, and a Rhaeto-Romanic storyteller not entirely averse to variation—told *Reinold la marveglia*.[23] The names and the plot are clearly derived from Musäus, but in contrast to Musäus, Spinas gives the three crucial episodes a nearly identical wording. Whereas in the first episode, Musäus chose indirect discourse and varied the narrative in other respects as well, the passages of direct discourse correspond to one another in the tale as told by Spinas:

"My dear sister Adelheid, if you are in there, come out, for here is your brother Reinhold the Marvel, who has come looking for you." Thereupon a woman stepped out of the cave and said: "What, you, my brother, the son of Count So-and-so?" "Yes," he said. "Then flee for God's sake, for when my husband comes—tonight he is still a bear—he will devour you. If you had come tomorrow, he would have been a man." He said: "Yes, but where shall I flee, for I don't know which way to turn? . . ."

And so on. The subsequent episode reads:

"My dear sister Louise, if you are up there, come down, for here is your brother Reinhold the Marvel, who has come looking for you." Thereupon a woman appeared at the rim of the nest, looked down, and said: "What, you, my brother, the son of Count So-and-so? Then flee for God's sake, for tonight my husband is still an eagle—if you had come tomorrow, he would have been a man—and if he catches you, he will pick out your eyes." "Yes, but where shall I flee, for I am totally lost in this forest and do not know which way to turn? . . ."

The third episode, which was again worded differently by Musäus, proceeds similarly. Not only the passages of direct discourse but also those of third-person narrative tend toward verbatim repetition: "No sooner had he left than the bear appeared" *(Bagn tgi lè sto davent reivigl igl urs).* "No sooner had he left than the eagle appeared" *(Bagn tg'el è sto davent, reiva notiers l'evla).* "No sooner had he left than the fish appeared" *(Bagn tg'el è sto davent, reival igl pesch).*

Rigid, verbatim repetition is an element of the folktale's abstract style. At first glance, however, such repetition seems to run counter to the normal tendency toward isolation. How could the sentences of an episode recur word for word in subsequent episodes if each were really isolated, without relation to the next? Here it becomes apparent that we must distinguish between external and internal isolation. One and the same stylistic impulse permeates the entire folktale. From this impulse all episodes arise; it keeps on forming the same characters, so that they all resemble one another, while at the same time each stands alone. But outwardly, to the eyes and ears of the audience, each part of the folktale is self-enclosed and self-sufficient. For this very reason, and only for this reason, the folktale can take the liberty of describing the same situation two or three times in precisely the same terms. If the individual episodes were not self-contained so that they seemed sealed to the outside, as it were, the former passage would have to be restored while being recalled, and this would result in either abridgment or variation. Slight variations occur frequently; they are even favored by accomplished storytellers, who like to bring their large vocabulary into play. But even episodes whose wording is varied are self-sufficient. An inner resistance to abridgment is still current among storytellers today. True storytellers do not find satisfaction in such phrases as "Everything happened just as before." Their objective is to conjure up an image, regardless of whether it is the same image used in the previous episode or a similar one. No allusion to previous episodes can accomplish this; only a full and complete narration will do, whether by exact repetition of the entire wording, or by variation through new words or through sentences of different construction.

Visible isolation, along with the invisible interconnection of all things (*Allverbundenheit*)—these may be considered the principal characteristics of the folktale. Guided by an invisible hand, isolated characters are joined in harmonious cooperation. These two aspects are interrelated. Only that which is not rooted anywhere, neither by external relationships nor by ties to its own inner being, can enter any association at any time and then break it off again. Conversely, isolation derives its meaning only from the capacity for extensive interconnections. Without this capacity, the externally isolated elements would lack support and fall apart.

The phenomenon of repetition first led us to an appreciation of this reciprocal relationship. Only because each episode, each character, indeed each type of conduct is sealed off from others is it possible and even desirable for identical events to be reported again and again in identical words. Abridgment and, to some extent, variation break down the self-sufficiency of the episode concerned by making it appear dependent on preceding ones. In reality, however, the episode is not dependent on what precedes it but on the same invisible formative impulse that created the prior narrative as well, which itself obeys strict laws. The subsequent scene is not a copy of the preceding one; it resembles the other so closely only because it originates from the same source. In relation to each other, the two scenes are isolated, but both spring from the uniformly creative will that permeates the whole. Unrelated to each other, they are nevertheless formed and sustained by one and the same center.

The entire abstract style of the folktale, as I have described it, is subject to the law of isolation and universal interconnection. The abstract style works out the individual elements of the tale plainly and distinctly, separates them with unnatural clarity, and imparts stability and well-defined contours to bodies and their movements. In short, it isolates things in a way that would be inconceivable in a realistic story. However, this very isolation makes possible that effortless, elegant interplay of all its characters and adventures with which the folktale delights us and which is as fully a part of its abstract style as is the tendency toward isolation.

If the princess wanders unawares to—of all places—her father's kingdom and arrives at its capital city at the very moment when he has died and when the officers of the kingdom have decided that the first newcomer should be made king, this is not chance, but precision. The same precision assures that the true bridegroom always returns on the very day on which the bride, after one or many years, is to marry another man. The wife of a man who has been spirited away to the otherworld arrives there after long wanderings at the very moment when he is about to marry another woman; on her way, the sun, the moon, and the winds give her just the things she needs to prevent this second wedding at the last minute. Stojscha, the hero of a Yugoslavian folktale, needs only to lie down and put one of his three kerchiefs on his face ("so that the flies will not sting him"—it would never occur to him to do this deliberately as a distinguishing sign), and directly there appears, on her way to fetch water, the very sister who once embroidered the kerchief.[24] The merchant's daughter sets out looking for a prince who has been wounded and spirited away. She "accidentally" overhears a conversation between a giant and a giantess as she goes along, and thus she learns the only means of curing her spouse.[25] Allerleirauh wanders all night long, then sits down in a hollow tree and falls asleep. No sooner has she woken up than the king, who happens to be hunting in that forest on this very day, meets her and takes her along with him (KHM No. 65). Tschuinis, the hero of a Latvian folktale, is sentenced to be hanged, "but it so happened that at that very moment a prince passed by the gallows" to ransom him.[26] A prince sets out "to look for a girl who comes from nowhere," for he does not wish to marry anyone else. "On his way he came to a large forest," and there he met a girl of radiant beauty; he "asked her, where she was from and what she was waiting for. She replied that she belonged to nobody, she was from nowhere, and she was waiting here for her good fortune. Thereupon he said: 'Oh! that's exactly the girl I'm looking for, a girl who comes from nowhere; but do you want to be mine?' 'I do.' So he took the ring off his finger and gave it to her, and she gave him hers."[27] The folktale does not make him ask several times in vain; the very first girl he comes upon is the one he is looking for.

The tsar's son who goes to look for the golden peahens "set out all alone on his journey into the wide world and after long wanderings came to a mountain range, stayed overnight with a hermit, and asked him whether he could tell him something about the nine golden peahens. The hermit replied: 'Ah, my son! You are lucky; God has shown you exactly the right way. It is no more than half a day's journey from here.' "[28] In this instance, too, we are not told anything about the prince having made previous inquiries; the folktale makes it appear as though the prince on his long journey (which he is undertaking without any companions) is now posing his question for the first time—and this hermit is the precise man who can give him the information desired.

In the Grimm brothers' folktale of *Rapunzel* (KHM No. 12), the thorns gouge out the prince's eyes; he then wanders about blind, and yet he manages to come upon the very place where Rapunzel and her two children have found shelter in a far-off land. Even though this ending does not originate in a true folktale but is the invention of a French lady of letters of the seventeenth century,[29] it graphically demonstrates a recurrent characteristic of the folktale. The blind man stumbles across whatever he is searching for; the person who is lost finds the way that leads him to what he needs. The peasant's boy marries the princess; the scurfhead marries the king's daughter; Cinderella marries the prince; and the outcast girl without hands wins a knight or a king. The youngest of three brothers, the simpleton, the scurfhead, the ashboy, Peau d'Âne,* the orphaned girl, the step-

---

*Literally "Donkey-Skin"; the heroine of the French version of AT 510B (*The Dress of Gold, of Silver, and of Stars*) that was put into rhyme by Charles Perrault in 1694. The English equivalent is "Cap o' Rushes" or "Catskin," the German equivalent "Allerleirauh."—*Trans.*

child, or (on the other hand) the prince or the princess—these are the heroes or heroines of the folktale. Of all people it is they, the isolated ones, who are blessed by fortune. Of all people it is they, because they are isolated, who are invisibly linked to the essential powers of the world.

Much has been made of the prevalence of chance in the folktale. One could also say that the folktale is a form of literature that knows no chance.

It has been called chance[30] that in the folktale of *The Twelve Brothers* (KHM No. 9) the heroine is sentenced to death and is led to the pyre at the very moment when the three or seven years of her brothers' enchantment have elapsed, so that they can rush up and pull their sister unharmed from the fire. But this exact dovetailing of the situations is nothing but a consequence of the folktale's abstract style. The two processes that to outer appearances are completely isolated—the heroine's royal husband has finally lost his trust in her, and the term of enchantment has finally elapsed—are coordinated in an invisible way. Their coincidence is not chance, but precision. One is tempted to say that the composer of the folktale has arranged it just so. But if we said that, we would depart from the principle of giving first consideration only to the work itself and its mode of operation. We do not inquire about the intentions of the authors of the tales, for it is difficult to determine to what extent they consciously construct their stories and to what extent they unconsciously trace out the objects of their vision. It is fascinating enough to try to penetrate the work itself and its mysteries; questions about its creator are not an immediate concern. When we question the work, the folktale, and note how it is recorded, we immediately perceive with absolute clarity that within the framework of folk narrative construction, the coincidence of the two events is quite natural. We do not perceive it to be "arranged" or "accidental," for it is completely in accord with the style that permeates the folktale as a whole. Such coordination is made possible through the elements that dominate everything else in the folktale as well: the tendency toward isolation and the capacity for all-encompassing interrelationships.

Isolation and the potential for universal interconnection are two correlates. It is not in spite of their isolation but because of it that folktale characters are capable of establishing contact with any other character. If they were bound by permanent human ties, as are the people and objects of legendry, they would not be free at any given time to establish the ties that are required by the situations in which they are placed. In legendry people are embedded in their family and in their village community. They have fixed habits of living and thought; they have emotional ties that are never broken. The inanimate objects of legendry derive from contexts that are in accord with their nature, and each object has its appropriate function. Bread, cake, and cheese exist to be eaten. Their amount can increase or decrease; at worst, they can turn into worthless or disgusting substances such as toads. In the folktale, on the other hand, there occur apples that summon mermaids, eggs that fulfill any wish, and pears that make people grow long noses that fall off again, as if a switch were turned on and off.[31]

In legendry a merman may dispense gold or pearls but never cheese, which is obtained from the little man who lives in the wild, or a crystal, which is obtained from the mountain dwarf, or a magic thread, which is obtained from the little woman who lives in the forest or bogs. Subterranean beings give a peasant tools and provisions, while the same beings give his wife yarn and bobbins and present a knight with weapons or jewelry and showpieces. Everything is coordinated with everything else. In the folktale a star may dispense cheese; a mule may give a straw hat; an eagle may give wooden clogs. A prince and a country bumpkin receive identical gifts of a magic sword, a magic horse, and a golden garment, and with identical ease they marry any maiden they want, whether princess or goose girl. The closest things or persons may remain unrelated, while distant ones may establish a connection, for everything in the folktale is equally close and equally distant. Everything is isolated, and precisely on that account it is capable of establishing any kind of relation. In legendry, when a person descends to the bottom of the sea or a lake, he or she does so to live with the merman or the water nymph or to assist the merman's wife in childbirth.[32] The folktale hero, on the other hand, unconcernedly follows a herd of cows or mares that are going to graze at the bottom of the sea.[33]

The individual elements of legendry are closely meshed; they are too specialized to fit in anywhere they might be needed. As parts of permanent communities, they are tied to a given place and are not ready to enter into new relationships that correspond to ever-changing situations. The elements of the folktale are completely isolated; they easily break away from any existing relationship and are free to enter into a new one. But the new relationship, too, remains a mere coupling and is broken as easily as it is established. The hero forgets parents and homeland unless the plot leads him back to them. The princess forgets her husband, the prince forgets his bride. Gifts are no longer mentioned as soon as there are no longer any tasks that call for them. Helpers disappear into the void as soon as the difficulty in question is overcome. The only remaining tie that binds the hero—marriage—is of interest to the folktale only so long as the bride and groom can again be separated. Once a marriage is firmly established, the story breaks off. A wedding is not the folktale's goal, only its endpoint.

Especially prominent manifestations of isolation and universal interconnection are gifts, miracles, and truncated motifs.

The gift is a central motif of the folktale. Since folktale characters lack an inner world of their own and as a consequence cannot really make any decisions of their own, the narrative must seek to propel them on their way through external impulses. A task set by the king, or a father's order, or a case of extreme need, or a young woman's test of her suitors leads the hero to undertake a journey out into the world. Tasks and dangers provide him with crucial opportunities. Gifts, advice, and direct intervention by otherworld beings as well as human beings help him on. In legendry a person who wishes to win a treasure or redeem the soul of someone who has died is on his own; the course and outcome of the undertaking depend on the strength or weakness of his character. In the folktale the hero would not attain his objective without help, in particular the help of otherworld beings. And this support is lavished on him. Otherworld beings come up to him out of nowhere and present him with their gifts. And the reason that he is able to secure the use of these gifts, at the same time as they are eluding the antihero, is often simply that he is the hero. He need not be any more ethical than his brothers or companions—he may even treat otherworld beings in a more niggardly fashion than they do, he may go back on his word,[34] or he may be an out-and-out sluggard—but it is still he and no other to whom a fish discloses a charm that will effortlessly provide him with anything he wants.[35] The heroes of the folktale meet the right helpers and press the right button to obtain help, whereas the antiheroes frequently do not encounter any helper, and if they do, they react wrongly and forfeit the gift. The hero is the lucky one. It is as if invisible ties linked him with the secret powers or mechanisms that shape the world and fate. Without his being aware of it, his behavior is shaped by cogent laws. As though drawn by a magnet, he, the isolated one, pursues his confident course and follows the precise line of conduct that the framework of his cosmos demands of him.

The gift the hero receives is the means by which he is linked to otherworld beings and human beings. The fact that it is given so regularly and that it is received by the hero so effortlessly demonstrates his capacity for establishing any kind of relationship whatever. If the folktale prefers to have its protagonists attain their objectives only through a chain of helpful measures, it does so not only as a means of prolonging, intensifying, and varying the plot, but also as a visible image of the way in which all things are interconnected. With ease, as though it were a matter of course, the hero establishes contact with any number of helpers. At the same time, however, gifts reflect the hero's isolation. His ties to the outer world are not direct or lasting but are based on a gift, preferably a distinctly visible, isolated object that does not become part of him but that he receives, uses, and subsequently discards as something external. In all essentials the folktale hero handles even intangible gifts as if they were objects. Personal characteristics, abilities, and injuries do not become part of his or her overall personality but play a role only if the external situation calls for them.

The gifts of the folktale, unlike those of legendry, do not arise from a relationship that has been previously established and that is consciously experienced and recognized, nor do they originate from otherworld beings familiar to the locale. They are given whenever a particular task calls for them, and they are offered—usually by total strangers—all of a sudden or as a result of an *ad hoc* relationship that is established quickly and rather sketchily. The hero does not receive them by virtue of any special ties—heroes do not have such special ties—but by virtue of his or her capacity for establishing any kind of contact. The gift, which itself is a self-contained, isolated figure, represents in sharp outline unknown spheres of existence and the latent ties between them and the isolated hero. Like the hero who receives it, the gift is of normal shape, neither dwarfish nor gigantic nor distorted; it has the appearance of a commonplace object, but its potential for effective action is enormous. Thus, the gift itself is the purest reflection of external isolation and potentially universal interconnection. It is invisibly linked with the whole cosmic system, just as the hero is linked through it. That the hero receives it—that he can and must receive it—is evidence of both the great privilege and the limitations of the folktale hero. He is blessed, and he is supported and propelled by forces that are superior or that serve a superior plan, without being chained to relative values by any subordinate link. Again on account of his isolation, however, the folktale hero is also totally at the mercy of powers that are completely unknown to him. He is not capable of intentionally establishing these beneficial connections but remains dependent on their being presented to him. For he is not a human being who seeks and anticipates, but a mere figure in the plot who neither sets his own goals nor attains them through his own efforts and accomplishments.

Miracles, too, are at the service of the folktale hero, but again not in such a way as to give him control over them. Unlike the magician or sorcerer of legendry or of the real world, he himself does not work miracles. He does not compel anything to occur. Miracles, too, happen to him. The folktale hero is not himself a magician; he receives magic objects that come from the beyond. He never obtains them by entreaty, he does not think about them at all—but whenever he needs them, they are granted. Miraculous gifts are merely an intensification of folktale gifts in general. It is sufficiently miraculous that the hero always receives the very thing he needs. The exact correspondence of gift and task, gift and predicament, as well as the dovetailing of all situations, is part of the folktale's abstract style, of which miracles are the ultimate, most perfect reflection. Everyday gifts—food that must be thrown to pursuing animals, for example, or pieces of clothing that are to catch the eye of the prince or of a female rival—are at least used for a purpose corresponding to their nature. However, the feather that does any kind of work;[36] the egg that fulfills any wish;[37] the horse that not only gives prudent advice but also builds bridges;[38] the magic charm that can bring about anything desired[39]—these are gifts that have no discernible relation to a context, and yet they point to latent connections. The fantastically marvelous gift is equal to any situation without being essentially appropriate to it. It is attached to nothing, and yet it has a capacity for establishing any kind of relationship; it is the purest manifestation of the principles of isolation and universal interconnection that animate the folktale from beginning to end.

In hagiography, miracles are conceived of and revered as revelations of an omnipotent God. In legendry, they are bewildering and obscure signs of a significant and dangerous otherworld, and they fascinate or frighten humankind. But in the folktale, miracles are an element of the plot, and it is within the plot that they have their meaning. For this reason they are accepted without surprise or agitation, as though they were a matter of course. The question of who brings them about or whose powers are thus implied has little interest; nothing is said of the source or origin of the miracle for its own sake. The legend and the saint's legend conceive of miracles as an exciting inroad of the numinous into the secular world. To the folktale, however, miracles are matter-of-fact occurrences (although not everyday ones). They fit freely and easily into the abstract style. The folktale conceives of *everything* as isolated and as capable of universal relationships, and miracles express both of these qualities with special clarity and vividness. The miracles of folktales are realized simply and directly, independent of external preconditions. Still, they abide by a hidden system of laws that is universally effective, even if nowhere explained by the folktale.

The folktale does not confirm or explain anything; it simply represents. Its characters do not know of the interrelationships of which they are part; they only let themselves be sustained by these interrelationships and thus they attain their goal. Otherworld beings do not function as parts of a harmonious whole that can be taken in at a glance. Since we perceive them only when they intervene in the action, we catch only a small part of their activity, but this part fits harmoniously into the plot structure. The folktale plot itself appears to be self-contained and yet is dependent on invisible systems. There is much that makes itself felt without becoming visible. Some things become visible but remain incomprehensible. The nature and standing of the actors are of interest only insofar as these matters are important to the plot. This is why there is an abundance of truncated motifs.

The truncated motif (*stumpfes Motiv*) is an integral part of the folktale. After all, *stumpf* means "encapsulated, isolated." All of the examples of the technique of isolation cited above are examples of the truncated motif as well: the magic mountain that suddenly is no longer of use; the courtship conditions that are unwittingly violated; the loss of the feet that in the very next episode is no longer taken into consideration, and so on. On account of their isolation, individual elements need not make themselves felt in all the ways we expect, but in one or several aspects they may remain truncated. Significant effects that we know to be wrapped up with them do not come about; the actors' origin, their history, and their previous and subsequent fate remain in the dark. When otherworld beings and their gifts project into the action of the tale, they play their part with great precision, but their origin and destination, the reason why they are able to intervene at the right moment, and their true nature in general are all matters that remain unexamined. Riches that are obtained merely serve to advance the action or bring an episode to a close; the folktale makes no use of the possibility of exploiting them further. The hero's special abilities may be attributed to his miraculous birth, to gifts presented by otherworld beings, or to a successful apprenticeship, but they may also remain totally unexplained. One person understands the language of animals because he has eaten magical food, another person understands it because a wise tutor has taught him, but a third simply understands it and we are not told why. What in one folktale is the gift of an otherworld being—a table that sets itself with food, a magic flute, or a magic sword—is in another folktale simply found.[40]

Even in instances when a donor appears, truncation is not done away with, it is only moved back a step. The donor himself is for the most part someone unknown: a little man, an old woman, a helpful animal, a dragon, a troll, a fairy. Unlike the donors who appear in myth or in saints' legends, he cannot be classified unequivocally within any familiar system. Angels, the devil, God, and the apostles do not truly belong in the folktale but are artificial substitutes for the folktale's real otherworld beings; their more favored place is in farcical folktales (*Schwankmärchen*), which generally are amenable to the mixing of elements. The invisible hierarchies to which the true otherworld beings of the folktale belong remain unknown. The fates of bewitched persons are made only partially visible. The folktale does not aspire to be systematic. All of the elements of its plot are sharply defined, but the lines leading up to them remain invisible, and in that sense one can speak of all folktale motifs as being basically truncated.

Until now scholars have not distinguished between truncated motifs and blind motifs, and the two terms have been used interchangeably. From the point of view of the folktale, however, a specialized use of the two expressions seems imperative. I shall employ the term "blind motif" for an element that is completely functionless, the term "truncated motif" for an element that, while not entirely lacking a function, remains unconnected in one or another essential respect.

Totally blind motifs are not especially common in the folktale. Brothers or companions that have no duties whatsoever, gifts that are not put to any use, and strange characters that do not play any role appear only infrequently. Ferdinand the Faithful finds a quill pen and picks it up at the behest of his magic horse, then loses it again, and a helpful fish later returns it to him, yet despite all these complex events, the quill remains without any function (KHM No. 126). Of the three magic halters that a Swiss simpleton receives from his dead father, he uses only the first two.[41] In addition to two other gifts that subsequently play an important role in the plot, the kind sister of a Danish version of *The Kind and the Unkind Girls* (AT 480) receives a third one: she is told that whenever she lets down her hair it will begin to dawn. This third gift does not have any influence on the story and never enters into the action.[42] The second of three brothers in a Carinthian version of *The Dead Man as Helper* (AT 505) plays no role of any significance, while even the oldest brother is no true protagonist but has only subordinate importance. In this tale an evil colonel makes the attempts on the hero's life that are usually made by the brothers.[43]

Most often, totally blind motifs of this kind are probably the result of faulty oral transmission.[44] A certain episode or feature is forgotten, but its agent is retained because he, she, or it is an integral part of a fixed stylistic formula: three brothers, three enemies, three princesses, three gifts. When one folktale is combined with another, certain characters become superfluous, but fixed stylistic formulas retain them just the same. It is immediately evident, however, that even though the origin of the blind motif can often be attributed to faulty oral transmission, forgetfulness, or the intermingling of tales, its tenacious retention cannot be explained in this way.

An element that has lost its meaning could easily be discarded. If it is embedded in a stylistic formula or if it has visually evocative qualities, even a person with little imagination should have no difficulty in providing it with a new justification in place of the forgotten one, for familiar motifs and ready-made figures of speech that could be used to this end are always available. But the folktale refrains from either dropping the element or justifying it anew. To the folktale even the element that has lost its meaning is meaningful, for it is suggestive of secret systems that project just this tip into the realm of the tale. Gifts that remain without function still reveal the hero as an individual who is specially endowed and who, in spite of his isolation, is in touch with secret powers. Brothers who do not play any role are significant at least as contrasting figures who are unblessed. In the folktale, blind motifs are not mere ballast but are a sign of interrelationships that are still operative even though unseen.

Truncated motifs reign supreme in the folktale. They are decidedly not the result of faulty transmission alone; from the outset they form an integral part of the folktale style. In the French version of *Cinderella* told by Perrault, the fairy godmother tells the heroine to hurry away from the dance before twelve o'clock. Móirín, the Irish Cinderella, is given a similar order by a helpful kitten (into which her dead mother has been transformed).[45] Aschenputtel, the Cinderella of the Grimm brothers, is not given this command by anyone yet acts as though this condition had been set (KHM No. 21).

No reasonable person will call the German tale mutilated on this account. The truncated passage need not be a result of imperfect transmission; it is representative of the true folktale. Without knowing why, Cinderella acts in accord with cogent laws. So does the merchant's youngest daughter, who incomprehensibly asks her father for a gift that is totally worthless but not easily attainable, a gift that without her foreknowledge will then bring her into contact with the animal prince.[46] A wise woman teaches Two-Eyes the charm that provides her with a table that sets itself; without having received any instructions, however, she recites a second charm with which she puts her sisters to sleep (KHM No. 130). How did she come by her knowledge? The folktale does not tell us. Nor are we told what gives the father of the bride of the animal prince the idea of providing his daughter with matches. He does not seem to know that with these matches the animal prince can be disenchanted.[47] A Serbo-Croatian folktale hero is informed by his horse that in order to accomplish his task he must ask the king for nine days' provisions, along with nine buffalo hides, nine balls of yarn, and nine needles. In addition, however, on his own initiative, he requests nine measures of millet.[48] How does he know that he will need these as well? Several times in a Bulgarian version of the tale of *The Lazy Boy* (AT 675) the tsar's daughter wants the hero to make use of his magic charm, but each time he replies: "Give me a fig, if you want me to say it." (As her sole dowry, the princess received a few clusters of figs from her father.)[49] We are not told why the hero wants a fig or what he subsequently does with it; the sexual significance that may once have underlain the image has vanished[50] and the motif lacks any foundation. But the folktale loves such free-floating motifs, for they point to regular patterns that are covertly operative.

The conduct of Cinderella, of Two-Eyes, and of the Lazy Boy can be seen as not arbitrary, but dependent on these hidden laws. The folktale actually seeks out the truncated motif. It speaks of another world as if it were drawing on a matter-of-fact familiarity with it, but unlike the legend or the saint's legend, it does not rivet its attention on the supernatural. Rather, it speaks exclusively of the events in which the hero is involved and which are subject to otherworld influences, whether supportive or antagonistic, by which the hero is affected without fully recognizing their nature and interrelationships. The folktale itself does not disclose these interrelationships. The hero does not perceive them, but he participates in them. He does not control them, but they help him on his way. Everywhere we see intervening in the plot for a brief moment characters whose own course remains inscrutable. Inexplicably, unknown forces exert their influence on the action. The serene, clear, and self-assured folktale thus abounds in partly truncated, truncated, and blind motifs, all of which are sharply outlined at the same time as they neverthe-less constantly point to a world that is never portrayed as a whole. While they make us sense the way in which all parts of this world are invisibly interconnected, they themselves only exist in appar-ent isolation.

The central representative of isolation and universal intercon-nection in the folktale is the hero. All figures depicted in the folktale, objects as well as persons, are isolated and capable of entering into any kind of relationship. But only for the hero does the latent capacity for establishing relationships turn into actual relationships. The anti-heroes sleep away their opportunities, fail to perceive them, waste them, or never encounter them at all. The secondary characters exist on the periphery and are important only as foils or as partners in the plot. The story spotlights the narrow path taken by the hero. It shows him to us as he moves along in isolation, equally ready to establish any essential relationship and to break off any relationship that has become inessential. To him, the tasks, difficulties, and dan-gers that confront him are nothing but opportunities. As he encoun-ters them, his fate becomes a significant one. Whatever assistance he receives does not serve to satisfy his desires—the folktale depicts anything but a land of milk and honey—but only helps him pursue his fated way.

By following his own course, the hero also rescues other people, often without intending to do so. Alternatively, he may help other people without any self-interest in mind, and precisely by acting in this way he may pave the way to his own goal. In the end the hero is forced to behead his helper—a white horse, for example—and to his surprise he thereby disenchants a prince who has been under a spell.[51] The princess throws the Frog Prince against the wall in order to kill him, but disenchants him through this very act (KHM No. 1). Con-versely, in order to ransom an abused corpse, the simpleton care-lessly gives away the goodly sum of money that was supposed to last him on his travels in search of the water of life. Precisely because he loses sight of his real goal and only does justice to the needs of the moment, he obtains—unawares and unintentionally—the only helper who can lead him to his goal and whose powers are sufficient to save him from the machinations of his false brothers.[52] At the very mo-ment when heroes act in total isolation, they unknowingly find themselves at the point of intersection of many lines and blindly satisfy the demands that the total structure places on them. They think only of others, and thus they reach their own goal. The folktale hero resembles those who find the Grail precisely because they are not searching for it. The folktale tends to frustrate enterprises that are carried out systematically and circumspectly: en route, the Uriah letter is rewritten by robbers who give it the opposite meaning.[53] On the other hand the poor peasant boy who sets out to solve the impossible task without assistance, without preparations, and without any specific skills is given help, and the powers guide him toward his goal. The blind, the disinherited, the youngest child, the orphan, the lost—these are the true heroes of folktale, for they are isolated and are thus freer than anyone else to engage in what is truly essential. As isolated individuals, they live as mere outlines or figures (*in Figuren*). Without knowing their true place, they act in a way that expresses an essential or unmediated relationship (*aus wirklichem Bezug*). The folktale gives perfect expression—not in fully concrete form, to be sure, but in abstract stylization—to what Rilke perceived and sought for but never attained.[54]

> *Heil dem Geist, der uns verbinden mag;*
> *denn wir leben wahrhaft in Figuren.*
> *Und mit kleinen Schritten gehn die Uhren*
> *neben unserm eigentlichen Tag.*
>
> *Ohne unsern wahren Platz zu kennen,*
> *handeln wir aus wirklichem Bezug.*
> *Die Antennen fühlen die Antennen,*
> *Und die leere Ferne trug. . . .*
>
> (Hail to the spirit that can unite us;
> for we do truly live in figures.
> And with little steps the clocks go on
> alongside our essential day.
>
> Without knowing our true place,
> we act out of real relationship.
> Antennae feel antennae,
> and the empty distance bore. . . .)

5

Sublimation
and All=Inclusiveness

The abstract, isolating, diagrammatic style of the folktale embraces all
motifs and transforms them. Objects as well as persons lose their individual characteristics and turn into weightless, transparent figures.

The motifs of which the folktale consists do not originate in the
folktale itself. Many are realistic motifs drawn from the sphere of
social life (*Gemeinschaftsmotive*): courtship, wedding, poverty, or-
phanhood, widowhood, childlessness, abandonment of children,
fraternal conflict, or loyalty of brothers and sisters, of friend and
friend, of servant and master. They reflect relationships between two
people, between a person and an animal, or between a person and
his environment, and they originate from everyday events. Most
likely they first found expression in simple factual accounts.[1] Aside
from these everyday motifs, the folktale makes use of supernatural
and magical ones such as the release of persons from a spell; the sum-
moning of distant helpers; and encounters or confrontations with
revenants, with otherworld animals, with all manner of dragons and
fabulous creatures, and with fairies, trolls, giants, and dwarves.
These motifs pertain to a reality that is experienced as numinous or
magical, and their true home is in legendary accounts. The folktale
assimilates them just as it assimilates the subjects of everyday life.
Both are given a form appropriate to the folktale, and only thereby
do they become "folktale motifs."

The magical origin of many elements of the folktale is demon-
strable. Rhyming incantations are spoken; charms are transmitted;
magic pictures, garments, and mirrors appear; blood-magic, name-

magic, and sympathetic magic are practiced. The tendency of things to go in threes (*die Dreizahl*), to which the entire folktale is subject, is vestigially of magical power. At the same time, however, one can immediately see that genuine magic no longer has any place in the folktale. Magic is inseparably bound up with psychological tension. It is realized through incantation, through an act of will. This is precisely what is lacking in the folktale.

When the hero rubs or warms the feather, hair, or scale that he has received from a helpful animal, his act does not involve the slightest effort of will aimed at forcing the animal to appear. The animal itself only seems to respond to a pre-agreed signal; it does not seem forced. Even in those instances in which the hero scorches the fin of the fish or the wing of the ant, as he has been told to do, we do not see the fish or the ant suffer from the heat. When the creature rushes up "at once," with mechanical promptness,[2] we do not by any means conclude that it was painfully coerced but take its appearance as a quite natural expression of the folktale's abstract style.

Nor does the folktale employ magic based on numbers. We never hear such orders as "You must say it three times." Every charm produces its effect as soon as it is uttered; every magical gesture takes effect with effortless surety. There is no need for strained repetition, for magical trebling. The triad has become a stylistic and structural formula. Similarly, incantatory rhymes adapt themselves easily and gracefully to the folktale style.

> "*Vör mi hell' un achter mi dunkel,*
> *dat kên Minsch sucht, wo ik hen funkel.*"[3]
>
> ("Dark behind me, before me bright,
> no one will look where I shine my light.")

> "*Weh, Weh, Windchen,*
> *Nimm Kürtchen sein Hütchen.*"[4]
>
> ("Blow, blow, little wind, I say,
> Take little Kurt's cap away.")

> "*Mazza bacucca,*
> *Batti batti sulla zucca.*"[5]
>
> ("Hammer, Emptyhead,
> Rap him on his gourd!")

The magic power that was originally inherent in the meter (*Wéh, wéh, Windchen*) is no longer much in evidence in the texture of the folktale. The folktale is unaware that magic requires *effort*. All magic is realized effortlessly. The little flute is sounded, and with every note there appears a gnome. Nothing illustrates the weakening of the element of magic more clearly than such playful pluralization. Comparative research has put us in a position to designate the three drops of blood in *The Goose-Girl* or the calling of the name in *Rumpelstiltskin* as magical motifs, but this is only because it has derived the concept of this magic from elsewhere. Such a concept could not have arisen from the folktales in question, for they bear hardly any trace of the truly magical.[6]

Originally mythic motifs have undergone this same weakening and transformation. Homer still emphasizes Odysseus' fear and trembling as the hero sets out for the realm of the dead. Folktale heroes enter otherworld realms (which they no longer experience as truly otherworldly) with equanimity. Scylla and Charybdis and the Clashing Rocks still call to mind the terrors of the ancient gates to the otherworld.[7] In the German folktale, on the other hand, the twin gates that the witch slams shut just graze the heels of the hero, who slips into the enclosure "just as the clock struck eight"—that is, at the utmost limit of the allotted time.[8] What was once a mythical experience has become a mere element of form that is used to show the extreme precision of events. In myths the hero is helped by a goddess who is devoted to him. In the folktales of antiquity she has already become a kindly little old woman.[9] In modern European folktales the grandmothers, wives, housekeepers, or even grandfathers[10] who are found in the company of otherworld monsters (or of robbers) no longer show any trace of the mythical helpers' strong ties of sentiment to the hero.

We have already seen that in the course of time everything truly numinous has disappeared from the folktale. Otherworld encounters take place, but the experience of otherness is lacking. Hans Naumann claims that in the black, white, iron, and stone characters depicted in the folktale, pre-animistic demons of the dead are to be recognized.[11] Giants and dwarves, too, are brought into relation with the realm of the dead. Originally, enchantment into a strange form was probably a veiled reference to death,[12] as was the act of falling asleep.

Frequently, animals are dead people who have changed form. But in the folktale, any such transformation is reported in a matter-of-fact manner, if at all, and it is never made to seem ghastly. The uncanny quality and the indefinable power of the numinous are absent. In the folktale, giants and dwarves, people made of stone or iron, and figures who are all black or all white do not give rise to the shudder that the presence of the supernatural excites. Rather, by virtue of the definition and clarity of their size, shape, color, and material composition, these beings have become representatives of the folktale's extremely stylized form.

Old rites, customs, and practices can be traced in the folktale, but only the ethnologist can detect them. Only the ethnologist will see the tower in which the folktale heroine is imprisoned in tales of the *Rapunzel* type (AT 310) as equivalent to the puberty hut of primitive cultures. Only the ethnologist will see the oft-repeated task of cutting down a forest in a single night and replacing it with a fruitful garden or a castle to be a survival of what was required of a suitor back in the times when fields were tilled with hoes: "To clear a field and build a house."[13] When a folktale hero is locked into a chest, trunk, or basket, this action may have its origin in an initiation rite. But all this is not directly evident in the folktale. Towers, chests, trunks, and extreme tasks all function as elements of the folktale's abstract style.

Sexual and erotic subject matter is equally emasculated in the folktale. Courtship, wedding, married life, and a desire for children are central motifs, but there is no true eroticism. When the swineherd asks the princess to bare her bosom and then show him her knee, neither he nor she betrays the slightest erotic feeling. "She undid her bodice at once, and when he had seen the birthmark on her bosom, he gave her the second piglet."[14] The two persons have nothing but their immediate objectives in mind (that is, they view them in isolation): he wants to accomplish the assigned task, and she wants to obtain the piglet. Of the desire to see or exhibit the body, to which we must attribute the origin of the motif, not the slightest trace has remained. Nudity, too, is portrayed in an entirely nonerotic manner in the folktale. As a counterpart to magnificent clothing, it is an element of a style that delineates things as absolutes.[15]

In the folktale, children are conceived with the same effortless ease with which they are given birth. There is no pain during their delivery, no excitement at their conception. "Lying on her back, the empress was fast asleep. The prince approached her gingerly, kissed her over and over, and lay with her; then he took the ring off her right hand and the stocking off her left leg and made a mark on her knee. He then hurried off to the galley, the crew quickly weighed anchor, and the boat sailed off."[16] Or in a Low German tale:[17]

When he saw the princess lying there, she looked so beautiful that he forgot all that the sentry had told him, and he went to share her bed. However, her bedclothes covered her from head to toe. At once he took out his knife, snipped off a little piece of cloth, and tucked it in his pocket. After he had lain with her a little while—though she never woke up on this account but remained fast asleep—he got up again. And he took a slip of paper and wrote down his name and where he was from and that he was the son of a certain king. And he put the slip of paper in a little crack under the table.

In a manner that is sharply imagistic (vividly outlined) but nevertheless totally nonsensual and unrealistic, a Danish folktale depicts the fateful events of a couple's wedding night: "Once upon a time there was a king who had a magnificent queen. When they were married and went to bed the first night, there was nothing written on their bed. But when they arose they found an inscription informing them that they would not have any children."[18] As a last possibility of sublimation, the folktale introduces—as usual—the miracle. The hero need only say a charm and the tsar's daughter, whom he sees standing at the window, is at once with child.[19]

Aside from the events that clearly pertain to the affairs of love, the folktale abounds with motifs and images that originally had an erotic meaning—the motif of the animal bridegroom, for example. "The princess told her father that she would only marry a man who could turn into a beast of prey or other animal."[20] The symbolism of folktales of the type of *Amor and Psyche* (AT 425A and related types) is weakened by the fact that at the crucial moment, every time, the animal bridegroom turns into a young man. The folktale no longer understands its own symbols (or, better, the symbols that it employs). This is especially evident in the dialogue concerning the lost key: without hesitation, the folktale has the hero ask the question that can be meaningfully posed only by a woman.[21] In like manner, even the Frog Prince's request to be allowed to share the princess's bed can be told and taken in quite innocently, by adults as well as children. If a real name is hardly ever ascribed to the disease from which the many sick daughters are suffering, this is not because the folktale deliberately intends to conceal. It is a stylistic tendency: the folktale does not individualize. The original meaning of the disease, however, is obvious: the princess suffers lovesickness and pines for her loved one. "On the same evening that he saw her picture, the princess saw his, and all at once she took to bed. 'Alas,' she said, 'Where can I find him?' And the doctors did not understand her malady."[22] Those who tell or listen to the folktale usually do not understand it, either. The folktale itself no longer understands its own meaning. For all of its motifs, from the numinous, magical, and mythic, to the sexual and erotic, to the ordinary ones of daily life, are equally emptied of their substance.

Ordinary motifs are portrayed in the same way as are all the others. Everything is presented to us in clear, neatly delineated images. Sensational and thrilling events are related as routinely as are the simple relationships and functions of everyday life. In a voice devoid of tragic overtones, the folktale tells of murder, violence, blackmail, betrayal, slander, incest, and the lamentable death of the princess's numerous ill-fated suitors. The ninety-nine heads that are chopped off and impaled on stakes have a purely ornamental effect; the rigidly formalized pluralization alone precludes all feelings of empathy or compassion. No fault can be found with the ill-fated unsuccessful suitors, all the same. The prince who rescues Sleeping Beauty is no more pure or noble than his predecessors; he only fares better because at this very moment the hundred years have elapsed, whereas all the preceding princes did not happen to hit upon the right moment and thus got fatally tangled in the thorns.

Generally speaking, the popular idea that the folktale identifies the good with beauty and success and the bad with ugliness and failure cannot be accepted without qualification. Such correspondences frequently occur, but they are not indispensable; the folktale is not bound to actual ideals of such a kind. The hero does not have to be a good-natured simpleton; he may also be a sly trickster. He is not forbidden to lie, to go back on his promises, or to engage in violence.

The princess in *The Frog Prince* is certainly very beautiful, but she is by no means a model of kindness when she finally tries to get rid of the frog by throwing it with all her might against the wall. In cold blood Aschenputtel (the German Cinderella) allows her two doves to pick out the eyes of her two stepsisters, one after the other. Snow White's evil stepmother (or mother) is anything but ugly; rather, she is "the most beautiful woman in the land" and is eclipsed only by Snow White herself. For the characters depicted in the folktale are not *types*, but mere *figures*. The type is still closely related to reality. The figure is nothing more than a vehicle for the plot; the only requirement it has to meet is to be distinctly visible and extremely well-defined. The folktale's millers, bakers, soldiers, and officers of state are anything but "typical" millers, bakers, soldiers, or officers of state. They do not typify a profession but exhibit traits that for the most part could be found as easily in one trade as in another. Consequently, their roles are easily interchanged: in one tale the coachman plays the same role that in another tale is played by the minister of state or the colonel. The golden spinning wheels, the glass shovels, and the golden geese of the folktale are not typical spinning wheels, shovels, and geese. The tools and objects of the folktale need not have their proper function but rather may produce any kind of magical or nonmagical effects that have little to do with the nature of these things in reality.

It is thus not only the numinous dimension of human experience that has vanished from the folktale, but also the worldly. The act of giving advice, an important element of human community life, becomes a mechanical device for promoting the plot. Just like tasks, conditions, acts of assistance, and gifts in general, acts of advice spur on the folktale hero, who has no inner promptings of his own. In contrast to what happens in real life, advice does not originate from an active relationship but rather may come into play with effortless ease at any stage of the plot. At any moment the folktale is prepared to introduce a character who can give advice. The folktale audience is accustomed to the frequent appearance of wise men, hermits, godmothers, servants, animals, and otherworld beings who possess special knowledge. Their helpful advice has come to be regarded as a familiar prop, a formula. In much the same way, we no longer perceive excess or immoderation in the excessively immoderate terms of courtship that are posed; rather, we matter-of-factly accept them as highpoints of the ornamentally clear folktale plot. Such courtship tests originate either from excessive jealousy on the part of the woman's royal father or from her own state of anxiety, whether this anxiety is an expression of her fear of marriage or her desire for a superior ("heroic") suitor, or both of these factors (as with the Brunhilde motif). But the folktale sublimates these dark psychological processes into brightly lit images that figure in the plot.

The antiheroes of the folktale are weightless counterparts to the hapless, tormented, grievously unsuccessful protagonists of legendry. The clairvoyants of legends (children born on a Sunday or during a special period in Lent) do not appear in the folktale. It is not those who are important, privileged, or marked who are singled out as the heroes of folktale, rather it is those who are carefree and isolated. Likewise, the special position of the youngest child has become an element of pure form. We may speak of "the weight of the stern" (*Achtergewicht*),[23] but within the overall framework of the folktale we recognize this as an expression of the principle of isolation. In the folktale, the real origins of this special position—the internal and external reasons why the youngest child is preferred and is discriminated against by its parents, sisters, and brothers—are no longer evident. Even the direct symbolism of the figure of the child (the child, orphan, foundling, or abandoned one as an embodiment of all that is isolated yet universally sheltered, of present weakness and potential strength, of all that finally fulfills its original promise)[24] is not felt with the same immediacy as it is in myth precisely because in the folktale the figure of the child, the youngest brother or sister, or the orphan is viewed as just one of many stylistic elements of similarly directed force.

The way that all folktale motifs are emptied of their usual substance is both an advantage and a disadvantage. The folktale loses in concreteness and realism, in nuance and in fullness of content, and in ability to express the deeper dimension of human experience and relationships, but it gains in formal definition and clarity. "Emptying" (*Entleerung*) also means sublimation. All elements become pure, light, and transparent and join in an effortless interplay that includes all the important themes of human existence.

The folktale's power of sublimation allows it to incorporate the world. The folktale becomes world-encompassing *(welthaltig)*. Albert Wesselski has claimed to be able to distinguish between realistic stories, legends, and folktales by correlating them with the respective motifs characteristic of each: realistic motifs with realistic stories, supernatural motifs with legends, and miraculous motifs with the folktale.[25] He fails to see that the folktale is not distinguished by a particular type of motif but by its special way of formulating its story. It takes its motifs from realistic stories, from legends, from myths, and at times directly from the real world as well, but it transforms all of them. By taking away their substance, sublimating them, and isolating them, it gives them the characteristic form of the folktale. There are no true folktale motifs; rather, any motif, whether worldly or miraculous, becomes a "folktale motif" as soon as it is incorporated into the folktale and is handled in the folktale's characteristic manner. Thanks to the folktale's abstract style, the search for eleven young women who resemble the princess down to the last hair, originally a worldly motif drawn from the sphere of social life, is no more or less "miraculous" than any motif that was originally numinous, such as an encounter with a dwarf or with a talking animal. As soon as they are taken up by the folktale, the numinous motifs found in legendry—journeys through the air on flying horses or pigs or encounters with otherworld beings or creatures of the underworld, for instance—assume a quite different aspect. Their materials are the same, but the new form gives them a folktale-like character. If the hero meets an old man who can give him special advice, originally this motif was not in the least miraculous. However, when it is assimilated to the abstract style (for the adviser knows precisely what kind of support the hero needs), it becomes much more "miraculous" and "folktale-like" than the far more fantastic motifs found in legends—encounters with disfigured corpses, for example.

There are realistic motifs *(Gemeinschaftsmotive)* and there are numinous motifs (Wesselski's *Wahnmotive)*, but properly speaking there are no miraculous motifs *(Wundermotive)*. Miracles are the culmination of the folktale's isolating and sublimating style. To all intents and purposes, any motif incorporated into a folktale becomes a miraculous motif.

The folktale prefers certain motifs because they are especially suited to its style. It delights in kings, princesses, orphans, and step-children, in radiant garments and humble nakedness. It presents its hero with all kinds of advice and gifts, preferably of a kind that will transport him effortlessly across the depthless surface of the plot. It likes to present contrasting figures side by side with the hero. Again and again, the action revolves around courtship, the acquisition of a kingdom, the release of persons from a spell, struggles with monsters, the accomplishment of difficult tasks, and the violation of prohibitions and conditions. But not one of these folktale motifs is essential to the folktale. The folktale can dispense with contrast figures. The hero does not have to be either a prince or a simple-minded peasant lad, just as the heroine need not be either a Cinderella or a princess. There may be no encounters with otherworld beings, and the elements of courtship, wedding, and kingdom may be lacking as well. In one instance, the hero's miraculous abilities may be the gift of an otherworld being, while in another instance they are a matter-of-fact part of him, and either way is in keeping with the character of the folktale.[26]

As far as its subject matter is concerned, the folktale's possibilities are essentially unlimited. Certain characters and developments for which it has an affinity occur again and again, either because they embody basic situations of human existence or because they adapt themselves with particular ease to the abstract, isolating style. At any time, however, other characters and developments may take their place without the folktale's losing any authenticity. Helpful animals most often lend assistance out of gratitude for a major or minor service rendered, but they may also step in and help for no discernible reason. Like gifts, helpers may disappear from the scene without a word of explanation as soon as they have accomplished their task; but they may also eventually be rescued by the hero, or a brief allusion may be made to their nature and fate. The anti-hero may bring about his ill fortune through some kind of failure or through some flaw in his character; then again, no reason for his lack of success may ever be given. In one instance the hero may reach his goal because he tells the truth and in another instance because he lies, and both instances can occur in the same tale.[27] The folktale hero may defeat the dragon either with outside support (as with the aid of a magic sword or animals) or by his own resources. Seemingly impossible tasks are usually carried out with the aid of helpers versed in magic, but occasionally they are accomplished by ordinary workmen.[28] Usually the hero is helped to the miraculous gift through an act of compassion, but sometimes through his very ruthlessness. The rescue of persons may be attempted and accomplished in a laborious way, or it may be carried out incidentally and without forethought. Usually the animal bridegroom is disenchanted through loving advances, but sometimes through callous mistreatment; the destruction of his animal skin may either bring about his redemption or prevent it.

The hero may be told how to select and handle his gift, but even without such advice, he acts with impeccable assurance. Sometimes there is a certain specific correlation between the gift's outward appearance and its function, or between the gift and its donor, or the gift and its recipient, and sometimes there is none. The hero may receive the gift either before or after the assignment of his task; he may know exactly what he needs it for, or he may not have the faintest notion about its purpose. To an otherworld being, an ordinary mortal's gift may be either significant or insignificant. After they have accomplished their special task most gifts are never mentioned again, but sometimes they are returned to the donor. The antihero (whether brother or comrade) may be sentenced to death for his treachery, or he may be given a princess or be appointed to a state office, or his subsequent fate may go entirely unmentioned. When the hero or antihero opens a forbidden door, this act of disobedience almost always inaugurates an unlucky turn of events; on a certain occasion, however, it may be precisely what is necessary and may lead to salvation.[29] In the end, the hero may return to his point of departure (his parents, or the taskmaster) or he may arrive at a distant, totally unknown place. Thus "anything is possible" in the folktale. Any element is acceptable to it. It is an inclusive form that incorporates the world.[30]

The folktale is a world-encompassing *(welthaltig)* literary form in the true sense of the word. Not only is it capable of assimilating and sublimating any element, it in fact reflects all essential components of human existence. Even a single folktale usually comprises both the microcosm and the macrocosm, private and public events, otherworld relationships and relationships with ordinary mortals. But when we consider a group of four or five stories (for all true storytellers have this many in their repertory) the whole range of human possibilities opens up before us. We find events and relationships that are characteristic of social life: courtship, betrothal, marriage; death of parents, of brothers and sisters, of a friend; and conflicts between children and parents or other close relatives (stepparents, parents-in-law, stepsisters and stepbrothers, or sisters-in-law), along with actions that range from pampering, solicitousness, and loyal support, through harsh lovelessness, persecution, defamation, and treachery, to abandonment, attempts at incest, and even murder by family members. We see people acquire knowledge and skills, win comrades and friends, enter into contact with all kinds of domestic and wild animals, meet with difficulties, succeed or fail in the service of a taskmaster or in the course of accomplishing important tasks, struggle with enemies, compete with rivals, become entangled in political intrigues (as when an officer of state or a colonel usurps the place of the hero), and intervene in great battles. The hero or heroine—whether prince or swineherd, tsar's daughter or ashmaid—acquires property, power, and family in the sublimated form of gold and jewels, a kingdom, and a princess. The folktale tells of obedience and disobedience, patience and crime, rewards and punishments, poverty and splendor, good fortune and misfortune, blessedness and failure. In addition, we hear of the diverse types of human conduct and interreaction: good deeds and evil deeds, acts and gestures of compassion as well as of hardheartedness, of modesty as well as of arrogance, of despondency as well as of fearlessness. Sometimes the characters are utterly alone, while at other times we see them in lively contact with their environment.

Side by side with the ordinary world exists the otherworld. The frequency with which the folktale makes use of otherworldly motifs is not surprising, for the confrontation with a totally different world is one of the basic concerns of human existence. None of the great European works of literary imagination fails to mention the realm of the dead. Homer, Virgil, Dante, and Goethe all have their heroes enter the nether world.[31] While individual folktales sometimes dispense with otherworldly motifs,[32] the folktale as a genre cannot do without them. In sublimated form, they are given a preeminent place. This is very much in accord with the role that the numinous plays in reality, a role that the more realistic legend attests to. The folktale hero enters otherworld realms. Still more frequently he is lent assistance by otherworld figures or has to struggle against them. His contact with them corresponds to what is possible in the real world through magic or mysticism. The folktale hero either forces the otherworld to yield its gifts or—as one of the blessed—he simply receives them. He rescues people who have fallen victim to the other-world (through bewitchment, for example) or he himself marries an otherworld spouse. He leads his bride back to his own world after she has been spirited away, or he himself enters her otherworld realm and stays there. In coping with the situations of the ordinary world, too, he makes use of powers that come to him from the otherworld.

Finally, in the folktale as a form we see united the decisive poles of existence: the confined and the expansive, stillness and motion, law and freedom, unity and multiplicity.[33]

The sharply *confined* form of all figures, the frame with which the folktale circumscribes events and objects (a room, a window, a fence, a tower, a castle, or a trunk), stands in contrast with the *expansive* plot, which leads to the farthest distances. Literally as well as figuratively, the hero reaches unreal heights: for days he climbs "mightily high" trees and thus arrives at strange towns, or his path leads him to the clouds. The poor peasant lad ascends the throne and marries the princess. Conversely, queens and princes suddenly plunge from their heights into the abyss. The hero reaches the depths of the sea, of hell, of the underworld.

The *stillness* of the folktale is rooted in the precision, clarity, and stability of its unambiguous form. Not only are the vehicles of the plot sharply defined figures (whether these are objects or persons); the story line, too, is impressively clear and emphatic. The plot progresses rapidly and resolutely. In an expansive *motion*, the characters are propelled across the depthless surface of the plot. In spite of their rigid form, they seem alive.

The characters' effortless mobility, given that anything con-ceivable can happen in the folktale, produces the impression of the greatest *freedom*. This freedom is not arbitrary, however. The folktale as a form is subject to stringent *laws*. Folktales are not the products of wild imagination; in regard to both their form and their choice of motifs, they observe binding laws, which—as with any genuine work of art—they carry out in a spirit of freedom. It is only through observing these laws that the folktale is brought into being.

In the folktale the *multiplicity* of things in the physical world is expressed in terms of formulaic plurality. Objects, characters, and periods (of days or of years) occur in twos, threes, sevens, twelves, or hundreds; episodes or elements of the plot occur in twos or threes. Such formulas convert multiplicity into *unity*. A similar effect is achieved by the folktale's goal-directed action and its tendency toward single-strandedness and toward unity of the hero and the plot. These features provide a solid center for the multiplicity of figures and episodes.

The elements that comprise the folktale are representative of the spheres from which they derive. They call these spheres to mind, but naturally they do not portray them, for these elements no longer possess the internal traits and the characteristic atmosphere of their original world. In the folktale they have turned into clear, weightless images. Earthy farm life and courtly manners, love and hate, the confusion of worldly affairs and the shock of numinous experiences, efforts of will and inner moods or humors—all these are distilled, made ethereal, stripped of their substance. A swineherd can become a king on the spot, for his previous milieu and his previous development have left no traces in him. The characters of folktale are not bound to any specific environment or to any individually developed inner life. Precisely for this reason, they can enter into any ties and play a part in any action.

The uniform style of the folktale sets into immediate juxtaposition the worldly and the numinous (this-worldly beings and other-worldly beings), the high and the low (princesses and peasant lads), the familiar and the alien (the hero's brothers and total strangers) within a single form. In this way the isolation and sublimation of the folktale's constituent elements create the opportunity for their "free" interplay. At the same time, however, this isolation and sublimation is the prerequisite for the folktale's ability to encompass the world. Only thus is the epic-like short form of the folktale able to become all-inclusive. No realistic, individualizing portrayal would be able to achieve such universality. That the folktale is an advanced form of artistic creation is evident from the surpassing skill through which it turns this necessity into a double advantage, for once its motifs are emptied of their usual power, they attain transparency and lightness. They not only become pure, clear, and radiant but are capable of effortlessly establishing contacts. In this way, even though sublimated, they still represent the diverse possibilities of actual existence. Although they themselves are scarcely real, they represent real things. The glass beads of the folktale mirror the world.

6

Function and Significance of the Folktale

Still the question must be posed as to the meaning and function of the folktale within the context of human existence. Only through the joint efforts of several scientific disciplines can this question be answered. The research of the folklorist, the psychologist, the student of comparative religion and mythology, and the sociologist must be taken into account side by side with that of the literary scholar. The art historian must be consulted as well.

At present, it is not yet possible to offer a comprehensive answer to the question of the folktale's function and mode and time of origin. Here I shall consider only what can be deduced from its form.

For the very *appearance* of the folktale should provide evidence as to its function. The form of a work of art of such extraordinarily wide diffusion is determined by two factors. It is dependent on what type of person creates and cultivates it. At the same time, much more significantly, it is dependent on the needs of the audience. Only a form that meets these needs could attain such great popularity and wide diffusion. The form of the folktale must correspond to its function. At least in approximate terms, therefore, we should be able to deduce its function from its form.

What are the human needs that the folktale satisfies by virtue of its inherent character? What does the folktale give its audience?

For a long time the reply of scholars in the field of folk narrative was: "exclusively entertainment."[1] This reply was based on the correct realization that in contrast to the legend, the folktale is a pure, purposeless literary mode.[2] Genuine literature, however, aims at more than mere entertainment. The term "entertainment" should not be taken too literally; one should not hold everyone who has used this term to its narrow denotation. Nevertheless, it is surprising how persistently people since Benfey's time have reiterated the opinion that the folktale aims at "nothing but entertainment."[3] Such a conception corresponds to the familiar view of folktales as "fantastically foolish stories" whose principal value for us consists in their preserving fragments of "the worldview of ancient humanity." As Panzer writes (sec. 37): "Viewed in this light, what at first glance appeared to be a ridiculous fabrication turns into a weighty source of historical information."

Literary scholars are interested in the folktale not for its value as an historical source, but as a narrative. They are concerned with comprehending the nature and function of this mode of storytelling.

The folktale is a world-encompassing adventure story told in a swift, sublimating style. With unrealistic ease, it isolates its figures and knits them together. Its sharp outlines and clarity of form and color go hand in hand with its emphatic refusal to explain its operative interrelationships in dogmatic terms. Both clarity and mystery are integral parts of it. What sort of place does an entity of this kind have in the context of human existence?

Orally transmitted folk literature can be divided into no more than a few types of narratives. From time immemorial, simple tales of personal recollection, stories told by way of gossip, comic stories, sagas (tales centering on the family, the court, and inheritance), legends, saints' legends, myths, and folktales have existed side by side.[4] Any real event, even if insignificant and incidental, has a tendency to be given verbal expression. Stories told by way of gossip (*Klatschgeschichten*) arise when people recount human experiences that are secondary or that are viewed only from the outside—recount them partly for their own sake, partly to measure them against an ethical standard. Jokes, on the other hand, delight in the violation of accepted rules, in the inversion of standards, and in the establishment of grotesque relationships. Sagas are based on reverence for the family. The family is their whole world, and they perceive, interpret, and judge everything from the family's point of view. Legends tell of what is extraordinary, strange, or unprecedented. They are affected by individual events, which they experience and view as something significant and which they portray as such. They try to show connections among things but do not give definitive answers, as do saints' legends, which unambiguously subsume individual events into a system of dogma. Myths trace the essential, constantly recurring processes of real life back to a unique, fundamental event, an event that becomes destiny. The folktale, by way of contrast, incorporates the motifs developed by these simple forms of narration, sublimates them, and turns them into the constituent parts of a far-ranging narrative that remains purposeful, however many episodes it may comprise.

All other types of narrative can easily and freely be traced back to a basic need of the human soul, to a uniform "spiritual activity" *(Geistesbeschäftigung)*, to use André Jolles' term. The folktale overshadows them all; its function is not immediately evident.

Not by chance has the folktale so frequently been compared with the legend and the saint's legend. These three forms surpass the others both in regard to their diffusion and diversity and in their importance. When legends are told at an evening social gathering they stand out as something more significant than ordinary stories;[5] folktales and folktale narrators enjoy special respect;[6] saints' legends are distinguished by an aura of the sacred. For centuries these three genres have coexisted without truly intermingling. Aside from occasional hybrid and mixed forms, the styles have maintained their purity. Each of the three forms has its own *raison d'être* and at the same time complements the others.

The legend tells of significant events and persons. It has its origin in thrilling events, and originally it embodies a belief in the reality of what is told. It is at once science and literature; that is, it is neither pure science nor pure literature, but rather is a prescientific, prepoetic entity that is complex and primitive.[7] It arises from the common people, and even today new legends come into currency. It draws on individual persons and individual phenomena for its subject matter, and its style of portrayal is individualizing and realistic. In a tone of either shock or amusement, it relates the incursion of a wholly other world, a subject of which it is especially fond. It presents its subject without interpretation, or if it makes an attempt at interpretation it does so in a groping, empirical, changeable way. It views both ordinary beings and otherworld beings above all as abandoned; they are either tortured or torturing, transgressors or fools. Not understood, interpreted without assurance, the Wholly Other projects into our world. Although events are profoundly experienced, they are not comprehended intellectually.

The saint's legend, on the other hand, invests everything with meaning. It relates everything to one and the same center, God. Whereas the legend confuses, amuses, frightens, and arouses humankind, the saint's legend clarifies and confirms. The legend poses questions; the saint's legend gives answers. But its answer is dogmatic; it systematizes otherworld phenomena and otherworld influences and gives them a significance whose content is narrowly circumscribed. Although the saint's legend may originate from the common people, it does so not directly, but under the influence of religious teachings. The Church also takes care to collect, maintain, and disseminate such tales.[8]

The folktale is free of such fetters. It is bound neither to reality nor to a dogma. Nor does it cling to individual events or experiences, for these are no more than its raw materials. Not only does the folktale not need the support of the Church; it continues to exist even in the face of clerical opposition. And yet, in its own way, it does give an answer to the burning questions of human existence, and this answer provides deep satisfaction.

In the folktale—perhaps for the first time—the world finds poetic expression. What in the real world is difficult, complex, and characterized by obscure interactions becomes in the folktale light and transparent and adapts itself with effortless ease to the interplay of all things. Whereas in the real world we see only partial developments and well-nigh incomprehensible fates, the folktale presents us with a world of events that is blissfully self-sufficient, a world in which each element has its exactly designated place. Furthermore, in the folktale we cannot see "behind things"; we only see the acting characters, not their whence and whither, their why and wherefore. But we see that it is always at the right moment in the plot that they make their appearance, only to disappear once there is no longer anything important for them to do. The interrelationships on which the total structure is based are illuminated just as little as in the real world; everything in the background remains in the dark. All that takes place in the illuminated foreground is so clearly depicted and so much in harmony with itself, however, that the portrayal fills one with blissful assurance. People who find themselves hurled into a threatening world whose meaning they do not know, people who in legends create the ghosts of this uncanny world out of their lyrical consternation—these people experience the transformation of this very same world in the quiet, epic vision of the folktale.

And the answer that the folktale gives to people who are suffering and anxiously questioning is more convincing and enduring than what is provided by the saint's legend. The saint's legend wants to explain, it wants to comfort; one senses its purpose. It demands faith in the truth of the story told and in the correctness of its interpretation. The folktale, however, demands nothing. It does not interpret or explain; it merely observes and portrays. And this dreamlike vision of the world, a vision that demands nothing of us, neither faith nor avowal, accepts itself so matter-of-factly and is given verbal expression so unerringly that we let ourselves be carried away by it in a state of bliss. In this sense folktales truly compose themselves, whereas saints' legends are purposefully premeditated, whether with the object of self-affirmation or with the object of strengthening others.[9] While the demand that saints' legends make on our faith also includes the possibility of doubt, even the inevitability of doubt, we willingly surrender ourselves to the pure, purposeless poetry of the folktale. The saint's legend wants to provide a definitive and binding account of the nature and meaning of supernatural powers (and thus also of events in the real world). The folktale leaves these powers unexplained at the same time as it shows their distinct and meaningful effects. It is precisely this relinquishment of explanations that engages our trust. Just as the folktale hero lets himself be moved and guided by unknown objects and characters without even asking about their nature and origin, we gratefully and unresistingly accept the help that the folktale gives us in our lives.

The folktale envisions and depicts a world that unfolds before us as the antitype of the uncertain, confusing, unclear, and threatening world of reality. Whereas the diversity of the real world is constantly on the verge of dissolution, whereas the forms of the real world blossom and wilt, and whereas the realistic legend never tires of representing this process of growth and decay, the folktale crystallizes forms and gives us clear lines and solid unwavering figures—not in lifeless stillness, however, but in purposeful motion. The persons and things it depicts do not wither. With decisive abruptness they may turn into other persons or things, but they do not fade away, they do not dissolve. The folktale's episodes do not break off or lose their sense of direction, but pure and sure they reach their specified goal. Behind the growing and withering forms of transitory reality, there are the pure forms—immutable, unmoved, and yet working. The folktale presents us with their image.

Only in a very special sense can the folktale be called a form of "wish fulfillment." By no means does it have the object of showing us the effortless satisfaction of primitive desires. Supplies of bread and cheese that are continuously replenished, balls of yarn that are never entirely unwound, treasures that people find, and helpers who assist them with their chores—these are the subject of the legend, not the folktale. Brownies who do the work of the tradesman or housewife at night, Alpine spirits who keep the herdsman company in mountain pastures, domestic spirits who bring good luck and prosperity to hearth, stables, and fields—these, to be sure, do arise from the wishful thinking of simple people. Whatever is difficult or laborious to obtain through daily work, the tellers of legends transform into the gifts of otherworld beings. The folktale, by contrast, does not dream of the fulfillment of everyday needs. It poses great tasks for its hero; it sends him off to encounter remote dangers, and his interest does not really focus on the treasure, the kingdom, or the spouse he finally wins, but on the adventure for its own sake. It is only the anti-heroes, the older brothers, who are satisfied when they find a mountain filled with silver or gold; the hero is impelled to go on, toward the adventure.[10] The folktale hero receives gifts so as to be able to accomplish his crucial tasks, not for his lasting comfort and enjoyment.

In actuality, the folktale gives its characters not things, but *opportunities*. It directs its characters toward places where something is to be accomplished, and it then showers its help on the person whom it finds to be ready for such an accomplishment—but only this person and no other. Gifts materialize precisely at the moment when hero and task coincide, and neither before nor after do they come into play. They do not serve to alleviate economic distress, but rather they either impel the hero into the adventure or direct him while he is engaged in it. They allow him to find and fulfill his essential destiny.

Although the folktale has been said to be the dream of "the power-less, the poor, and the oppressed, to whom the idea of mastering the world through action is alien,"[11] this view is hard to comprehend. The folktale hero is active and enterprising. Unlike the passive and brooding individuals depicted in legendry, he sets out into the world and acts. But the folktale is aware that an individual's own activity must be complemented by blessings in the form of impulses and assistance. No one is the sole architect of his own fortune. One cannot accept the thesis advanced by such scholars as Mackensen and Berendsohn to the effect that in view of the objects of its "wish fulfillment," the folktale must be regarded as "literature of the poverty-stricken" *(Armeleutedichtung)* that originates from "the lowest strata of the population."[12] To judge from its overall makeup, the folktale is not "the embodiment of the longings of simple people" (Spanner, p. 10); it is a vision of much more general significance.

Nor can the folktale simply be labeled "prescriptive" or "normative" literature *(Seinsollensdichtung)*. It does not aim to show us how matters should be in the world. On the contrary, it takes on the task of perceiving and giving verbal expression to what really happens in this world. It has no interest in depicting a world that is merely possible, a world of a kind we would wish for or demand. It does not want to construct an ideal. Imbued with true faith, it represents the world as the world unfolds to its vision. In its view, things become light, weightless, and transparent as the deceptive veil of apparent reality falls away. Whatever in the real world is bound in a complex net of interdependencies and reciprocal ties appears in the folktale in its ultimate isolation and capacity for universal interconnection.

The folktale contains within itself the antifolktale.[13] Side by side with the hero appear the antiheroes, the unsuccessful ones, while at certain stages of his path the hero himself may act inappropriately. Indeed, there exist early and deviant forms of the folktale that depict the failure or even the demise of the protagonist. But even in those stories in which the hero constantly errs and eventually falls from grace, as happens in the tales of *Godfather Death* (AT 332) or *The Fisher and His Wife* (AT 555), the predominant element for the audience is still the basic possibility of establishing fruitful contact with supernatural powers.[14] Almost spontaneously, in its fully developed forms, the folktale depicts this fortunate contact as a reality. The folktale only fulfills itself when, through the technique of isolation, it brings about the possibility of establishing all-inclusive ties. Consequently, in the fully developed form of the folktale it is quite naturally the hero who is assured of such contact who is given the central role. With some justice, his partners have been called mere foils, helpers, or opponents, whose *raison d'être* derives from their relationship to the hero. However, this view probably undervalues the secondary figures at the same time that it overvalues the hero. For he, too, is nothing but a flat figure. He, too, has no interest for his own sake, but (just like the secondary figures) is only of interest as a participant in the plot.[15] Within this plot, however, the minor figures maintain a certain independence that goes beyond their necessary relation to the hero. Like the mistakes of the hero himself, they represent important possibilities of existence that are meaningful not only in regard to interrelationships or contrast, but that on principle must not be absent from a form of literature that is world-encompassing. Hero, antihero, helper, and opponent are integral parts of the vision of the world that is presented by the folktale.

The folktale does not have its origin in a desire to transfigure the world or make it more beautiful. Of itself, the world is transfigured in the folktale. The folktale *sees* the world just as it depicts it. Fearful things are not excluded from its framework; like everything else, they are assigned a very specific place, so that everything is in order. In this sense, and only in this sense, the folktale may be called a form of wish fulfillment. It shows us a world that is in order, and thus it fulfills man's last and eternal wish. The folktale wants to fulfill this wish truly, not with pale substitutes. It does not want to invent things that do not exist and never could exist in the real world; rather, it sees reality become transparent and clear. It does not conjure up a beautiful world in which we might temporarily refresh ourselves while remaining oblivious to everything else; rather, it believes that the world is truly the way it perceives and portrays it to be.[16]

Since this process of vision and portrayal occurs as a result of necessity and comes into being spontaneously, we must not call the folktale polemic literature (*Tendenzdichtung*). Without any axe to grind, the folktale relates what presents itself to its poetic eye.

The folktale is normative, but not in the sense that it presents us with a merely possible world that, unlike the real world, represents the way things should be, so that the real world can be contrasted to it. The folktale does not show us *a* world that is in order; it shows us *the* world that is in order. It shows us *that* the world is the way it should be. At one and the same time, the folktale depicts the world as it is and as it ought to be.

André Jolles (pp. 199 ff.) rightly emphasizes that the folktale is not concerned with the ethics of action. It is not virtue that is the distinguishing characteristic of the folktale hero. But Jolles contrasts the ethics of action ("What am I to do?") with an "ethics of events," which "responds to the question: 'How should things happen in the world?' . . . This hope concerning the way matters should actually unfold in the world . . . is the spiritual concern of the folktale." The folktale represents "a form in which the events that comprise the course of action are arranged in such a way that they fully meet the requirements of naive morality, and thus are 'good' and 'right' according to our innate sense of absolute justice."

This concept of the folktale, in which the term "good" is practically a synonym for "just," is too narrow. The folktale is concerned with far more comprehensive matters than satisfaction of a naive sense of justice. Adventures, tasks, possibilities, dangers and supportive measures, failure and success, special abilities and their lack—all these are important for their own sake, not only as a means of showing the workings of justice. In all its richness, the world of the figures that the folktale presents to us—from the stars and the minerals and all the various objects to flowers, animals, human beings, and spirits —is of value in itself, and what holds it together is not the "justice of events," but the *rightness of events* in general. It would be a waste of effort if the folktale so painstakingly worked out the whole finely tuned system of order that it has at its disposal only to show "the justice of things." By simpler and more convenient means—namely, by means of the quasi-realistic story—this justice could be portrayed more convincingly than is done in the folktale. To the naive reader, the quasi-realistic story falsely presents as real what he or she sadly lacks in the world of experience. The naive reader can identify with the hero, and the happy ending affords him or her vicarious satisfaction of the need for enjoyment and justice. But from the outset, the folktale abjures the satisfaction of merely partial needs. It does not aim at deception. Not for a moment does its abstract portrayal leave us in doubt about the fact that it intends to portray what is essential, not merely what is real.

To Jolles, the presence of miracles in the folktale represents nothing more than "the only possible certitude that the immorality of reality has ended." Here the inadequacy of his view is especially evident. At the same time that a realistically designed story with a happy ending can dispense with all otherworld elements, it can portray "the justice of things" effortlessly and convincingly. However, the folktale miracle loses all its magic if it is degraded to the role of being a guarantor of naive morality. It shines in all its magic when it is comprehended as a visual embodiment of the twin features of isolation and universal interconnection. The folktale loves miracles for their own sake. By no means does it bring miracles into play only when they appear to be necessary or at least conducive to the portrayal of "the justice of things"; on the contrary, it introduces them everywhere and repeatedly, for it regards the miraculous as the most radiant and unequivocal manifestation of the all-pervasive principles of isolation and universal interconnection. For the folktale, showing "the justice of things" is only a secondary concern, not an ultimate objective. Rather, the folktale seeks to portray—profusely, repetitively, and in many variations—the miraculous contacts that the hero succeeds in establishing with the fundamental powers of existence in the course of his adventures and tasks. "Justice" and a happy ending are inseparably linked with the folktale only because they are the necessary consequences of this contact.

Jolles' explanation of the folktale's avoidance of specific indications of time and place is equally one-sided and insufficient. In his view, the folktale dispenses with such information and with the naming of historical persons only because historical locales, times, and persons stand in close proximity to "immoral reality." In my own view, the absence of all three sorts of information is an integral component of the abstract, isolating style. This style is not a means to any particular end; it is the living form the folktale takes. It is a natural development and produces a strong artistic effect on the audience. To regard this form or any of its components as no more than a means of satisfying naive morality would be an unpardonable impoverishment of the conception of the folktale.

Rather than regarding the folktale as a portrait of the real world in its essential nature, Jolles sees it as something to be contrasted with the world. The spiritual concern that animates the folktale negates "the world as a reality that fails to satisfy the demands of ethical behavior; instead, it affirms the existence of another world in which all requirements of naive morality are met." In this way Jolles degrades the folktale to the level of a fantasy that merely substitutes for reality. On the contrary, the folktale is not "diametrically opposed" to the real world; it sees this world become transparent. It attempts to perceive the world's true nature, and in deep trust it lets us share its vision—a vision in which the folktale itself believes. Jolles fails to perceive this faith the folktale has in itself, and thus he comes to regard the folktale as mere wish fulfillment.

Robert Petsch's opposing view seems to me more valid: "The folk clearly recognize the fact that here the world is portrayed as it actually should be and (in the optimistic point of view that is expressed in the folktale) as *at bottom, in fact, it really is.*"[17] What, when unmediated, is a spectacle only for an infinite mind, the folktale turns into a spectacle for finite minds.[18] The folktale is a counterpart of reality only insofar as it presents a contrast to its outer appearances, not its true nature. The true nature of reality is exactly what the folktale attempts to perceive and depict. The folktale conceives of itself and presents itself as a means of perceiving the essence of the real world.

This extended discussion of André Jolles' views has been necessary since it is to this scholar in particular that folktale research is deeply indebted. While we must reject as too narrow his view that the spiritual purpose underlying the folktale is a realization of the requirements of naive morality, methodologically Jolles made an important contribution in two ways. First, he posed in all seriousness the question of what constitutes the spiritual concern that is operative in the folktale; that is, he dared to consider the folktale as the expression of a specific spiritual activity. He thereby took sharp issue with the stock view of folktales as mere entertainment. Second, in his attempt to define the nature of this spiritual activity, Jolles did not get lost in the consideration of motifs but viewed the folktale as a whole.[19] He thus cleared the way for an analysis of the folktale *per se.* Taken alone, the origin, history, and content of individual motifs do not permit any conclusion as to the ultimate meaning of the folktale as a form. Every single element of the folktale—the presence of miracles, for example—must be capable of being explained by reference to the character of folktale narrative, not only as a relic of archaic customs or modes of experience.

As a narrative type, the folktale simultaneously entertains and illuminates the nature of existence. It does not require one's belief in the physical reality of the story told; indeed, it prohibits such belief. The abstract style and the several ironic formulas of opening and closing make us feel that the world of the folktale is fundamentally distinct from physical reality and that the two spheres never blend. Nor does the folktale consciously interpret the world. Unlike the legend or the saint's legend, it does not explain or interpret, and it dispenses with any systematic representation. It merely portrays. As a truly poetic work, however, it demands faith in the inner truth of what it relates. It does not present itself as idle play but gives visual expression to an experience of the world.

Robert Petsch, who considers the essence of epic poetry to be "the interweaving of the adventurous with the meaningful," has called the folktale "the archetype *(Urform)* of human narrative art."[20] And indeed, the folktale manifests itself as a pure, epic vision. Whereas legends originate from inner agitation, the folktale springs from inner calm. Only because the folktale creator is himself unmoved can he perceive and portray movement with such clarity and sureness. The folktale is filled with epic light, epic serenity. It combines epic movement and epic clarity, each in the most sharply defined form. The relative self-sufficiency of each episode and the relative insignificance of the ending are both epic phenomena.[21] The truncated nature of many motifs testifies to their inner force: they exist for their own sake, as representatives of an unspecified part of the world. The all-inclusiveness of the folktale signifies the fulfillment of an epic drive toward the perception and portrayal of the world. By sublimating its motifs and emptying them of their substance, the folktale establishes an objectivity that is characteristic of epic poetry. In place of epic expansiveness, however—a trait that is not essential to the epic, only optional—the folktale favors epic terseness.

The folktale's abstract portrayal of events and figures imparts to it both clarity and assurance. The nimble movement and rapid progression of the plot, together with the hero's far wanderings, give it an effortless ease. Constraint and freedom, stability and movement, firm form and a nimbly progressing plot combine in the folktale to constitute an artistic unity and produce a magical sense of form in the minds of the listening audience. In both its form and its content, the folktale provides "a reply to the demons."[22] Its general aspect is determined by the clarity of its lines and the sharp definition of its characters, along with its concomitant refusal to arrange or systematize its characters and events into some comprehensive scheme. The isolating, diagrammatic style produces an effect that is wholly unique: at the same time that the operative interrelationships are left completely undefined, the greatest certainty prevails. The absence of a comprehensive view in no way prevents the hero from establishing contact with the essential powers of existence. It is as though the folktale wished to give us assurance: even if you yourself do not know whence you come and whither you are going, even if you do not know what forces are influencing you and how they are doing so, even if you do not know what kind of relationships you are embedded in, you may rest assured that you *do* stand in the midst of meaningful relationships.

We can immediately see how strongly and convincingly the folktale conveys this message, as well as how uniquely its means are suited to this end, when we compare genuine folktales to an artful tale such as Apuleius' story of "Amor and Psyche." Although the events of this story correspond to those of the tale-type of *The Monster (Animal) as Bridegroom* (AT 425A and related types), the otherworld beings that it depicts, whether good or evil, are precisely identified and systematized. This robs Apuleius' tale of all credibility. The story becomes the poet's plaything, as the gift-giving and obstructing powers are made into divinities in whom he himself does not believe—divinities who clearly belong to a fabricated system. By contrast, the profound seriousness of the folktale is evident in its very refusal to engage in classification. The folktale says no more than it knows, and it knows only what it perceives. It does not fabricate anything. It is not a playground for willful fantasies. It faithfully portrays humankind and the world the way it perceives them to be, in images.

It is possible to call the folktale a symbolic literary form,[23] but only in the sense in which all literature is symbolic. The special events that it relates not only have a literal meaning but conceal and manifest something of general significance. If a swineherd and a princess are mentioned, they signify not only a swineherd and a princess, but human beings in general. Illness is not only illness, but calls to mind suffering in general. When uninitiated listeners hear how a girl has been saved from being killed by a dragon, doubtless they first imagine this literal event and nothing more. But through the literal image they also become aware of certain psychological processes. The soul's distress, the soul's liberation, the power or the powerlessness of gigantic, instinctive forces—all of these concerns are manifested in such images. At the same time, such images can preserve the dim memory of cruel rites of sacrifice. The relationship of human beings to the daemonic powers of nature makes itself felt as well, as does the relationship of human beings to each other. Depending on their individual situation, listeners sense some or all of this. Unconsciously or semiconsciously, they do not regard the images that fill their mind's eye to be merely pictures, but always metaphors as well. It is only when the image is consciously interpreted that its poetic effect is destroyed.

A folktale can be interpreted, but any single interpretation will impoverish it and will miss what is essential. By being sublimated, all elements of the folktale are so fully divested of their separate characteristics and so completely removed from the sphere in which they originated that they can come to symbolize other spheres as well. What was once an erotic symbol can come to be a sign of something quite different.[24] In the folktale, the desire of the merchant's youngest daughter for a snake or for a flowering branch embodies above all the heroine's unexplained ability to hit upon what is truly essential and to establish secret interconnections of which she herself is not aware. At the same time, this desire may signify tenderness and modesty, or alternatively willfulness, capriciousness, affectation, and false humility. The erotic potential of the image may make itself felt, but it need not. The question about the lost key originally had a sexual significance, and the illness from which the princesses suffer is lovesickness (see pp. 70–71 above). In the folktale, however, these features do not have to be understood in a sexual sense, nor do they need to be unconsciously experienced as sexual or erotic symbols. Depending on the character of the listener, the beautiful and pure princess can be experienced as a symbol of what is pure and good and yet in need of salvation—experienced, not consciously interpreted, for she is a symbol, not an allegory—or she can be taken as the human soul in general, which longs for unification with the realm of the spirit. But she may also simply be understood as a young woman who wants to be conquered and saved by a man. The prince can be taken as signifying active spiritual powers. The stars, stones, flowers, and animals in the folktale, as well as its garments, rings, staffs, coffers, eggs, and interior spaces, signify first of all themselves. Beyond that they are representatives of the visible world of the cosmos and of human affairs. But they may also signify facets of the unconscious inner world of human beings. What is unconscious and ineffable finds visible expression in them.[25] In this sense they are not symbols that conceal, but symbols that reveal.[26] At the same time (in their sexual sense, for example) they may also conceal.

Any one-sided interpretation of a folktale is arbitrary. This does not mean, however, that scholars must entirely forego the act of interpretation. It is an essential aspect of the folktale as a form, as this form has presented itself to our sight, that by means of isolation, abstraction, and sublimation, it turns every one of its elements into a diagrammatic figure—that is to say, it frees it from its solid roots, from its definite and unequivocal nature as an individual person or thing, in order to transform it into an image that is capable of being comprehended in a multitude of ways. For the eye and for the senses in general, concrete individual persons or things are characterized by indefiniteness and ambiguity, for their contours blur and the infinitude of their interior space cannot be taken in perceptually. For the senses, the abstract and linear is what is simple and unequivocally defined. For the mind, however, concrete unique entities are immutable and unequivocally defined; their ultimate nature can never be perceived only because our windows of perception are not equal to this task. In themselves, individual things are well defined to the last detail, differentiated in a characteristic way, and constrained to a unique configuration. The abstract figure, on the other hand, can be taken in by the mind in various ways. Since it is not charged with any particular content, it can convey the most diverse meanings.

The weightless figures of the folktale have the property of not demanding a specific interpretation. They actually prohibit specific interpretations and allow for (and even call for) diverse ones. They cause various soft but clear tones to sound in harmony in the minds of the listening audience. Without the listener's being aware of it, they present him or her with a visible image of an array of invisible phenomena. As soon as listeners take the figures in, unconsciously they cannot help charging them with a personally appropriate content—usually several levels of content, in fact. This is the freedom that the folktale gives listeners and that is destroyed only through their conscious, one-sided interpretations. The intellectual authority that the folktale exerts over its listener consists in the fact that his or her own experience must be adjusted to conform with the strict form of the folktale, and thus it is subjected to an intellectual order.

On account of the characteristic lightness and agility of all its figures, the folktale is inclined toward the farcical tale *(Schwank)*. The inner freedom that the folktale has acquired in handling its elements tempts it to play with them in a high-spirited manner. Profound seriousness turns into jest and mockery. Its sovereign free play with its constituent motifs turns into a burlesque sort of random play. Miracles follow upon the heels of miracles, and they are wasted on undeserving heroes. Alternatively, miracles are replaced by acts of deceit, while the hero's worldly wiles take the place of gifts from otherworld beings. The *Schwank* deliberately draws out the hero's capacity for all-encompassing relationships to a ridiculous extreme, and thus it derides the folktale's deep faith. The *Schwank* depicts not "the rightness of things," but the humor of things. Many tales whose basic structure is like that of a genuine folktale have *Schwank*-like overtones in the verbal form in which they are recorded. Even serious folktales like to give individual elements a comic appearance, for the form of the folktale is so highly developed that further development along its own lines is impossible; the only way open is that of deviation toward the burlesque.

The folktale's fully developed form marks it as the end product of a long period of literary evolution. Legends, saints' legends, and realistic stories (in Wesselski's sense) take individual motifs as their subject and remain bound to them. The legend strives to give verbal expression to a particular experience of real life. Each of its constituent elements is so charged with tension and so vividly animated that the narrative itself cannot unfold freely, and so the legend remains a short form with no more than a single episode and with a tendency toward the fragmentary. Its poetic power is exhausted in a titanic effort to deal with an individual person's unprecedented experience. The folktale, by contrast, does not itself labor to create the elements of which it is constructed; rather, it obtains them from all quarters, divests them of their original experiential content, and in a sovereign and masterly manner uses them in its own way. This produces an impression of weightless simplicity. Lightness and masterly simplicity, however, are the distinguishing characteristics of late forms.

It is not by chance that in Germany it was the Anacreontic movement (Wieland, Musäus) that rediscovered the folktale.[27] This movement likewise represented the end product of a long development. In a masterly fashion it played with unchanging motifs that were emptied of their substance, and like the folktale it presented the appearance of childlike simplicity. No one considers it primitive or naive on this account. We know that it stood at the end of a period of evolution; it was not in the least naive, and its simplicity was artful. In regard to the folktale, no independent field of scholarship can provide us with information bearing on the circumstances and time of its origin. To judge from its internal formal characteristics, however, we can be sure that the folktale too is neither primitive nor naive, but is a highly developed form of art.

The Romantic movement itself, to whose love of the folktale we are so deeply indebted, is likewise a late form. On the other hand, the authors of the *Sturm und Drang*, who cultivated a decidedly early form of poetry, felt an affinity for the legend rather than the folktale (as in Goethe's *Faust* and Bürger's *Lenore*). The folk legend represents an early form of literature. It is primitive and combines literature and science, or rather it is a complex, prepoetic, prescientific entity. The folktale is pure literature and on this account alone cannot be primitive. It is the undifferentiated whole that is primitive. The folktale must have emerged at a stage of human development when individual spheres had already become clearly separated and when literature disengaged itself from any necessary relation to actual affairs and to "science." As primitive entities, legends can still arise from the folk at any time, but folktales are not created by the folk.

As to the time of origin of the folktale, formal analysis of the kind I have offered provides little information. While undoubtedly it is the product of an advanced culture, it could well have developed in very early times. Since in our time the true folktale audience consists of children between the ages of four and nine, or at most up to the age of twelve or thirteen,[28] an early date seems likely. The great need of children to listen to folktales and the fidelity with which they cling to their wording, even if they have heard the story only once, show them to be the most legitimate folktale audience today. This does not mean that folktales were originally created for children, but only that (in accordance with basic phylogenetic law) these stories evidently correspond to an earlier stage in the development of humankind.

The research of C. W. von Sydow and W. E. Peuckert[29] makes such an early time of origin appear likely. Psychological folktale research, whether of the psychoanalytic or of the eidetic school,[30] has arrived at the same conclusion in its own way. Von Sydow views the folktale as an Indo-European inheritance. Peuckert even considers that it originated in pre-Indo-European times and associates it with the agrarian and urban civilization of the Eastern Mediterranean and the Near East,[31] in a post-totemic period characterized by a matriarchal kinship system. During the preceding totemic period, in his view, there flourished the "mythtale" (*Mythenmärchen*) with its unlimited magical causality.[32] Hermann Bausinger believes that folktales come into being "wherever wish and reality have separated," wherever the "magical world" (quoting Peuckert) has passed and yet is still familiar as "the good old times" that can be kept alive in stories.[33] Guided by very different considerations, Otto Rank likewise places the folktale, which he believes is preceded by the totemic myth, in the period of transition from a patriarchal kinship system to a more advanced form of social organization. Otto Huth traces the origin of the folktale back to the late Stone Age and claims to recognize in it premythic, megalithic "mystery legends" (*Mysterienlegenden*).[34] Jan de Vries, on the other hand, regards the folktale as an expression of an aristocratic way of life and conjectures that the folktale has emerged whenever a mythic culture has been replaced by a more rationalistic one, as happened during the Homeric era or the Italian Renaissance, for example.[35]

In itself, my own formal analysis does not yield any conclusive arguments for or against precise datings. However, when Peuckert suggests that the folktale is to be ascribed to a period at the end of a "magical" world and at the beginning of a "rational" one because, while still employing many magical motifs, it has already begun to play with them, his argument is not convincing. The folktale plays with all its motifs, not only the magical but also the numinous, the sexual, and the worldly in general. Without exception it divests them of their power and sublimates them. No partial explanation for this phenomenon is needed,[36] and no partial conclusion is to be drawn. The abstract style "empties" motifs and sublimates them. In the hands of a superior artist, it can certainly do so even during a period when the corresponding subjects are still in full bloom in real life.[37]

The depiction of the mother/child relationship in folktales allows neither the conclusion that the folktale has been composed for children from the outset, nor the conclusion that the folktale is literature for and by women.[38] It does appear to show, however, that the folktale filters down from a higher to a lower level. The folktale may be literature for primitive people, but it is not literature by primitive people.[39] We may assume that as pure literature it is the creation of true artists, from whom it is passed down to the folk. It arises from an act of genuine poetic vision. One can speak with justice of the folktale's "dreamlike" vision, but undoubtedly these visions are the waking dreams of the poet rather than ordinary sleep-induced dreams. Certain motifs, perhaps, could have their source in sleep-induced dreams.[40] The all-inclusive character of the folktale permits it to assimilate elements from this sphere of human existence, too. Moreover, we may recall how relatively unemotional is the manifest content of dreams,[41] as well as how relatively lacking in imagination dreams are (as is shown by their typical motifs).[42] Both features are characteristic of the folktale also. The lack of emotionality in the folktale goes much further than in sleep-induced dreams, however, for folktales extend the principle of depthlessness to the realm of psychology. In this respect the folktale more closely resembles the poet's waking dream, from which it may well have originated.[43]

Common people are the carriers and cultivators of folktales, but they hardly ever create them.[44] It seems to me that the folktale is a gift from visionary poets to the people. Who its original creators were escapes our knowledge. To what extent they presented the tales to the people in a form appropriate to them and suitable for oral transmission, and to what extent the tales were polished to their characteristic form by the process of oral transmission, we cannot easily say.[45] My own formal analysis, by which I have tried to demonstrate the folktale's very pronounced stylistic tendencies, leads me to suspect that the true authors of folktales must be credited with more than is generally assumed.

Until now, students of the folktale have been inclined to ascribe its individual stylistic characteristics exclusively or primarily to the conditions of oral transmission.[46] Once one takes seriously the realization that, like other basic literary forms, the folktale is an expression of a spiritual activity, such a mechanistic explanation of an artistic phenomenon is no longer sufficient. Legends, saints' legends, family sagas, and stories told by way of gossip are orally transmitted as well, and yet their style is quite different from that of the folktale. This is not only because as an episodic story, the folktale requires a rigid, formulaic style that can serve as a mnemonic aid to the storyteller, whereas the legend, as a nonepisodic entity, does not require such a style. Rather, the difference in style must be the expression of a different stylistic impulse.[47]

Everything alive lives both in and of itself and also through the support of its environment. Every living thing grows in accord with immanent laws and yet at the same time must adapt to its surroundings. But the immanent law is primary. Poetry can exist only if its own spirit conforms to the external conditions of its existence. The folktale realizes its own form and yet is dependent on the external possibility of being passed on from mouth to mouth. But its own character is primary. Just as the form of a plant cannot be "explained" from its location, its climate, and the composition of its soil, but only from its own developmental law, the style of the folktale cannot be deduced from the mode of transmission. A plant will only thrive where external conditions are in accord with its own law, and the folktale only flourishes where the external world is ready and able to receive and transmit it in a manner compatible with its true nature. The primary factor is the inner need that its creator, preservers, and listeners feel for it. Its suitability for oral transmission is secondary. For the folktale to survive as a living form, both elements are equally important, the internal and the external. Spiritually, however, the inner law takes precedence. We can understand the folktale and its function in the world of human beings only if we comprehend its characteristics from its own frame of reference and only from its own frame of reference. That these characteristics at the same time render possible its oral mode of transmission is the sort of fortunate circumstance that is necessary wherever life is to emerge.

There are two possibilities. Either the folk so unerringly polish a literary work that is presented to them that this work both comes to suit their inner needs and fits the mode of oral transmission, or from the outset this work is presented to the folk in a form that conforms to their needs and their narrative capabilities. At the present time it is impossible to say which view best accounts for the origins of the folktale. It would be welcome, however, if folktale scholars were to give more serious consideration to the second possibility than it has as yet received. For it is very possible that while the actual creators of folktales are, like Homer, heirs of a long line of development, their creations, as the final fulfillment of this development, are preserved quite pure and unchanged as they are handed down by oral transmission.

The aim of my study has not been to formulate conclusions as to the mode of genesis and time of origin of the folktale. Such conclusions have had to be drawn with the greatest caution and only in passing. Rather, I have attempted to describe the nature of the European folktale and to comprehend its function. While it goes without saying that the style of the folktale varies from narrator to narrator, from people to people,[48] and from epoch to epoch, there still exists a basic form to which the folktale as a narrative type aspires. This basic form is hardly ever perfectly realized, but it is present invisibly behind every folktale. Present-day storytelling takes playful liberties with it and sounds variations on it. Every individual folktale contains features that do not fully correspond to it. Through the comparison of many narratives, we have been able to comprehend what is truly characteristic of the genre. When a certain folktale gives specific information about place, time, and historical persons, it still remains a folktale so long as it maintains folktale structure and style in other respects. But specific places, times, and personal names are alien to it. They do not belong to the true folktale style, which is of an abstract nature. A Lithuanian tale speaks as follows of three sisters, for example:

After a few months had passed, the two sisters became the maidservants of their hated sister, and her good fortune made the fearful flame of hatred and envy flare up in their hearts. In spite of this, the queen's humility and love did not die out, but the flame of hatred in the hearts of the sisters grew stronger and stronger. The two maidservants of the queen were tormented by the fire of envy. For envy never gives the heart rest. It showed itself everywhere and grew stronger and stronger. For there is nothing that can satisfy the heart burning with envy, until it finds a cure. . . .[49]

All this is empty embellishment and is completely unlike the true folktale. But in the next sentences, when the thread of the story is resumed, the pure folktale style soon reestablishes itself. (The parts that are still not characteristic of folk narration are italicized; they become increasingly rare as the true folktale style reasserts itself as if spontaneously.)

After the three sisters were wed, a year passed *as quickly as an hour*, and the queen gave birth to a son. Then *the queen's sisters had a lucky opportunity to pacify their hearts. Namely,* the two envious sisters put the prince in a little kettle and threw him into a ditch that ran through the royal palace. Then they showed the king a piece of wood that they had wrapped in swaddling clothes and told him his wife had given birth to it.

The sisters, about whose inner feelings the narrator had wasted so many words, now do not betray the slightest emotion over what could not help but be a hair-raising deed. They are now portrayed in an entirely depthless manner and carry out their cruel plan with utter lack of concern. Their last gesture underscores the heartless determination with which they act: they replace the living child with a hard, unfeeling piece of wood, which they calmly show to the king without any hypocritical outpouring of indignation.

At the end of a Norwegian folktale the king returns to his castle after a long absence:[50]

At first the queen did not recognize him, for he had grown so gaunt and pale, what with his long wanderings in deep sorrow. But when he showed her the ring, she was overjoyed, and they celebrated their proper wedding so that it was the talk of the whole land.

That the king in his wanderings was consumed with sorrow and that he had turned gaunt and pale does not have the ring of the true folktale. On closer examination, one realizes that the narrator inserted these words because he misunderstood the folktale style in another respect as well: he thought that he had to explain what to the genuine isolating folktale style is a matter of course, the queen's failure to recognize the king. The need for a token of recognition, which at the same time is an externalization or projection of an inner relationship that in the true folktale cannot be portrayed in any other way, needs no justification.

Additional examples of departures from the principles of isolation and depthlessness in the folktale have been adduced above (on pp. 14, 19–20, 25, and 39–40). Rationalizations for the presence of universal interconnections are especially frequent in Serbo-Croatian folktales: "You are lucky, God has shown you exactly the right way." "He unceasingly prayed to God, and God kept him safe and sound this night as well."[51] In the true folktale world, God need not be troubled to put everything in order, for this order comes about by itself. Our criteria enable us to distinguish between the genuine *(echt)* and the ungenuine *(unecht)* in the folktale—terms that are not equivalent to "original" *(ursprünglich)* and "reworked" *(nicht ursprünglich)*. A number of scholars have demonstrated that Wilhelm Grimm, too, deviated in some respects from the true folktale and developed his own style.[52] By tracing the history of the tale of *Rapunzel*, one can show how a genuine French folktale changed its style at the hands of a literate lady-in-waiting at the court of Louis XIV, then was thoroughly purified by Jacob Grimm and thereby brought back closer to the style of the true folktale. Subsequently it was sentimentalized by Wilhelm Grimm through the introduction of words expressing emotion. When it returned to circulation among the folk, the process of stylistic self-correction began, and the story was freed from the adornments of the French fairy-tale style even more distinctly than it had been at the hands of Jacob Grimm.[53]

The European folktale has presented itself to our eyes as an episodic, world-encompassing adventure story recounted in an abstract style. It comprehends the world. It does not show the world's innermost interrelationships; it shows its meaningful play. To the folktale, all of the elements of the world have become light and transparent. Not only their magical aspects have vanished, but their mythical, numinous, and everyday aspects have disappeared as well. It is precisely this fact, however, that underlies the unique magic of folktales and the magical effects that they produce. The folktale enchants all the things and events of this world. It releases them from their weight, their rootedness, and their normal constraints and transforms them into a different, more intellectual form. It not only speaks of magic, it practices it. It brings to pass the act of redemption that reality seems to demand of the mind and of language. It sublimates and spiritualizes the world.

The folktale is the "glass bead game" (*Glasperlenspiel*) of past ages.[54] Like the bow and arrow, tomahawk, and saber, in our own time it has been demoted to the level of the nursery. It no longer satisfies us, for we consider it too simple, too "simple-minded." It no longer embraces all aspects of our world. We generally consider it insufficiently rich and insufficiently differentiated. We are no longer satisfied by its answers to ultimate questions. The folktale depicts human beings as favored individuals who are showered even with *opportunities*. But people today want to define both themselves and the world. They want to have more than just passive experience of the transcendent powers; they want to gain knowledge of them. They perhaps long not so much to be singled out for favor as to be self-determining individuals who consciously and perceptively choose their own goals and paths. For this reason the legend, however more primitive an entity than the folktale, is more compatible to modern man in its outlook.

The folktale represents a comprehensive and self-contained poetic vision. At the same time that the legend is complex, limited, and relatively unformed, it points beyond its own framework. The folktale reveals to us a poetic vision of the nature of the world, without inquiring about the nature and characteristics of individual powers. The legend, by contrast, calls particular things into question. It is fascinated by the inhabitants of this world as well as by those of the other world; it "explains" in its own way; it gives partial answers. Particular things never relinquish their hold on it. Bent on perception and interpretation, it pushes into the dark. The legend illuminates fragmentary areas, or it would like to illuminate them. The folktale, imbued by poetic faith, presents a provisional view of humankind and the world as a whole. As pure literature, it remains on the level of pure potentiality. In a primitively ambitious way, on the other hand, any legend is an attempt at a more impressive and at the same time more real illumination of existence. Legends do not provide an overall perspective, but they take pains over particular phenomena. They do this as a form of literary science, for literature and science are still combined in them in an undeveloped state. For this reason, legends are primitive entities. But the separation of what was once a primitive whole cannot be achieved definitively. Once an unconsciously undifferentiated unity has unfolded into parts and has attained self-awareness, it strives for new unity at a higher level.

Are you seeking what is noblest, what is greatest? The plants can show you.

What a plant is spontaneously, you can become by choice—it is that.

The primitive legend points to the state to which development aspires. What was once a gloomy, undeveloped unity aspires to return to unity without giving up its own nature or its own inherent laws. This higher unity can only be a many-faceted whole. We are dreaming of a new union of literature and science. After differentiation has taken its course, what in the primitive legend was a forced and involuntary conjunction will take the form of a free, rich, and harmonious union.

The modern age has made immense advances, but only in circumscribed areas. As an entirety it has not yet found its own style. Technology and certain scientific disciplines have pushed far ahead. Morality, civilized conduct, and art have not shown an equivalent development. "God has not kept pace." "In regard to civilized conduct, God has fallen behind."[55] At the same time, we yearn for a new harmony and its artistic expression. The age of the folktale is past; but like the legend, the folktale seeks to assume a new existence on a higher level. Just as the old folktale adopted the subject matter of

primitive legendry in sublimated form, the new folktale will have to
be able to assimilate the insights of modern science.

Poets and scientists are dreaming of "a new alphabet, a new language of symbols through which they could formulate and exchange
their new intellectual experiences."[56] In this future "glass bead game,"
science and art, fragmentary perception and comprehensive vision,
and actuality and potentiality would come together as a unity, and
the ancient contrast between folktale and legend would cease to exist. Like the legend, this form would combine literature and science
in one, and like the folktale, it would offer a playful overview of
human existence. We do not know whether this new folktale will remain merely the dream of poets. In the meantime the old folktale
lives on, for children a comfort and joy, but for us a promise of
possibilities whose fulfillment is still to come.

7
Folktale Scholarship

The folktale enjoys the attention of a great range of disciplines. In our time it has been a subject of research particularly among the fields of folklore, anthropology or ethnology, psychology, and literature. Folklorists analyze folktales as documents of cultural and intellectual history and observe their role in the community. Psychologists take the narratives as an expression of internal mental processes and investigate their influence on listeners or readers. Literary scholars attempt to determine what makes a folktale a folktale; they wish to comprehend the essential art of the genre as well as of individual tales, and like folklorists, they pose the question of the origin and history of the different folktale types. The folklorist is interested first of all in the function and biology of the form; the psychologist is interested in it chiefly as an expression of the needs of the human soul; the literary scholar is concerned primarily with the form itself and its place within the world of literature.

My own book has attempted to provide a sort of phenomenology of folk narrative as we find it in Europe. I have offered a literary interpretation of the folktale whose goal has been to establish the essential laws of the genre. The existence of hybrid forms that stand between the folktale and the legend, the folktale and the saint's legend, and the folktale and the fable is just as evident as is the comparable overlapping of the genres of lyric and epic poetry or epic and dramatic poetry. There exist both epic dramas and lyric dramas, but the concepts of the drama, the lyric, and the epic are nevertheless clearly distinct from each other, not only in the imagination of literary theorists, but also in the perception of authors and those who enjoy the works. A multiplication of genres and a tendency toward specialization are an achievement of more advanced cultures. An undifferentiated whole is a more primitive state: in the field of biology, within the seed all parts are as yet undivided from one another, whereas the mature plant is richly and clearly segmented. The narratives of primitive tribes often consist of myth, legend, folktale, and fable all in one, while a division into different genres is still in its infancy. In Europe, which in other spheres as well has achieved a degree of specialization that is unique (even if frequently adopted by others), narrative genres are more clearly differentiated than elsewhere.

The characteristics that I have identified are evident from the comparison of many narratives. An individual folktale may sometimes deviate from the ideal type—here or there it may contain an intricate descriptive passage or direct expressions of emotion—but if in all other respects it complies with the rules of the genre, then it will still fall under the heading of "folktale." Nothing alive is schematic, and yet everything alive strives for a certain form. No single narrative will rigidly follow all rules of the genre, but many narratives approach the strict form and approximate it. It is not only scholars, with their habits of comparison and analysis, who will develop a fixed concept of the type, but habitual listeners to folktales, who know many narratives, also carry such a concept within them. They will nevertheless enjoy the particular variations and cheerful flourishes of any one narrator, for such variations reveal a measure of freedom that we sense is beneficial. Compulsion and freedom coexist in a multiplicity of ways in the folktale. In addition, a basic structure remains perceptible to the listener's consciousness even if characteristics subject to national and geographic, individual, or temporal influences work together to shape the narrative. If folktales always gravitate toward a certain intrinsic form in spite of all liberties taken, they do not do so because the author or narrator is aware of the demands of the genre and consciously manipulates certain rules, but rather because, as I have tried to demonstrate, the genres reflect and satisfy certain needs of the human psyche.

There remains a question as to whether my description of the basic structure of the folktale truly encompasses the folktale that is alive in oral tradition, or whether in the end it is only valid for the literary folktale and pertains only to the style of Wilhelm and Jacob

Grimm and the many who have followed in their footsteps.

Anyone who wants to discover the distinct character of the European folktale must not rely exclusively on recordings made by the collectors of today, who are equipped with tape recorders and publish their recordings or shorthand notes unaltered. Narrative tradition in modern Europe is on the decline, as is shown, for example, by the folktales recorded even before World War II by Melchior Sooders in remote Haslital.[1] What is valid for the modern narrator may not necessarily have been true for a narrator who was still a member of an active storytelling community of adults. The expectations and needs of that earlier audience would have influenced narrative style in another manner than today, when an isolated narrator is influenced by an audience of children or even by the presence of the folktale scholar, to whom he may at last again tell one of the beloved old tales. When oral narrative tradition was widespread it also produced a much larger number of talented narrators than can be found today.

We must therefore remain dependent on the records of the nineteenth century. In part these are highly reliable. Wilhelm Grimm, however, who was left to edit the later editions of the *Kinder- und Hausmärchen* almost by himself, dealt very freely with his sources and stylized them according to his artistic sensibility. Moreover, the Grimm brothers frequently combined several variants and picked out from each of them the episodes and features they liked best—a method that recently has been recommended for modern editions as well, although not in such an extreme form. The folktale has "no proprietor," according to a Greek folk saying. Only after the collector has heard the same tale from many narrators can he "determine the locale where the general sensibility of the folk spiritually and artistically resides and in which it creates."[2]

This unexpected dissenting voice against word-for-word publication deserves to be heard. We would not wish to do without verbatim recordings; they correspond to the principle of true-to-life faithfulness that is part of twentieth-century science, and they are instructive for folkloristic, psychological, and literary purposes. But Milliopoulos, whom I have just quoted, speaks in favor of a point of view that has recently been neglected and that deserves to be drawn upon as a supplement to the principles of publication that are customary today. Just as the narrator has often heard his story from several persons and then attempts to bring the form to a state of perfection himself, so too the collector and publisher naturally take it upon themselves to generate the ideal form that results almost spontaneously from a comparison of different versions. This procedure should not become a general editorial principle, of course; the scholarly publisher must not himself assume the role of "proprietor" of the folktale. And the ideal form could only be attained by comparing similar narratives, not by combining relatively dissimilar variants, as the Grimm brothers permitted themselves to do.

Wilhelm Grimm's stylistic recasting was largely responsible for the creation of the literary folktale *(Buchmärchen)*, an elevated folktale, so to speak, that we may clearly distinguish from freely inventive stories of deliberate artfulness *(Kunstmärchen)*.[3] Literary folktales have an important function in that they fill the gap created by the disappearance of the oral tradition and have become the living possession of both children and adults. They cannot be considered fully representative of the true folktale, however. From the outset I have therefore drawn on the *Kinder- und Hausmärchen* only for supplementary purposes. But whatever is common to the narratives of the sixteenth, nineteenth, and twentieth centuries—whatever can be observed in the folktale of *The Little Earth Cow* (which is clearly more faithfully recorded than the corresponding tales by Basile and Perrault)[4] and what is evident also among the narrators studied by Gottfried Henssen or Leza Uffer and is likewise found in nineteenth-century editions—such features obviously pertain to the style of the folktale as a genre.

Recordings made during the twentieth century enable us to confirm our observations in many ways. When the Grimms' folktales returned to the folk, they tended to become purified and in many ways have again approached the abstract style that was weakened by Wilhelm Grimm. In the Grimms' account, Cinderella first receives "a dress of gold and silver," then "an even more splendid one," and finally one "that was so magnificent and shining that nothing like it had ever been seen" (KHM No. 21). But in a version told by the North German farm laborer Egbert Gerrits, the first dress has silver stripes of two fingers' breadth, the second has gold stripes of two fingers' breadth, and the third has both gold and silver stripes.[5] This is at the same time more abstract, more ornamental, more sharply linear, and more graphic than the Grimms' account—for our term "abstract" is not to be understood as the opposite of "graphic." On the contrary, an abstract (that is, nonrepresentational) depiction provides more suggestive visual images than does a realistic mode of depiction that singles out each thing for individual treatment.[6] Almost spontaneously, Gerrit's account restores the sort of clearly defined progression of elements (*Steigerung*) that strives for clear and simple visibility and that had become effaced in the Grimms' mistier, more poetical phrasing. This progression assumes the form of a type of variation that separates elements precisely, not indefinitely.

In the tale of *Rapunzel* (KHM No. 12), in Wilhelm Grimm's phrasing, "The prince became overwhelmed with grief, and in despair he jumped from the tower." According to our definitions, this manner of expression does not correspond to the style of the true folktale. In oral tradition it corrects itself. In two later narratives derived independently from Grimm, one recorded in Danzig, the other in a Swabian enclave of Hungary, the passage is corrected in the same way. The schoolchild from Danzig narrates: "When she [the witch] saw that it was a prince there, she threw him down." The Swabian narrator relates: "She gouged his eyes out and threw him down."[7] Thus both times psychological suffering is replaced by an external blow; the inner impulse is changed into a clearly visible external process. It is not surprising, in addition, that the sentimental and conceptual expressions that were added by Wilhelm Grimm (Jacob had avoided them in the first edition) disappear in folk retellings as well.[8] In the Swabian/Hungarian version, the term "sorceress" (*Zauberin*) is replaced by "witch" (*Hexe*), a term that is authentic to the original account as we find it in the Mediterranean variants of the folktale of *Rapunzel*.

Therefore one may indeed say that in the oral tradition of the folk, the folktale style passes through a process of self-correction (*Selbstberichtigung*) that is analogous to the self-correction of the structure of the narratives that has been identified by Walter Anderson.[9] The closing part of the Grimms' tale of *Rapunzel*—a passage that ill accords with the expectation of the folktale audience and that originated from the fantasy of a maid of honor at the French court in the late seventeenth century—does not imprint itself on the memory; it shrinks or undergoes a fundamental reworking. Almost without exception, popular oral versions of this folktale type (AT 310) conclude with the magic flight of the couple. The three enchantments that deceive the pursuing witch lend structure to the concluding episode and constitute sharply outlined visual images that contrast clearly with each other in the true manner of the folktale. The change of style in the tale of the animal-as-bridegroom that derives from Musäus (see pp. 47–50 above) is a further example of the self-correction of internal and external form in oral folk narrative tradition.

The fate of the tales of Grimm and Musäus when returned to oral tradition shows in what sense the folktale may be called a collective composition (*Kollektivdichtung*). Folk narrators collaborate. Just as folksongs undergo not only deterioration but transformation as they are sung by the folk, folktales as well are not simply marred or, on the other hand, slavishly preserved. They frequently approach the ideal form in retellings as they approximate to the essential folktale style ever more closely, while elements foreign to the folktale are eliminated, replaced, or transformed. This occurs not because of technical factors involved in the mode of transmission, or at least not exclusively so, but according to the inner necessities of the narrator and the audience. Just as from the beginning, a song composed by an individual has to conform to a certain model if it is to become a folksong, the same is true of a narrative that is to be adopted and carried on by the folk. From the outset, in this sense, folksongs and folktales issue "from the collective whole."[10] In the interplay between the technical needs of transmission and spiritual and artistic needs, as in the interplay between creative authors and re-creative narrators, a kind of collective work of art comes into being that in many ways resembles the farcical tales, legends, and saints' legends recounted by the folk, but that as a whole clearly has a character of its own.

The surprising consistency of the folktale style and the way in which its various elements create a unified and harmonious effect, as this book has tried to point out, give the folktale the right to be called a poetic composition. Its origins and historical development are difficult to clarify, but its effect is that of a genuine work of art. Behind it exists an artistic impulse that is not only personal but that, in the sense indicated, transcends personality.[11]

The literary scholar is interested first of all in the artistic effect of folktale narrative, and from the beginning he tries to infer this effect from its form. At the same time, however, he understands the folktale as a declaration, a predicating statement whose general character arises directly out of its form. The basic characteristic of the folktale's style is the isolation and effortless connection of all its elements, and its hero represents an image of humankind, ultimately isolated, but capable of universal relationships. The intrinsic truth of this image of humanity is self-evident: ultimately, human beings stand alone, yet help comes to them again and again, and they often permit themselves to be sustained by forces that they do not grasp in their total context any more than the folktale hero comprehends the universe of the otherworld beings he encounters.

Legends embody an alternative image of humanity that is also true in its own way. In them, people are depicted as observers and as beings who reveal themselves and push forward into the unknown. To all outward appearances and in their disposition, they are rooted in the community, but emphasis is placed on their loneliness during the decisive events. Loneliness and isolation are two different things. Lonely people feel lonely and abandoned only because they are adjusted to human society. One may not speak of the folktale hero's loneliness, however, but rather of his isolation, for he is depicted as a flat figure rather than as a complex human being with manifold real connections. Although isolated, he is not abandoned; on the contrary, he is capable of coming up with the contact he needs anywhere, and always at the right moment. The essentially lonely human beings of legendry are often fearful, and they often fail. The folktale shows another potential of human conduct, the possibility of acting and behaving as if one were sure of making the contact one needs. In these two genres, so closely related in the narrative repertory of the folk, we see expressed not simply pessimism and optimism. The differences between the genres are based not only on a different predisposition, mood, or worldview on the part of various authors or narrators, but on the human condition as such. Human beings are outwardly bound to the community as well as internally self-dependent and imperiled, just as legends depict them. At the same time, as portrayed in the folktale, they can be in happy contact with the essential powers of existence and can go their way with calm assurance in spite of all the mistakes they make and all the blows of fate that befall them. In its fascinatingly sharp-focused manner of narration, the folktale not only offers confidence and security to its present-day audience of children. It shows them, even in a world threatened by the sinister forces of mass mentality and nationalism, an image of human beings isolated in their essence and destiny, and yet on this very account knit together by all-encompassing ties and capable of making universal contact.

In its manner of narration, in its internal and external form, and in its style, we see in the folktale an expression of a definite human and artistic attitude. We have identified its characteristics mainly by contrast to the legend and the saint's legend. It is certainly no accident that in all three forms, however, supernatural elements occur side by side with everyday ones. In their own way, all three narrative genres testify to the different means by which people come to terms with their world, to which "otherworldly," "mythical" reality belongs just as much as does everyday reality. Although myths in the narrow sense are clearly distinct from folktales (the myth can speak exclusively of gods or other supernatural beings, and human beings need not appear in it, whereas the hero of a true folktale is always a human being), in recent years attention has been drawn more strongly to the characteristics that are common to both narrative genres, as the point of view of Wilhelm and Jacob Grimm, who believed in the descent of folktales from myths, has been approached again from different directions. "The folktale is the playful daughter of myth," says Friedrich von der Leyen.[12] According to Karl Justus Obenauer, "A folktale in the narrower sense comes into being when the laws of epic narrative generate this apparently artless form out of the collective repository of half-mythical, half-magical images."[13]

Jan de Vries, who agrees with me in emphasizing the playful and sublimating style of the folktale,[14] postulates the development of this form wherever a culture based on myths develops into a more rational one. The folktale as a genre may arise sooner or later depending on the stage of development of a people. Among the Greeks this may have taken place during the Homeric era, when people turned aside from mystery cults based on emotion and began facing the gods with an almost ironic liberty. In medieval France the change may have occurred when the heroic *chansons de geste* gave place to the courtly romance. De Vries defines myth as a representation of the deeds and sufferings of a god, while he sees heroic legends and folktales (both originally cultivated by an aristocratic society) as two kinds of desacralized myth embodying diachronically and then synchronically different human attitudes: the tragic, which emphasizes destruction and sacrifice, and the comic, which highlights the hero's powers of transformation and regeneration. De Vries sees myths, heroic legends, and folktales as comprising three genres that are sharply distinct from one another in spite of similar themes and similar plot structures, and he sternly warns against assuming the existence of folktales during a given period on the basis of mere "folktale motifs," for these may be components of myths as well. De Vries' assumption of the temporal and geographic polygenesis of the folktale as a genre can be taken for granted, as can his acceptance of various possibilities of diachronic succession and synchronic coexistence among different genres. Epic poems and dramas, as well, have arisen successively among various peoples at various times and have still developed into synchronically coexistent genres.

As far as the still undisclosed prehistory of the folktale is concerned, the hypothesis of its descent from the narratives of shamans —a proposal first made by Leo Frobenius and Karl Meuli[15]—has recently been raised again by Mircea Eliade, Friedrich von der Leyen, and Luise Resatz.[16] Eliade sees embodied in the folktale, despite its sublimating narrative style, the structure of a very serious and difficult adventure, the adventure of initiation—that is, of a ritual transition from ignorance and immaturity, through a symbolic death and resurrection, into the state of an initiated adult ("*à l'âge spirituel de l'adulte*"). According to this view, a folktale is a kind of reduced ceremony of inauguration, an initiation rite transposed into the sphere of fantasy. "The tale takes up and prolongs the process of initiation on the level of the imagination" (*Le conte reprend et prolonge l'initiation au niveau de l'imaginaire*). From my own point of view I see this as quite possible. In the folktale, serious things are taken lightly. This statement is not meant to be derogatory (as in general the concepts that I have raised are not merely negative: "loss of weight" and "emptying" simultaneously denote sublimation and spiritualization, while a "depthless" representation of reality can operate more suggestively than a three-dimensional representation, and so on). What is achieved in the practice of magic and in cult actions can become an element of existence on the purely spiritual level in the imagination and in internal contemplation. The folktale comes into being side by side with contemporaneous rites of initiation, and it persists after these have ceased, so that their original seriousness shines through its bright and weightless form and can still be perceived. Its abstract style, which on the one hand produces the effect of effortlessness, can at the same time (as Otto Huth has emphasized)[17] be a sign of what originally were ecstatic experiences. The folktale is perhaps really something like "a lighthearted doublet of myth and initiation rite," as Eliade has claimed:

Without being aware of it, rather with every intention of simply amusing themselves or relaxing, the people of today still profit from the imaginary initiation that folktales bring about [*"de cette initiation imaginaire apportée par les contes"*]. . . . Today, people have begun to be aware that what we call initiation pertains to human life in general and that all existence is built on an unbroken series of "trials," "death-like incidents," and "resurrections"— regardless of the kind of terms in which modern usage reproduces these originally religious experiences.

Modern folklorists' discovery that primitive habits and concerns live on in all human beings, even in the middle and upper social and cultural classes of contemporary Europe,[18] must be taken into account by students of the folktale, too. It is significant that folktales capture the interest of the educated even more during rationalistic eras than at other times. Light reading matter that ostensibly serves the purpose of mere entertainment can secretly satisfy suppressed internal expectations. In the sublimated figures and events of the folktale, the intensity of feeling that was originally linked to them continues to operate below the surface. But reality has become play; everything appears in a lighter, airier combination than in real life, or even in the legend and the saint's legend, and for this very reason everything is taken in more easily by hearers and readers and is thus assimilated more completely. The folktale is what Adalbert Stifter had hoped his own poetry would be: "as simple, clear, transparent, and soothing as the air";[19] but along with its pure and strong fragrances we inhale the sublimated essences of life.

Psychological folktale scholarship seeks to uncover the suprapersonal mental processes that are mirrored in the folktale. Just as

dreams were Freud's chief path to the discovery of the individual unconscious, C. G. Jung and his school have seen folktales and myths
as the chief means to the discovery of the collective unconscious.
During the twelve years that elapsed after the first publication of the
present book, a number of informative essays on the psychology of
the folktale were published. As elsewhere in this short survey, we
can only single out a few examples.

In an inquiry included in the fourth edition of Charlotte Bühler's
well-known work *Das Märchen und die Phantasie des Kindes* (Munich,
1958), Josephine Bilz interprets the events of folktales as a representation of the processes of maturation. The role reversal that we often
find in children's play as well as in the folktale (for example, between
the children and the witch in *Hansel and Gretel*) and the equally
common instances of a person's being taken away (for example, in
Rapunzel or *Rumpelstiltskin*) indicate a change of form, a transition
from one stage of development into another (such as the change of
an infant into a schoolchild, a schoolchild into a young adult, or a
person's entry into marriage or motherhood, among others) that is
always accompanied by distress and that manifests itself in night-
mares and fantasies of abduction. Yet Bilz sharply distinguishes
dreams, with their undifferentiated "archaic raw material," from the
artistically arranged narrative of folktales. Jung and his students also
see in the folktale the mirroring or the preformation of a process of
development, more specifically the process of integration that occurs
in mid-life. To Jung, the journey of the hero or heroine to an underworld or supernatural world or into a distant realm, or his or her
marriage to an animal, are symbols of a turning toward the unconscious that leads to a dangerous but vital confrontation between the
conscious and the unconscious. If all goes well, this process results in
synthesis and spiritual integration. According to this view, the brother
who is "left behind" in the well-known tale of *The Two Brothers*
(KHM No. 60; AT 303) is representative of a component of the human
soul that has a deeper familiarity with the powers of the unconscious
and can therefore bring about the rescue, like the helpful animals of
other folktales. The individual characters of a folktale are thus seen
as components of the human personality, and in essence the folktale
represents a psychological process. The abstract stylization of the
tale, together with the figurative quality of its human beings and

animals, is called on to witness that tales do not deal with fully individualized persons or the portrayal of an external world; rather, they represent an internal reality. Even if this conclusion cannot be proven absolutely, one still must grant that precisely because the folktale never directly expresses the psychological, its characters and events can easily be taken as symbolic images of inner potentialities and processes.

In spite of a number of forced interpretations, the monumental work of Hedwig von Beit and Marie-Louise von Franz offers a wealth of material and of interpretations of individual tales and contains many interesting viewpoints and instructive hints.[20] We may take as an example their interpretation of the oft-cited amorality of the folktale. According to von Beit and von Franz, sympathy for the hero's false brothers or evil sisters signifies weak toleration of corrupt impulses in one's own soul, while a sense of loyalty directed toward the fighting giants means surrendering one's powers to the primitive forces of the unconscious. Laziness on the part of the hero can mean a refusal to conform to conventional values and can hint at a connection with the unconscious. The laziness of the unkind sister in *The Kind and the Unkind Girls* (AT 480), however, is evidence of a corrupted lapse into the unconscious. (As we have seen, the Janus face of all phenomena and attitudes in the folktale recurs again and again.) The concept of the folktale as a representation of internal processes thus leads to a re-evaluation of certain features that others have viewed as immoral.

Jung and his students have astutely illuminated one side of the folktale. They themselves know that the folktale is not completely explained by their work. A poetic composition can never be fully analyzed. The folktale must be interpreted on different levels, and the confrontation of human beings with the external world and with the cosmos is mirrored in it just as much as is the confrontation of human beings with themselves.

The true guardians of the folktale are neither literary scholars nor psychologists, but folklorists. The products of their devoted collecting activities are continually brought to light in new scientific and popular publications, while at the same time thousands of manuscripts have been made available in the folklore archives of many

European countries. More and more, the principle prevails of publishing the tales word-for-word as they were collected. As one example we may cite Kurt Ranke's excellent, richly documented, and fully annotated edition of the folktales of Schleswig-Holstein.[21] For Ranke, "the many less talented narrators have the same claim to be counted among the supporting base of the tradition . . . as do the few good ones." Gottfried Henssen proceeds from a similar point of view in his edition of the narratives of Mecklenburg. Here and there he simply prints the bare notations of the collector, Richard Wossidlo. Still, he gives a place of honor to talented narrators.[22] The folktales and other narratives of a single outstanding storyteller (whose version of Cinderella we discussed on pp. 110–111 above) are edited by Henssen in his book *Überlieferung und Persönlichkeit: Die Erzählungen und Lieder des Egbert Gerrits* (Munich, 1951).

The monumental series *Märchen der Weltliteratur*, edited by Friedrich von der Leyen and published by Diederichs Verlag, is being edited anew and supplemented volume by volume. In addition, in the years since World War II another, smaller collection entitled *Das Gesicht der Völker* has been published by Erich Röth Verlag. Both collections are addressed to the general public and therefore single out for inclusion tales that are especially well narrated, while often the editor or translator either takes small liberties in rendering the text or relies on a text that has already been reworked. Since 1956, previously unpublished folktales have been printed in their original language and in translation in the annual volumes published by the Gesellschaft zur Pflege des Märchengutes der europäischen Völker (now titled simply the Europäische Märchengesellschaft).[23]

In an extensive collection of Swedish folktales that is appreciated as much by scholars as by general readers, Waldemar Liungman has published tales as yet mostly unprinted that, in large part, he collected himself.[24] In France, in 1955, Paul Delarue founded the series *Contes des cinq continents* (Paris: Éditions Érasme), a great undertaking that bears comparison with the *Märchen der Weltliteratur*. Even more important is his series *Contes merveilleux des provinces de France* (Paris: Éditions Érasme), each of whose volumes appears in a popular as well as a scholarly edition (since 1953) and contains mostly unpublished material. Delarue's life work was crowned by the publication of a comprehensive, extensively annotated catalogue of the French folktale, the first volume of which was published shortly after his death.[25]

In the 1950s both Austria and Italy came into possession of their representative anthology of folktales, their "Grimm," in the form of Karl Haiding's *Österreichs Märchenschatz* and Italo Calvino's *Fiabe italiane*.[26] Both works contain valuable scholarly notes, while the first includes a large number of tales that Haiding recorded himself. Since both books are addressed to a large general public, the wording and even, in part, the contents of the tales are adapted. Unfortunately, Calvino often takes liberties by adding poetic embellishments and insertions and thereby exceeds the limits of the permissible.

In many of the editions mentioned, as well as in other editions, much attention is paid to what has been called the "biology of the folktale" (*Märchenbiologie*); that is, the personality of the male or female narrator and the role of the folktale and the act of narration in the life of the individual and the community. Since the appearance of M. Asadowskij's *Eine sibirische Märchenerzählerin*, FFC No. 68 (Helsinki, 1928),[27] a number of other independent studies have been devoted to the life of folk narratives and to the narrative repertory, narrative style, and way of life of individual storytellers. Representative of this direction in scholarship are such persons as J. H. Delargy (Ireland), Gottfried Henssen and Hermann Bausinger (Germany), Leza Uffer (Switzerland), Karl Haiding and Elli Zenker (Austria), and Milko Matičetov and Maja Bošković (Yugoslavia). Representative titles are *Lebendiges Erzählen* by Bausinger (Diss. Tübingen 1952) and *Von der Gerbärdensprache der Märchenerzähler* by Haiding, FFC No. 155 (Helsinki, 1955).

The compilation of catalogues and type and motif indexes is one of the most impressive achievements of scholars in the field of folk narrative. Of international importance is the Tale-Type Index compiled by Antti Aarne and expanded by Stith Thompson. It distinguishes between "animal tales," "ordinary folktales" (including under this rubric tales of magic, religious tales, novellas, and tales of the stupid ogre), and "jokes and anecdotes" (including tall tales).[28] The index reduces to certain basic types the narratives that exist all over the world in innumerable variants. Thus, one finds the tale of *The*

Two Brothers (mentioned above on p. 117) listed as Type 303 *(The Twins or Blood-Brothers)* in the section "tales of magic" under the key word "supernatural adversaries," with cross reference to Type 300 *(The Dragon-Slayer)*, which can exist as part of the same tale. Aarne gives a concise summary of the contents of the tale and Thompson carefully divides it into episodes. The famous incident in which the second brother places a sword between himself and the queen or princess who mistakes him for her husband is listed as the third element of the fourth episode, *The Chaste Brother:* "At night he lays a naked sword between himself and her."

Much more extensive than the Tale-Type Index is Thompson's Motif Index,[29] which distinguishes about forty thousand motifs under headings such as *Animals* (B), *Tabu* (C), *Ogres* (G), and *Unnatural Cruelty* (S). Our sword motif—"Sword of Chastity," T 351—is found in the section titled *Sex* (T) under the subheading "Chastity and celibacy" in the subcategory "Chaste sleeping together" (T 350–356). Thompson's Tale-Type Index and Motif Index are cross-referenced and, furthermore, include references to Johannes Bolte and Georg Polívka's five-volume *Anmerkungen zu den Kinder- und Hausmärchen der Brüder Grimm* (Leipzig, 1913–1932), which designates the structure of many thousands of international folktale variants by labeling their constituent motifs with letters and numbers (for example, A^4BC^3DE or B^1CDE^1F). The Motif Index also contains bibliographical references to special studies dealing with particular motifs. Although the Tale-Type Index and Motif Index were originally intended as an aid to the research of the Finnish School (see p. 123 below), both works have attained a value of their own as a grandly planned alphabet of the themes and types of folk narrative, and both can serve as models for analogous undertakings in the realm of higher literature.

To folklorists we likewise owe the most important reviews of scholarly research that have appeared since World War II. They are the work of Will-Erich Peuckert,[30] Lutz Röhrich,[31] and Kurt Ranke.[32] Since 1957 Ranke has published *Fabula*, a trilingual journal for narrative research that regularly informs of new publications, adds supplementary type indexes to previously published collections, prints original essays, and publishes texts and special studies in two auxiliary series. The two series complement the Finnish series *Folklore Fellows Communications* (FFC), which since 1910 has published studies on the folktale and other folkloristic subjects, mostly in German, with some in English or French. A great collective of scholars of all orientations under the leadership of Ranke is now preparing an international *Enzyklopädie des Märchens* that is to replace Lutz Mackensen's unfinished *Handwörterbuch des deutschen Märchens* (1930–40).[33]

Among individual folkloristic achievements, Lutz Röhrich's weighty book *Märchen und Wirklichkeit* deserves special mention.[34] It not only summarizes the customs, rites, beliefs, and habits of thought that are mirrored in folktales and at the same time discusses elements of their ethnic, social, historical, and geographic background, thereby taking into consideration survivals of former culture as well as the culture of today; it also asks the fundamental question, Why are human beings generally so receptive to the folktale? As a folklorist, Röhrich finds the motif more important than the style ("The genres change but the motifs remain constant"), and he emphasizes the relation of the folktale to reality more than its relation to the fantastic. He assumes that the folktale has had a fantastic and inventive side from the beginning, too, of course. A story in which a relation to reality has not yet been wedded to literary composition could scarcely be considered to fall under the heading of folktale. Indeed, the basic motifs of human existence can be traced in the narrative literature of all times, and motif-complexes as well can be preserved for a long time and can migrate from one genre to another without breaking apart—but not without changing their appearance. The internal compulsion to develop characteristically differing genres belongs just as clearly to the history of the human spirit as does the impulse to create certain groups of motifs. Röhrich rightly holds that only the concurrence of many criteria permits us to call a narrative a folktale. But instead of following Röhrich in denying the possibility of a definition, I would hold that the concept of the folktale must comprehend both content and form. In my own view, the folktale is a narrative of adventures that represents in short form, sublimated and organized, the essential relations of human existence.[35] With the terms "sublimation" and "all-inclusiveness" *(Welthaltigkeit)*, in the sense I have used them in this book, I believe I have defined the folktale insofar as the areas of form and motif are concerned, while the term "narrative of adventures" *(Abenteuererzählung*, from *ad* +

ventura) at the same time encompasses the protagonist, the human hero who sets out journeying from home and reacts to and comes to terms with whatever he encounters. At the time of this writing, Röhrich's informative and cautious book is the most important contribution to the interpretation of the folktale through cultural and religious history and vice versa. In this regard it follows a scholarly direction that Will-Erich Peuckert identifies as the most essential and fruitful for folklorists.

The works of the so-called Finnish school, applying the historic-geographic method, are often regarded as purely folkloristic. This school endeavors to find evidence of the paths of migration of individual folktale types and to locate their centers of origin. Through careful comparison of all known variants, it attempts to establish a family tree of subtypes and finally to identify an archetype, or at least a basic form.[36] As Will-Erich Peuckert and others have pointed out, this endeavor conceals an essentially literary concern. If today the zeal for such studies has diminished and interest in them has waned, this is not simply because they have become very time-consuming and difficult due to the wealth of material available, nor only because the belief in the possibility of constructing a reliable archetype has been shaken, but also because of a shift in interest (evident in other disciplines as well) from the investigation of relations of interdependence to the investigation of the phenomenon itself. The existence of an enormous number of variants can divert attention from the individual narrative, whose intrinsic value is felt more keenly today. However, the great monographs retain their value independent of the specific goals and dogmas of the Finns and Swedes. They do not yield a stylistic history of the different folktale types, but they do give us a structural history, insofar as this can be attained. No one who engages in the study of an individual folktale would wish to forego these extensive investigations of narrative types. Since World War II the *Cinderella* cycle (AT 510 and related types), the tale type of *Amor and Psyche* (AT 425A and related types), and the tale type of *The Kind and the Unkind Girls* (AT 480) have been analyzed in exemplary manner by Anna Birgitta Rooth, Jan-Öjvind Swahn, and Warren E. Roberts.[37] The monograph on the tale-complex of *The Dragon-Slayer* and *The Twins or Blood-Brothers* that we have mentioned repeatedly in this chapter was written earlier by Kurt Ranke.[38]

A comprehensive survey of the origin, diffusion, and paths of migration of all the most important folktales and folktale-like narratives told by developed and undeveloped peoples is provided by Stith Thompson in *The Folktale*, a standard work whose second edition was published in New York in 1951.[39] It contains an index of tale-types and an index of motifs that give the reader an introduction to the contents and design of the great type and motif catalogues by Thompson that were discussed earlier.

Friedrich von der Leyen takes into consideration all directions of folktale scholarship in his booklet *Das Märchen*, with whose fourth edition (Heidelberg, 1958) Kurt Schier collaborated. It reviews the most important achievements, goals, and methods of folktale research and appropriately characterizes the different forms taken by the folktale in different societies, much as von der Leyen did at greater length in his two volumes *Die Welt der Märchen* (Düsseldorf, 1953 and 1954), which rely mainly on the series *Märchen der Weltliteratur*.

In his book *Das Märchen: Dichtung und Deutung* (Frankfurt, 1959), the literary scholar Karl Justus Obenauer first of all inquires into the meaning of the folktale, discusses such matters as number and animal symbolism, and offers a number of interpretations of particular tales. Worth final mention is Wilhelm Schoff's book *Zur Enstehungsgeschichte der Grimmschen Märchen* (Hamburg, 1959), which describes the informants of the Grimm brothers, honors their contributions, and makes public original drafts and tales from the Grimms' legacy that until 1959 had only been published in scholarly journals if at all.

Thus our short survey of folktale scholarship since World War II fittingly concludes with the founders of folktale scholarship, Jacob and Wilhelm Grimm—folklorists, literary scholars, and interpreters of myths all in one. Today, only the cooperation of different scholarly disciplines can do justice to the folktale. Anyone who studies the folktale carefully from his or her area of specialty serves the other disciplines as well. Literary scholars, insofar as they interpret the folktale justly, are also performing folkloristic work, and folklorists perform the work of literary history. Psychologists likewise render services to both sciences and may themselves rely on folkloristic and literary research. Neither individual scholars nor the different disciplines have any reason to regard each other with distrust, for they

achieve their best in cooperation. Specialization has
since the time of the Grimms. One quality is just a
it was then, however: a love of the subject. J̶̶
Grimm were not only scholars, they were also lovers of the folktale.
If scholars of today feel the same deep respect for individual narratives, then they do no damage when they probe into them with the
sharpest instruments at their disposal. If examined ably, the folktale,
an archetype of the art of narration, may provide us with information concerning the nature of literature and of human beings.

In its various modes and in its different versions, the folktale
expresses not only a variety of universal human needs and attitudes
but also a living diversity of epochs, nationalities, landscapes, social
strata, and personalities. Each single folktale has its own meaning
and can be analyzed and interpreted according to different points of
view. At the same time, when taken as a harmonious group, folktales present an encompassing image of humankind and the world.
Attempts at psychological or anthropological interpretation of particular tales (as undertaken by Jung and his school) and the attempt
to grasp the nature and character of the genre (as I have ventured to
do in this book) are not mutually exclusive; rather, they supplement
each other. Any particular tale possesses the value and charm of the
unique. It also has the advantage of belonging to a viable suprapersonal genre and of participating in this genre's inner necessities. At
the same time as the folktale leads us into the midst of the rich nuances
of the life of the folk and the individual, it thus leads us to the great
constants of the human condition.

Supplement: Structural Folktale Scholarship

In the 1960s and 1970s, structural folktale scholarship began in earnest under the influence of Vladimir Propp's book *Morphology of the Folktale*.[1] Published in 1928, but translated into English only in 1958 and into other languages even later, Propp's structural analysis is a kind of counterpart to the stylistic analysis attempted in the present book and deserves to be summarized and critically evaluated briefly here.

Propp's fundamental discovery was that there exist innumerable wondertales—his investigation is concerned only with these, not with novellas, religious folktales, or farcical folktales—that have completely different content, but similar structure. Just as in language there exist innumerable sentences of wholly different content but the same construction, he sees the structure of folktales as constant and invariable and their content as variable.

Comparison with the verbal sentence suggests an objection to Propp's theory: namely, that to reverse the terms of the discussion, one and the same statement can be formulated in sentences of completely different construction. In this event the content remains constant, while the variable element is the structure (the order of the parts of the sentence, for example, or the construction of principal or dependent clauses). American scholars have gone as far as to oppose to Propp's thesis the idea that it is ultimately a question of point of view whether one designates content or structure, the actors or the actions, as the constants or the variables.[2] Indeed, instead of speaking of constants and variables, we might perhaps better speak of structure-forming and non-structure-forming elements, terms that Propp himself uses in the afterword to the Italian edition of his work (*elementi costruttivi* and *elementi non costruttivi*).[3]

I would grant to Propp that in the folktale, and not just the wondertale alone, actions are of greater consequence and of higher relevance than the persons who carry out these actions. Propp makes this clear by the following comparison (pp. 19–20):

1. A tsar gives an eagle to a hero. The eagle carries the hero away to another kingdom.
2. An old man gives Súčenko a horse. The horse carries Súčenko away to another kingdom.
3. A sorcerer gives Iván a little boat. The boat takes Iván to another kingdom.
4. A princess gives Iván a ring. Young men appearing from out of the ring carry Iván away into another kingdom. . . .

In these examples the actions are obviously more important than the agents. The subjects can be substituted for one another, but the predicates remain the same. In place of the tsar, one can readily substitute the tsar's daughter or grandfather or a magician; as a means of conveyance, an eagle, a horse, a boat, or a magic ring can serve equally well (whether directly or, as with the ring, indirectly). The proceedings remain the same.

Again a reference to linguistic facts is useful. The construction of sentences is much more consistent than their content, for there are vastly more sentences with the same structure than with the same message. Moreover, linguistic scholarship has long since recognized the primary importance of the predicate among the various parts of the sentence. Correspondingly, in the folktale and in other kinds of narratives as well, the structure is more constant than the statement—the "content," or theme, or substance—even if this is not true to the extent as the verbal phrase, for Propp underestimates the significance and the impressive constancy of the dramatis personae. Actors can be substituted for one another more readily in the folktale than, for example, in the legend, and magic objects or magical events do not occur in every wondertale. But the genre as a type cannot be imagined without kings, princes, princesses, witches, or magic objects. These figures and objects recur with just as remarkable constancy as do any stereotyped events and sequences. They contribute their part to giving the wondertale its specific character. If kings, princesses, and witches were systematically replaced by figures of everyday life, while magic horses or rings were replaced with airplanes, the narrative structure could be retained but the character of the genre would be decisively changed. Its symbolic power would be weakened and would be of a different sort.

If dissimilar characters or incidents have the same effects—that is, have the same function within the narrative—Propp speaks of them as *transformations*. A command, a request (to fetch something), a task, or an act of expulsion are only variations or transformations of the basic element "sending away." The term "transformation" suggests that a certain form is to be regarded as the original one. In the previous example, according to Propp, this would be the command (accompanied by threats and promises).[4] The archaically religious, the heroic, or the fantastic form of an element is to be regarded as primary and the realistic or rationalistic form as secondary.[5] (With this thesis, contained in his essay on transformations, Propp departs from mere description and proceeds to historical and genetic conjectures, on which he elaborates in his later book on the historical roots of the folktale.)[6] As another example of possible transformations Propp cites the element of "reversal": a female figure is substituted for a male, or vice versa, or a locked hut is replaced with one with a wide-open door.[7] An object can take the place of a person: a precious (perhaps magic) object that is the goal of a quest is a transformation of a golden-haired princess who is the goal of a quest.[8] A magical aid can have the same function as a supernatural helper (pp. 45–46). The absence of an element can be a kind of transformation as well, as when we find a test without a tester (p. 49). When Propp declares that from a structural point of view there is only a single type of wondertale, one that is represented most accurately by the dragon-slayer type,[9] then he evidently regards all other wondertales as transformations of this tale (to which he therefore also ascribes chronological priority).

One danger in this approach, as the last examples have shown, is that of forcing the material into preconceived molds. If a person wants to reduce everything to one basic element, even the most dissimilar things will seem to be "nothing but a transformation."[10] To do justice to Propp's position and intention, however, one must realize that what matters to him is the effect of each element on the plot. Seen from this point of view, a quest for the water of life can indeed fulfill the same essential function as a quest for a princess, while a final wedding can fulfill the same function as a simple material reward. Propp logically uses the term "functions" (more precisely, "functions of dramatis personae")[11] to designate the basic elements of the plot of the wondertale that he declares to be constant. Since the unexplained use of the word "function" seems strange, Alan Dundes has suggested replacing it with the term "motifeme,"[12] while others speak of "function slots."[13] Both of these terms indicate that we are dealing with structural molds that can be filled in various ways. For example, the motifeme of *interdiction* (in Propp's terms, the "function" of interdiction) can be fulfilled by a warning not to go out into the street or by a warning not to enter a certain chamber. Dundes terms these specific motifs "allomotifs."

Since Propp views an element's function as what is significant (here we speak of narrative function, not symbolic function—the ambiguity of the word makes Dundes' terminology preferable), we can see that he is concerned with the relative placement of elements and with the ordering of each element within the whole. Propp transcends the motif hunting of atomistic scholarship.[14] His attempt accords with one of the essential requirements of our century, which has adopted as one of its leading concepts the maxim, "The whole takes precedence over its parts." Propp's theory of transformations, which he developed from the model of Goethe's morphology,[15] corresponds to present-day needs and a general human striving to reduce diversity to unity. Through his acknowledgment of Goethe, Propp reveals that he sees similar forces operating in the formation of folktales and in nature at large (he speaks of "iron laws"),[16] so that folktales almost seem to compose themselves, as was previously observed by the Grimms. "The realm of nature and the realm of human activity cannot be separated," writes Propp.[17] "There exists something that they hold in common: similar laws that can be studied by related methods"—that is, with "exact methods" like those that are used today in the humanities and social sciences as well as the natural sciences.

Although Propp strictly confined his research to the Russian wondertale, he was convinced that with insignificant modifications his results, as far as they were correct, were also valid for non-Russian materials (p. 100). One of his most important theses is that the number of "functions" is limited. He mentions thirty-one possible functions, and other scholars have tried to reduce this number.[18] He regards the one absolutely necessary function to be the element of lack or villainy (a situation of lack, or an injury caused by a villain). He thus arrives at the following definition: "Viewed morphologically, any narrative can be called a wondertale (*Zaubermärchen, conte merveilleux*) that develops from an act of injury or a state of lack, through certain mediating functions, to an eventual wedding or other concluding (or extricating) functions."[19]

Within the framework of such a definition, it would be preferable to exclude wedding as a mere motif, whereas injury and lack are clearly motifemes. More important is the question of whether the definition is too broad. Propp does not specify the minimum number of functions that are necessary to constitute a wondertale.[20] The sequence of *lack* leading to *lack liquidated* is a formula that is valid not only for the wondertale but for many other narratives and real-life situations as well. Modern biology regards the human being as a being living in lack (*Mangelwesen*) who precisely on this account seeks to come into possession of what he lacks, and who therefore advances further than other forms of life that are more self-sufficient in themselves. The experience of a human being or a folktale hero is a little like the experience of Saul, "who went to seek his father's she-asses and found a kingdom."[21] The formula of *lack* (or injury) followed by *lack liquidated* (or injury redressed) designates a basic phenomenon. As Paul Helwig writes, "Life is what comes about when obstacles are interposed between the onset of a desire and its gratification."[22] Not only human beings but all other forms of life live in the rhythm that is encompassed by the formula of lack and lack liquidated. An essential accomplishment of Propp's definition seems to me to be that without intending to do so, it reveals the folktale hero as a representative of the human race, or even of living beings in general. On the other hand, for this very reason the definition is too broad.

Propp himself states that his definition can also be applied to myth, for example.[23] Eleasar Meletinskij reminds us that myth is often concerned with the liquidation of an element of lack affecting the group (a "collective" lack).[24] The mythic hero must fetch the earth up out of the water or bring back the sunlight, for example. Propp moves the folktale, which he believes must derive from myth, too close to the latter. Meletinskij, taking issue with Lévi-Strauss and Greimas, but implicitly affecting Propp as well, points out important differences between the two genres. While tests (or trials) are characteristic of the wondertale, they play an unimportant role in myth.[25] In the folktale the gifts of otherworldly helpers are only a means to fulfill tasks and gain supremacy in contests that finally lead to the realization of a goal (a royal wedding, for example). In myth and in mythological narratives, by contrast, the goal is, for example, to obtain valuable resources of nature and culture or to gain the favor of guardian spirits. Marriage (with an animal spouse, for example) can sometimes be a means of reaching this goal: what in the folktale is an end is a means in myth and in mythological narratives.[26] A nonstructural distinction between the two genres is that in the folktale, as already mentioned, the motif of lack regularly affects an individual, while in myth it affects a group. In addition, mythic events can very well take place exclusively among supernatural beings, while this would be unthinkable in the wondertale, which regularly features human heroes, heroines, and partners.[27] The last two points make it clear that nonstructural as well as structural distinctions can be essential and can appear with clear consistency.

Of the thirty-one functions established by Propp, a few may be mentioned as examples. *Lack* corresponds to *lack liquidated; interdiction* is followed by *violation;* an attempt at *deceit* is followed by the act of *being deceived* (whereby, as an interesting stipulation, the hero can become the accomplice of the antagonist); a *test* is followed by the *receipt* of a magic agent; a *contest* is followed by *victory.* The combination of events into binary pairs is obvious and in part is almost given by definition. How far Propp is correct in postulating that the sequence of functions is always basically the same is subject to dispute.[28]

The thirty-one functions are distributed among seven leading dramatis personae: the antagonist (or villain); the donor (who presents the magical gift); the helper; the object of a quest (such as a princess); the dispatcher; the hero; and the false hero (or antihero or usurper). In reality these are roles rather than characters, as on the one hand a single character can assume multiple roles, while on the other hand several characters can share a single role.

The mere enumeration of the functions and roles distinguished by Propp, even apart from their syntagmatic linking, reveals something of the character of the wondertale. Propp's definition should be broadened by specifying the minimum number of connecting links that are necessary (the "mediating functions" between lack and lack liquidated) and should be completed by discussion of the characteristics that constitute the folktale *style*. As the definition stands now, even if one were to integrate into it the seven-role model—here again Propp does not specify a minimum number of roles—it is valid for other narratives besides the wondertale and even for nonliterary life processes, as we have seen.

Propp considered his structural research a necessary prerequisite for historical and genetic folktale research, as well as for stylistic analyses, since first one must establish what the folktale really is.[29] I find this view almost as mistaken as the Finnish school's concept that only after identifying the original form of the various folktale types can one attempt to interpret them.[30] While strict definitions are always problematical, there exists an adequate preexisting consensus concerning the concept of the wondertale and the folktale in general. In fact, Propp himself bases his work on tales numbered 50 to 151 in the Afanas'ev collection, and he thereby accepts Afanas'ev's prior decision as to which narratives are to be regarded as wondertales. Stylistic investigations can be undertaken independently of structural research, and the same is true of historical and genetic investigations. Although Propp categorically claims that synchronic research must precede diachronic, in his later study of the historical roots of the wondertale he makes conspicuously few references to his structural analysis.

In its own right—to defend Propp against himself—Propp's structural analysis is no mere preliminary study. Alan Dundes, Reinhold Breymeyer, and others have pointed out a few of its many possible implications.[31] Here I shall only mention their call for an extension of structural research along the lines of Propp's model to classics of world literature, to legends and farcical tales, and to proverbs, riddles, games, films, and comic strips. American, French,

East European, and Israeli scholars have addressed such problems and in the process have also had occasion to evaluate critically some of Propp's theses.[32]

One final word about the term "morphology." The word suggests that—true to Goethe's saying, as cited by Propp, that "the study of form is the study of metamorphoses" (*Gestaltenlehre ist Verwandlungslehre*)—Propp's work is concerned not just with syntagmatic structural analysis but also with the discovery of transformations (metamorphoses) on the basis of paradigmatic evidence as well. Thus, one may say that Propp's *Morphology of the Folktale* is a work of far-reaching importance. Because it approaches the folktale from a completely different direction and in a different manner than I have taken in the present book, it has deserved special independent consideration. Propp's structural analysis and my stylistic analysis work hand in hand to complement one another.

Notes

TRANSLATOR'S PREFACE

1. The change of ethical coloring can clearly be seen, for example, in the 1807 edition of "The History of Jack and the Beanstalk" (Opie, pp. 164–174), in which certain changes in the plot and persistent editorial footnotes remind the reader that good boys should live at home in obedience to their mothers, whereas the Jack of the true folktale succeeds precisely be-

cause of his independence in leaving home and mother.

2. The distinction between the fairy tale and the oral folktale and the afterlife of both forms in the mass media are addressed from a Marxist perspective by Jack Zipes in his book *Breaking the Magic Spell: Radical Theories of Folk and Fairy Tales* (Austin: Univ. of Texas Press, 1979).

3. *The Uses of Enchantment: The Meaning and Importance of Fairy Tales* (New York: Knopf, 1976).

4. Dégh's book was first published in Berlin in 1962 under the title *Märchen, Erzähler und Erzählgemeinschaft dargestellt an der ungarischen Volksüberlieferung;* its English translation, by Emily M. Schossberger, was published in 1969 by Indiana University Press, Bloomington. It is well supplemented by Dégh, ed., *Folktales of Hungary,* trans. Judit Halász (Chicago: Univ. of Chicago Press, 1965), which includes many tales collected by Dégh from the narrators discussed in *Folktales and Society.*

5. See, for example, Roger D. Abrahams, "Folklore in Culture: Notes Toward an Analytic Method," *Texas Studies in Literature and Language,* 5 (1963), rpt. in *Readings in American Folklore,* ed. Jan Harold Brunvand (New York: Norton, 1979), pp. 390–403; and Dan Ben-Amos, "Toward a Definition of Folklore in Context," *JAF,* 84 (1971), rpt. in Brunvand, pp. 427–443. An outstanding example of a functional and contextual approach to a genre other than the folktale is Henry Glassie's *All Silver and No Brass: An Irish Christmas Mumming* (Bloomington: Indiana Univ. Press, 1975); while in *Deep Down in the Jungle: Negro Narrative Folklore from the Streets of Philadelphia,* 2nd ed. (Chicago: Aldine, 1970), Roger Abrahams discusses certain types of folklore not as texts, but as performances taking place within the context of Black life in the inner city. In his recent textbook *The Dynamics of Folklore* (Boston: Houghton Mifflin, 1979), Barre Toelken discards the conventional generic approach to folklore in favor of an approach that stresses process, performance, and community.

6. See Isabel Gordon Carter, "Mountain White Folk-Lore: Tales from the Southern Blue Ridge," *JAF,* 38 (1925), 340–374, featuring verbatim texts; Richard Chase, *The Jack Tales* (Cambridge, Mass.: Houghton Mifflin, 1943), and *Grandfather Tales* (Boston: Houghton Mifflin, 1948), featuring his own retellings; and C. Paige Gutierrez, "The Jack Tale: A Definition of a Folk Tale Sub-Genre," *North Carolina Folklore Journal,* 26 (1978), 85–110. In the same September issue of *North Carolina Folklore Journal* are four other studies relating to the Jack tales. Vance Randolph has published many folktales from the Ozarks in his own retellings in four collections: *Who Blowed Up the Church House? and Other Ozark Folk Tales* (1952), *The Devil's Pretty Daughter and Other Ozark Folk Tales* (1955), *The Talking Turtle and Other Ozark Folk Tales* (1957), and *Sticks in the Knapsack and Other Ozark Folktales* (1958), all published by Colum-

bia University Press, New York. The standard bibliographical guide to North American and British folktales published before 1966 is Ernest W. Baughman, *Type and Motif-Index of the Folktales of England and North America* (The Hague: Mouton, 1966).

7. Most of these tales are unpublished; a few have appeared in the pages of *Tocher*, an invaluable little journal devoted to the presentation of material from the Archive of the School of Scottish Studies, Edinburgh.

8. *A Dictionary of British Folk-Tales in the English Language* (Bloomington: Indiana Univ. Press, 1970–71). The four volumes are divided into Part A: Folk Narratives (including a volume of "Fables and Exempla and Fairy Tales" and a volume of "Jocular Tales, Novelle, and Nursery Tales") and Part B: Folk Legends (including another pair of volumes divided by subject, according to whether the legends center on the activities of devils, fairies, ghosts, giants, and so on). The inconvenience of the editor's alphabetical arrangement of tales within each subcategory is diminished by the inclusion of two indexes of tale-types and migratory legends, one in Part A, Vol. I (pp. 35–77) and one in Part B, Vol. I (pp. xxv–xxxix).

9. These include volumes of the folktales of England, Ireland, France, Germany, Norway, Hungary, Greece, Israel, Egypt, China, Japan, Mexico, and Chile.

10. For the first three volumes of the *Enzyklopädie des Märchens* (see Chapter 7, note 33 below), Lüthi has provided brief articles on terms that play a key role in his discussions of the folktale style: *Abstraktheit, Affekte, Allverbundenheit, Altern, Blindes Motiv, Dekorative Züge, Detail, Dialog, Distanz, Drei, Dreigliedrigkeit, Dynamik, Eindimensionalität,* and *Einsträngigkeit.* For forthcoming volumes, articles are in preparation on *Extreme, Flächenhaftigkeit, Isolation, Stil, Stumpfes Motiv,* and *Sublimation.* —*Trans.*

11. For further information on terminology, see Lauritz Bødker, *Folk Literature (Germanic),* International Dictionary of Regional European Ethnology and Folklore, Vol. II (Copenhagen: Rosenkilde and Bagger, 1965), especially the items Fable (p. 94), Fairy Tale (p. 96), Folktale (pp. 106–109), *Geschichte* (pp. 122–123), *Kunstmärchen* (p. 168), Legend (pp. 173–174), *Legende* (pp. 175–177), Local Legend (p. 181), *Märchen* (pp. 184–188), Migratory Legend (pp. 198–199), Myth (p. 205), Novella (pp. 215–216), *Sage* (pp. 255–259), Saint's Legend (p. 262), *Schimäremärchen* (pp. 265–266), *Schwank* (pp. 267–269), *Schwankmärchen* (p. 269), Tale of Magic (pp. 291–292), *Volksmärchen* (p. 322), *Volkssage* (p. 323), and *Zaubermärchen* (p. 329).

INTRODUCTION

1. Jakob Minor, ed., *Novalis' Schriften* (Jena: Diederichs, 1923), III, 4 (No. 6) and III, 327 (No. 919).

2. The obscurity of the Grimms' *Deutsche Sagen* should be lessened somewhat by the publication of *The German Legends of the Brothers Grimm*, 2 vols., trans. and ed. Donald Ward (Philadelphia: Institute for the Study of Human Issues, 1981).—*Trans.*

3. Walter Berendsohn, *Grundformen volkstümlicher Erzählerkunst in den Kinder- und Hausmärchen der Brüder Grimm* (Hamburg: Gente, 1921), p. 35; see also Chapter 5 below, notes 26 and 32.

4. C. W. von Sydow, "Kategorien der Prosa-Volksdichtung," in *Volkskundliche Gaben: John Meier zum siebzigsten Geburtstag dargebracht*, ed. Harry Schewe (Berlin: de Gruyter, 1934), pp. 257–261; cf. Chapter 5 below, note 6.

5. Lutz Mackensen, "Das deutsche Volksmärchen," in *Handbuch der deutschen Volkskunde*, ed. W. Pessler (Potsdam: Athenaion, 1934), II, 317; cf. Will-Erich Peuckert, *Deutsches Volkstum in Märchen und Sage, Schwank und Rätsel* (Berlin: de Gruyter, 1938), p. 11.

6. Mackensen, in Pessler, p. 306.

7. August von Löwis of Menar, ed., *Russische Volksmärchen* (Jena: Diederichs, 1927), p. x (from the series *Märchen der Weltliteratur*, henceforth abbreviated MdW).

8. Günter Otto, *Bäuerliche Ethik in der schlesischen Volkssage* (Breslau: Maruschke and Berendt, 1937), p. 5.

9. Robert Petsch, "Die Kunstform des Märchens," *ZfV*, N.S. 7 (1935), 4. Cf. also the views that I have presented in my dissertation *Die Gabe im Märchen und in der Sage* (Bern: Francke, 1943), henceforth abbreviated *Gabe*. All three works just cited regard as transient those legends that only tell of gruesome, exceptional, or strange events rather than of the numinous. On this point see also Rudolf Otto, who understands "the fearful and the sublime" (*das Fürchterliche und das Erhabene*) to be an analogous means of expressing the idea of "*das Tremendum*"; see his *Das Heilige*, 2nd ed. (Breslau: Trewendt and Gramer, 1918), trans. by John W. Harvey as *The Idea of the Holy* (London: Oxford Univ. Press, 1923), pp. 12–14. For contrasting views see Friedrich Ranke, "Volkssagenforschung," *DVfL*, 19 (1941), pp. 1–36 of the Referatenheft; and Peuckert, p. 105; cf. also S. Singer, who places legends involving the miraculous (*Wundersagen*) and legends involving natural events (*natürliche Sagen*) side by side as groups of equal importance in his book *Schweizermärchen* (Bern: Francke, 1903), p. 10.

10. André Jolles, *Einfache Formen*, 2nd ed. (Halle: Niemeyer, 1956).

11. Albert Wesselski, *Versuch einer Theorie des Märchens*, Prager deutsche Studien, 45 (Reichenberg: Kraus, 1931), p. 100; R. Petsch, "Die Lehre von den 'Einfachen Formen,' " *DVfL*, 10 (1932), 366; Friedrich Ranke, "Märchenforschung," *DVfL*, 14 (1936), 262; Friedrich Ranke, "Aufgaben volkskundlicher Märchenforschung," *ZfV*, N.S. 4 (1933), 208; and Mackensen, in Pessler, pp. 315 and 319.

CHAPTER ONE

1. Paul Zaunert, ed., *Deutsche Märchen seit Grimm*, MdW (Jena: Diederichs, 1919), I, 137.

2. Gian Bundi, ed., *Märchen aus dem Bündnerland* (Basel: Schweizerische Gesellschaft für Volkskunde, 1935), p. 2.

3. Johannes Bolte and Georg Polívka, *Anmerkungen zu den Kinder- und Hausmärchen der Brüder Grimm*, 5 vols. (Leipzig: Dieterich'sche Verlagsbuchhandlung, 1913–32), II, 536 (henceforth abbreviated *Bolte-Polívka*).

4. Paul Zaunert, ed., *Rheinlandsagen* (Jena: Diederichs, 1924), I, 273; Gustav Jungbauer, *Böhmerwaldsagen* (Jena: Diederichs, 1924), p. 192; Paul Zaunert, ed., *Deutsche Natursagen* (Jena: Diederichs, 1921), I, 115; and cf. Hanns Bächtold-Stäubli, ed., *Handwörterbuch des deutschen Aberglaubens* (Berlin: de Gruyter, 1927–42), VI, 419; VIII, 669; IX (part 2), 594.

5. On this matter cf. Peuckert, p. 14.

6. Bundi, p. 1; Zaunert, *Deutsche Märchen seit Grimm*, I, 4; cf. Käte Müller-Lisowski, ed., *Irische Volksmärchen*, MdW (Jena: Diederichs, 1923), No. 20.

7. Zaunert, *Deutsche Märchen seit Grimm*, I, 5; rpt. in Max Lüthi, ed., *Europäische Volksmärchen* (Zürich: Manesse, 1951), pp. 306–307 (cf. Chapter 3 below, note 22).

8. From this Peuckert draws the conclusion that modern tales of magic (*Zaubermärchen*) could not have originated in a totemistic society. Totemism would have given rise to "mythtales" (*Mythenmärchen*), in which magic "is . . . an everyday affair, like eating, drinking, and sleeping" (pp. 14–15).

CHAPTER TWO

1. Cf. *Gabe*, sections 2 and 3, particularly pp. 28 and 46–50.

2. Max Boehm and F. Specht, eds., *Lettisch-litauische Volksmärchen*,

MdW (Jena: Diederichs, 1924), No. 1; see also E. Róna-Sklarek, ed., *Ungarische Volksmärchen* (Leipzig, 1909), pp. 196–197; and cf. p. 44 above.

3. For example, in KHM No. 31. It is intriguing how, in a German folktale recorded in the sixteenth century, the little earth cow (*Erdkühlein*) advises the heroine to shed tears when a certain future course of events comes to pass; see Karl Goedeke, *Schwänke des 16. Jahrhunderts* (Leipzig: Brockhaus, 1879), p. 12, rpt. in a slightly modernized edition by Ninon Hesse, *Deutsche Märchen vor und nach Grimm* (Zürich: Europa, 1956), p. 20. For commentaries on this "oldest version of the tale of *Cinderella*" see Albert Wesselski, *Deutsche Märchen vor Grimm* (Leipzig: Rohrer, 1938), pp. 304–309, and Ninon Hesse, "Das Erdkühlein," *Neue Zürcher Zeitung*, April 3, 1960 (No. 1118). The tale was first printed under the title "Ein schön History von einer Frawen mit zweyen Kindlin" in Martin Montanus, *Ander theyl der Gartengesellschaft* (Strassburg, c. 1560). [Lüthi discusses this tale in detail in Chapter 5 of *Once Upon a Time: On the Nature of Fairy Tales* (pp. 71–81).]

4. Zaunert, *Deutsche Märchen seit Grimm*, II, 169.

5. Axel Olrik, "Epische Gesetze der Volksdichtung," *Zeitschrift für deutsches Altertum*, 51 (1909), 1–12 (point 8). [An English translation of this important article, with critical commentary, is included in *The Study of Folklore*, ed. Alan Dundes (Englewood Cliffs: Prentice-Hall, 1965), pp. 129–141.]

6. Zaunert, ed., *Deutsche Märchen aus dem Donaulande*, MdW (Jena: Diederichs, 1926), p. 83.

7. Otto Sutermeister, *Kinder- und Hausmärchen aus der Schweiz*, 2nd ed. (Aarau: Sauerländer, 1873), No. 6; cf. *Gabe*, pp. 128–129.

8. Charlotte Bühler, *Das Märchen und die Phantasie des Kindes*, 4th ed. (Munich: Barth, 1958), p. 54. Cf. p. 53 (*Affekt*).

9. August Leskien, *Balkanmärchen*, MdW (Jena: Diederichs, 1919), p. 194 (Serbo-Croatian).

10. *Russische Volksmärchen*, No. 2.

11. An example is cited on p. 25. If in a Hungarian folktale it is said that the devilish king "became so furious that he exploded on the spot" (*Ungarische Volksmärchen*, p. 167), then this is another demonstration of the tendency of the folktale to let inner emotions appear on a level where they can be taken in by the eyes, thus translating the invisible into an image and thereby integrating it into the course of the action.

12. Wilhelm Wisser, ed., *Plattdeutsche Volksmärchen*, MdW (Jena: Diederichs, 1919), p. 243.

13. Cf. *Gabe*, pp. 109, 119–126.

14. Heinz Rölleke, *Die älteste Märchensammlung der Brüder Grimm:*

Synopse der handscriftlichen Urfassung von 1810 und der Erstdrucke von 1812 (Geneva: Martin Bodmer, 1975), p. 108.

15. For Perrault's text of this tale in comparison with the versions of Basile and the Grimms, see Fritz Ernst, *Dornröschen in drei Sprachen* (Bern: Huber, 1949).—*Trans.*

16. See *Gabe*, pp. 103, 129 ff.

17. See *Gabe*, p. 49.

CHAPTER THREE

1. *Balkanmärchen*, pp. 179–180 (Serbo-Croatian).

2. Gerhart Hauptmann, *Ausblicke* (Berlin: Fischer, 1924), p. 22.

3. For example, Klara Strobe, ed., *Nordische Volksmärchen*, MdW (Jena: Diederichs, 1919), II, No. 24 (Norwegian).

4. *Russische Volksmärchen*, No. 43.

5. *Balkanmärchen*, No. 17 (Bulgarian).

6. Emmanuel Cosquin, ed., *Contes populaires de Lorraine* (Paris: Vieweg, 1886), I, No. 1.

7. Friedrich S. Krauss, ed., *Sagen und Märchen der Südslaven*, II (Leipzig: Friedrich, 1884), No. 131.

8. Bolte-Polívka, I, 208.

9. See *Gabe*, pp. 55–56.

10. P. Kretschmer, *Neugriechische Märchen*, MdW (Jena: Diederichs, 1919), No. 31 (Cretan).

11. *Balkanmärchen*, No. 29 (Serbo-Croatian).

12. *Russische Volksmärchen*, No. 4.

13. For example, *Balkanmärchen*, No. 7 (Bulgarian).

14. A. Löwis of Menar, ed., *Finnische und estnische Volksmärchen*, MdW (Jena: Diederichs, 1922), No. 26 (Finnish).

15. *Ibid.*, No. 30 (Finnish).

16. *Balkanmärchen*, Nos. 2, 6, 12, 18 ("Everything there was black—the people, the animals, even the tsar himself").

17. *Nordische Volksmärchen*, II, No. 7 (Norwegian). A Russian folktale begins: "There once was a tsar, a mighty lord, who lived in a region as flat as a tablecloth" (*Russische Volksmärchen*, No. 43).

18. See *Gabe*, p. 95.

19. If he does not remain a truncated motif, in relation to which see pp. 60–64. In the Swiss folktale "Hans Tgavrêr," the princess wants to give the hero a hundred soldiers to take along on his journey. " 'Certainly not, I shall go alone,' said Hans. 'No, I will not let you go like that,' she answered. So in the end he decided to take forty men along with him"—but

even these he soon sends back home, and only then can his adventures begin. Leza Uffer, ed., *Rätoromanische Märchen und ihre Erzähler* (Basel: Schweizerische Gesellschaft für Volkskunde, 1945), No. 21, rpt. in Lüthi, *Europäische Volksmärchen*, p. 279, and in Uffer, *Die Märchen des Barba Plasch* (Zürich: Atlantis, 1955), p. 72.

20. *Balkanmärchen*, No. 17 (Bulgarian).

21. See *Gabe*, p. 135 (in allusion to *The Frog Prince*, KHM No. 1).

22. Zaunert, *Deutsche Märchen seit Grimm*, I, 1, rpt. in Lüthi, *Europäische Volksmärchen*, p. 301. The narrative was first printed in U. Jahn, ed., *Volksmärchen aus Pommern und Rügen*, I (Soltau: Norden, 1891).

23. See *Gabe*, pp. 61–62.

24. See *Gabe*, pp. 30–31.

25. For example, *Balkanmärchen*, No. 23 (Serbo-Croatian); see p. 41 above.

26. Not only in Grimm but in the Yugoslavian folktale as well: *Balkanmärchen*, No. 34 (Serbo-Croatian).

27. Zaunert, *Deutsche Märchen aus dem Donaulande*, pp. 62 ff.

28. Zaunert, *Deutsche Märchen seit Grimm*, I, 1 (see note 22 above).

29. See, for example, Cosquin, I, 32, 34.

30. *Russische Volksmärchen*, No. 4.

31. *Balkanmärchen*, No. 29 (Serbo-Croatian).

32. *Deutsche Märchen seit Grimm*, II, 285.

33. *Balkanmärchen*, No. 56.

34. I am using the term after the model of Wilhelm Worringer in his 1907 Bern dissertation, *Abstraktion und Einfühlung*, published in Munich by R. Piper & Co. in 1908 and frequently reprinted thereafter, most recently in 1959. For basic remarks pertaining to this work, see *Gabe*, p. 28 n., and my article *Abstraktheit* in the *Enzyklopädie des Märchens*, I (Berlin and New York: de Gruyter, 1977), cols. 34–36.

35. See further Mackensen, p. 309. That the original magic and power of the sacred numbers still find a faint echo in the folktale is emphasized by Karl Justus Obenauer in *Das Märchen: Dichtung und Deutung* (Frankfurt: Kostermann, 1959), pp. 93–127.

36. This principle is beautifully illustrated in the Lotharingian folktale of "Le Roi d'Angleterre et son filleul" (Cosquin, I, 32 ff.; German trans. in Lüthi, *Europäische Volksmärchen*, p. 150).

37. Giuseppe Pitrè, ed., *Novelle popolari Toscane*, I (Rome: Soc. Editrice del Libro Italiano, 1941), 3.

38. See pp. 9, 12–17, and 22–23 above. Occasional attempts at maintaining parallel plot lines, as with the simultaneous departure of two or three brothers, disappear before the dominant preference of the folktale for plots of a single strand (*Einsträngigkeit*). A modern narrator from Lor-

raine enjoys to the full, with heavy-handed transitions, the unaccustomed refinement of a double-stranded plot: "Now we leave the lad in the garden and go back, we return to Rosamunde and see how things are going there." Or: "Now we leave the pilgrims again and follow the lad." See Angelika Merkelbach-Pinck, ed., *Lothringer erzählen*, I (Saarbrücken: Saarbrücker Druckerei, 1936), 226, 230. For a similar effect see Plasch Spinas, another present-day folktale narrator, in Leza Uffer, ed., *Rätoromanische Märchen*, No. 21, trans. in Lüthi, *Europäische Volksmärchen*, p. 279): "Now let us leave him to prepare the sticks while we return to the princess, because he needed about three weeks to cut sticks for all the goats." See also a modern Greek tale: "Now let us leave the princess to wail and to search for him everywhere, and let us turn to the sugar merchant and his wife" (*Neugriechische Märchen*, No. 53). Cf. Bolte-Polívka, IV: 22-24.

39. *Balkanmärchen*, No. 2 (Bulgarian). In the frame story of *The Arabian Nights*, it is king Shahriar who every night for three years takes a beautiful girl as his wife, but has her head cut off at dawn; this is at once more rational and more realistic than the unreasonable and unexplained nonviolent death of the husbands in the Bulgarian folktale.

40. For example, *Balkanmärchen*, Nos. 42 and 43 (Serbo-Croatian), *Russische Volksmärchen*, No. 41.

41. *Lettisch-litauische Volksmärchen*, No. 1 (Latvian).

42. *Balkanmärchen*, No. 36 (Serbo-Croatian); *Lettisch-litauische Volksmärchen*, No. 1.

43. *Finnische und estnische Volksmärchen*, No. 31 (Finnish).

44. *Balkanmärchen*, No. 35 (Serbo-Croatian).

45. *Ibid.*, No. 33 (Serbo-Croatian).

46. *Ibid.*, No. 17 (Serbo-Croatian).

47. *Irische Volksmärchen*, No. 21.

48. Zaunert, *Deutsche Märchen aus dem Donaulande*, p. 315; cf. *Gabe*, p. 63.

49. *Balkanmärchen*, No. 26 (Serbo-Croatian); cf. Zaunert, *Deutsche Märchen seit Grimm*, I, 133.

50. *Lettisch-litauische Volksmärchen*, No. 26 (Latvian).

51. *Nordische Volksmärchen*, II, No. 4 (Norwegian).

52. *Irische Volksmärchen*, No. 20.

53. *Lettisch-litauische Volksmärchen*, No. 26.

54. *Ibid.*

CHAPTER FOUR

1. KHM No. 165; Sutermeister, No. 19. I have investigated the tale

from different points of view in *Gabe*, pp. 8–17.

2. *Lettisch-litauische Volksmärchen*, No. 1 (Latvian).

3. *Plattdeutsche Volksmärchen*, p. 230.

4. KHM No. 21; see Chapter 7, note 5.

5. *Balkanmärchen*, No. 23 (Serbo-Croatian). Cf. p. 31 above.

6. *Lettisch-litauische Volksmärchen*, No. 7 (Latvian).

7. *Balkanmärchen*, No. 10; cf. Cosquin, I, No. 3, where after receipt of the gift the unvarying question is asked: "*Qu'en ferai-je?*" ("What shall I do with it?").

8. *Balkanmärchen*, No. 7 (Bulgarian).

9. *Russische Volksmärchen*, No. 4.

10. *Deutsche Märchen seit Grimm*, I, 1 (see Chapter 3, note 22 above).

11. *Sagen und Märchen der Südslaven*, II, No. 131.

12. Löwis of Menar, *Die Brünhildsage in Russland* (Leipzig: Mayer & Müller, 1923), pp. 38–39 and 42.

13. Zaunert, *Deutsche Märchen seit Grimm*, II, 282.

14. For example, *Finnische und estnische Volksmärchen*, No. 15 (Finnish).

15. *Nordische Volksmärchen*, II, No. 37 (a nice example of how the "legend motifs" of the changeling and of the devil-as-bridge-builder are given a new style in the folktale).

16. Cosquin, I, No. 1.

17. *Neugriechische Märchen*, No. 1.

18. *Balkanmärchen*, No. 9 (Bulgarian).

19. A. Genzel, in his otherwise valuable unpublished thesis "Die Helfer und Schädiger des Helden im deutschen Volksmärchen," Diss. Leipzig 1922, p. 155.

20. Kurt Ranke, *Schleswig-Holsteinische Volksmärchen*, II (Kiel: Schleswig-Holsteinische Universitätsgesellschaft, 1958), 212 ff.

21. J. K. A. Musäus, *Volksmärchen der Deutschen*, ed. Moritz Müller (Leipzig: Brockhaus, 1868), II, Part 3, "Die Bücher der Chronika der drei Schwestern." [This important collection was first published in 1782–1787.]

22. According to a gracious communication by Dr. Georg Fausch, whose folktales collected in the Apulian alps are included in his 1962 Zürich dissertation "Testi dialettali e tradizioni popolari della Garfagnana" (see especially the tale "Raíno").

23. *Rätoromanische Märchen und ihre Erzähler*, No. 8, pp. 164–187; cf. Leza Uffer, *Die Märchen des Barba Plasch*, pp. 112–129. I should like to thank Professor Uffer for information that he has graciously given me; my thanks also must go to Dr. V. Novak and Dr. M. Matičetov, both from Liubljana, who were kind enough to point out to me that the Serbian folk-

tale collector Wuk Stephanowitsch Karadschitsch, whose narrative of Stoj-scha and Mladen (*Volksmärchen der Serben* [Berlin, 1854], No. 5, rpt. in *Balkanmärchen*, No. 24) served in the first edition of this book as an example of word-for-word repetition, stylized his recordings for the printed version and thus consciously created the verbatim reiteration. I have therefore dismissed the Serbian example from the present edition; it was not difficult to replace it with two other versions of the same tale type (AT 552), both trustworthy twentieth-century publications (by K. Ranke and L. Uffer).

24. *Balkanmärchen*, No. 24. That she does not recognize him directly, but by means of the scarf, is characteristic of the isolating manner of representation of the folktale. The folktale places an object between two persons that can be detached from them, most often a gift, and this object is the vehicle of their contact. An immediate recognition of the identity of the other person would give the folktale figure too much psychological roundness. When the persons depicted in the folktale separate from each other, then they "forget" each other without any need for a drink of forgetfulness, such as is found in mythical narratives: "As soon as the princesses returned home to their father, they lost all thought of him" (Cosquin, I, No. 1). It is on this account that the folktale is fond of introducing tokens of recognition that are exchanged between two persons and without whose mediation, often, no recognition would be possible (cf. pp. 17–18 above).

25. In an Italian tale referred to in Cosquin, II, p. 221.

26. *Lettisch-litauische Volksmärchen*, No. 7 (Latvian).

27. *Balkanmärchen*, No. 30 (Serbo-Croatian).

28. *Ibid.*, No. 23 (Serbo-Croatian); cf. pp. 31 and 41 above.

29. Cf. M. Lüthi, "Die Herkunft des Grimmschen Rapunzelmärchens," *Fabula*, 3 (1959), 95–118 [and see Lüthi's other studies of *Rapunzel* cited in Chapter 6, note 53].

30. Genzel (note 19 above); cf. pp. 29 and 31–32 above and *Gabe*, pp. 128–129.

31. Zaunert, *Deutsche Märchen seit Grimm*, II, 254, 277, and Bolte-Polívka, I, 472 ff.; cf. *Gabe*, pp. 19, 50–51.

32. Cf. *Gabe*, pp. 41, 103.

33. Zaunert, *Deutsche Märchen aus dem Donaulande*, pp. 269, 288.

34. For example, in *Nordische Volksmärchen*, II, No. 7 (Norwegian).

35. *Balkanmärchen*, No. 5 (Bulgarian).

36. Bolte-Polívka, II, 231.

37. Zaunert, *Deutsche Märchen seit Grimm*, II, 254.

38. See *Gabe*, pp. 32–33.

39. *Balkanmärchen*, No. 5.

40. KHM Nos. 54, 91, 111; Bolte-Polívka, I, 470, 474; II, 31; Zaunert, *Deutsche Märchen seit Grimm*, II, 58, 260; Bundi, *Märchen aus dem*

Bündnerland, pp. 115, 125; *Neugriechische Märchen,* No. 6.
    41. Bundi, p. 55.
    42. *Nordische Volksmärchen,* I, No. 4; cf. KHM No. 135.
    43. Zaunert, *Deutsche Märchen aus dem Donaulande,* p. 136.
    44. See also Antti Aarne, *Leitfaden der vergleichenden Märchen-forschung,* FFC No. 13 (Hamina, 1913), pp. 25–28.
    45. *Irische Volksmärchen,* No. 20.
    46. KHM No. 88; Bolte-Polívka, II, 232; *Plattdeutsche Volksmärchen,* p. 266; Sutermeister, No. 37; Zaunert, *Deutsche Märchen seit Grimm,* I, 113; Bundi, p. 40; Cosquin, II, No. 63; cf. *Gabe,* p. 26.
    47. Sutermeister, No. 37.
    48. *Balkanmärchen,* No. 42.
    49. *Ibid.,* No. 5.
    50. See the article *Feige* in the *Handwörterbuch des deutschen Aberglaubens,* II, 1305 ff.; cf. pp. 69–71 above.
    51. Zaunert, *Deutsche Märchen seit Grimm,* I, 5 (see Chapter 1, note 7 above).
    52. Zaunert, *Deutsche Märchen aus dem Donaulande,* pp. 57, 118.
    53. The motif of the Uriah letter gets its name from David's letter to Joab, 2 Samuel 11, 14–15. Lüthi discusses the motif in *So leben sie noch heute: Betrachtungen zum Volksmärchen* (Göttingen: Vandenhoeck and Ruprecht, 1969), pp. 71–76.—*Trans.*
    54. Rainer Maria Rilke, *Sonnets to Orpheus,* Part I, sonnet 12, trans. M. D. Herter Norton (New York: Norton, 1942), p. 39. See also Hermann Pongs' characterization of the goal of Rilke's self-realization as "total isolation and total interrelation" (*Ganz-einsam-sein und Ganz-im-Bezug-sein*) in *Das Bild in der Dichtung,* 2nd ed., II (Marburg: Elwert, 1963), 322.

CHAPTER FIVE

    1. Albert Wesselski, to whom we owe the well-coined term *Gemeinschaftsmotiv,* sees in such realistic stories (*Geschichten*) the original "primary form" (*einfache Form*) that precedes all others, whether folktale, myth, or legend; see his *Versuch einer Theorie des Märchens,* pp. 10 ff. The question of what forms preceded the folktale, however, still requires detailed and solid investigation. On this point see R. Petsch, "Die Kunstform des Märchens," *Zeitschrift für Volkskunde,* N.S. 6 (1935), 1 ff. [Wesselski's theories are the subject of a monograph by Emma Emily Kiefer, *Albert Wesselski and Recent Folktale Theories* (Bloomington: Indiana University Press, 1947).]
    2. For example, in *Balkanmärchen,* Nos. 6 and 10 (Bulgarian).

3. *Plattdeutsche Volksmärchen*, p. 127.

4. KHM No. 89; see also F. von der Leyen, *Das Märchen: Ein Versuch*, 4th ed. with the collaboration of Kurt Schier (Heidelberg: Quelle and Meyer, 1958), pp. 172–173, where the example of *Rapunzel* has to be dismissed, however, since the *Rapunzel* verses were composed by Jacob Grimm. See Chapter 4, note 29, and Chapter 6, note 53.

5. Pitrè, I, 192.

6. This vitiation of the magical element in the folktale suggests that C. W. von Sydow's term "chimera tale" or "chimerate" (*Schimäremärchen*) might be preferred to the term "magic tale" (*Zaubermärchen*) (see p. 2 above); however, von Sydow's term does not do justice to the inner necessities that govern the folktale plot.

7. See Karl Meuli, "Odyssee und Argonautika," Diss. Basel 1921, pp. 87 ff. and 104, rpt. in his *Gesammelte Schriften* (Basel: Schwabe, 1975), II, 653 ff. and 666.

8. Zaunert, *Deutsche Märchen seit Grimm*, I, 11; cf. KHM No. 97, and see p. 31 above.

9. See Ernst Howald, *Der Mythos als Dichtung* (Zürich: Max Niehans, 1937), pp. 84 ff.

10. *Neugriechische Märchen*, p. 76.

11. Hans Naumann, *Primitive Gemeinschaftskultur* (Jena: Diederichs, 1921), pp. 41–50.

12. As is clearly recognizable, for example, in Cosquin, I, No. 3.

13. Peuckert, pp. 20 ff.; cf. Cosquin, I, 40.

14. Krauss, *Sagen und Märchen der Südslaven*, II, No. 131.

15. On the erotic signification of nudity as well as of magnificent garments, see Otto Rank, *Psychoanalytische Beiträge zur Mythenforschung* (Vienna: Internationaler Psychoanalytischer Verlag, 1919), essay 10: "Die Nacktheit in Sage und Dichtung."

16. In the folktale, events that in the real world spring from impassioned experience thus become calm and collected actions that seem ornamental in their abstracting isolation and clear delineation. (The technique of stylized *pluralization*—see pp. 33–34 and 68 above—finds its counterpart in the technique of stylized *isolation*; that is, the concentration of an unmanageable number of events or persons into single, clearly visible acts or figures.)

17. *Plattdeutsche Volksmärchen*, p. 158.

18. *Nordische Volksmärchen*, I, No. 1.

19. *Balkanmärchen*, No. 5 (Bulgarian).

20. *Neugriechische Märchen*, No. 26.

21. See, for example, Merkelbach-Pinck, *Lothringer erzählen*, pp.

232-233; cf. Peuckert, p. 28, as well as p. 14 above.
  22. *Neugriechische Märchen*, No. 26.
  23. See Olrik (Chapter 2 above, note 5), and cf. pp. 53-54. [According to Olrik's "Law of the Weight of the Stern," the last item in a series of persons or things will be the one of most sympathetic interest.]
  24. On this point see Carl Gustav Jung and C. Kerényi, *Essays on a Science of Mythology*, trans. R. F. C. Hull, Bollingen Series 22 (New York: Pantheon, 1949), on the divine child archetype.
  25. Wesselski (see note 1 above) distinguishes *Gemeinschaftsmotive* ("realistic motifs"), which are recognized by both the narrator and his audience as perfectly possible in reality, from *Wahnmotive* ("supernatural motifs"), which are considered to be only half true, as well as from *Wundermotive* ("miraculous motifs" or "fabulous motifs"), which are not taken as true at all. According to whether a narrative uses exclusively "realistic motifs" or also "supernatural motifs" or "fabulous motifs," he terms it a realistic story (*Geschichte*), a legend, or a folktale. His mistake is obvious. According to this theory, one and the same narrative could be a folktale for one people, a legend for another, and even a realistic story for another (cf. Friedrich Ranke, "Märchenforschung," *DVfL*, 14 [1936], 265). Indeed, even for one and the same people a narrative could be a legend for one particular social class (or at a particular time) but a folktale for another, more enlightened class. Because many things that seem impossible to us (such as shape-changing, as of human beings into donkeys) seem quite possible to primitive peoples and to children, just as they did to medieval Europe and as they do to a large part of the Orient today, one could not speak of the narratives of these peoples, classes, or times as "folktales," but rather only as "stories" or at the most as "legends." "India, the fairy-tale land, does not know the fairy tale" (Wesselski, p. 87, quoted by Ranke, p. 264).
  Wesselski's criterion is a purely external one. He distinguishes between the genres of realistic story, legend, and folktale according to whether or not their contents command belief. Without the narrative itself being changed, it is classified into different categories according to the attitude of the narrator and the audience. A numinous motif—the value-laden term "supernatural" should be avoided—could indeed spontaneously call for a completely different construction than would suit a worldly motif. The sense of excitement that one feels in the presence of the numinous will assume a different verbal expression than a social event of less keen suspense. But then the difference will be directly evident from the form of the narrative, and the question as to the belief or disbelief of narrator and audience will not have to be posed at all. In addition, there is no need to

postulate a third category of motif, the "miraculous motif," side by side with the two categories of the numinous and the worldly (Wesselski's *Wahnmotiv* and *Gemeinschaftsmotiv*). Whether a given thing is to be termed "fantasy" or "miracle" depends on the judgment of the observer. In the folktale, we cannot distinguish between realistic motifs that command belief and miraculous motifs that do not, as Wesselski would have it. Rather, worldly relations are represented just as unrealistically as are numinous ones, because the motifs do not create the form, but the literary form shapes the motifs.

26. In his book *Grundformen volkstümlicher Erzählerkunst in den Kinder- und Hausmärchen der Brüder Grimm* (Hamburg: Gente, 1921), Walter Berendsohn unintentionally carries to a ridiculous extreme Folkers' definition of the legend as "explanatory" (J. Folkers, "Zur Stilkritik der deutschen Volkssage" [Diss. Kiel 1910]) by unhesitatingly calling any part of a folktale that is meant to explain the origin of a thing or a quality as an "origin legend" (*Ursachensage*) and as therefore not folktale-like (pp. 41–42, 45, 50–54, 57, 59, 67, etc.). He does not recognize that a motif of legendry that has been taken up and recast by the folktale thereby loses its original character and becomes an integral part of the folktale, just like any other motif. He is completely mistaken when he states that the folktale acts out of character when it offers an explanation for the hero's miraculous capabilities. On the contrary, the folktale has a strong tendency to trace such capabilities back to gifts (see pp. 56–58 and 72 above as well as *Gabe*, pp. 91 ff.), while at other times it may leave such capability or knowledge unexplained. Either way is in keeping with the character of the folktale. Indeed, part of the essence of the folktale is that it can realize either possibility. Berendsohn's work suffers from the basic error that he is trying to grasp the essence of the folktale by investigating its content. In his view, "The folktale is a love story with obstacles that finds its conclusion in the final union of the couple. . . . The essential content of the folktale lies in its otherworld motifs (*Jenseitsmotive*). . . . A narrative in which the protagonist does not penetrate into the magic-filled realm of the soul or does not receive decisive help from the otherworld is no true folktale, even if it incorporates some of the folktale's stylistic traits" (p. 35).

27. For example in Sutermeister, No. 19.

28. For example, Cosquin, I, 36, and KHM No. 65.

29. For example, *Nordische Volksmärchen*, I, No. 2 (Danish).

30. Cf. the section on "Märchen" in Jolles' *Einfache Formen*.

31. Cf. also Howald, *Der Mythos als Dichtung*, p. 106: "The first surprising fact is that of all the legends we have investigated, the further we penetrate into them, the more they point outside this world and bear every indication that once upon a time they took place in an "other" world. It

seems as though our real world were no place for these adventures, but that in former times, whoever wanted to achieve something extraordinary had to leave our world and had to search for the entrance to another one."
   32. For example, the Grimms' tale *Allerleirauh* (KHM No. 65). Cf. also pp. 32 and 74 above. By contrast, in the Grimms' version of *Little Red Riding Hood* (KHM No. 26), the act of entering into the stomach of the wolf still seems to point back to the underworld. Berendsohn's view that there is no such thing as a folktale without otherworldly motifs (see note 26 above) is questionable. Individual folktales are not tied to specific motifs. Quite naturally, though, it is a rare exception if in a given tale otherworldly motifs of some kind do not occur side by side with worldly motifs; the very term *Zaubermärchen* leads us to suspect this. Novellas often make do without otherworldly motifs (as in the stories of the princess who must solve a riddle [AT 851]). If these stories are nevertheless called folktales, then this is because we experience the overall style of a narrative, not the content of its motifs, as its distinguishing feature.
   33. In relation to these categories, see Theodor Spoerri, *Die Formwerdung des Menschen* (Berlin: Furche, 1938), pp. 222–223.

CHAPTER SIX

   1. Friedrich Panzer, "Märchen," in *Deutsche Volkskunde*, ed. John Meier (Berlin: de Gruyter, 1926), section 1; cf. section 40; the article is reprinted in *Wege der Märchenforschung*, ed. Felix Karlinger (Darmstadt: Wissenschaftliche Buchgesellschaft, 1971), pp. 84–120.
   2. Cf. Friedrich Ranke, "Sage und Märchen" (1910), rpt. in his *Volkssagenforschung: Vorträge und Aufsätze* (Breslau: Maruschke and Berendt, 1935), and in his *Kleinere Schriften*, ed. Heinz Rupp and Eduard Studer (Bern: Francke, 1971), pp. 189–203.
   3. Thus Johannes Bolte, "Name und Merkmale des Märchens" (Bolte-Polívka, IV, 36), and Richard Hünnerkopf, "Volkssage und Märchen," *Oberdeutsche Zeitschrift für Volkskunde* (1929), p. 2. Cf. also Obenauer, pp. 292 ff.
   4. See Otto, *Bäuerliche Ethik*, pp. 4–5, 9, 11, 25, and Jolles, *Einfache Formen*.
   5. See Otto, *Bäuerliche Ethik*; Otto Brinkmann, *Das Erzählen in einer Dorfgemeinschaft* (Münster: Aschendorff, 1933); and Gottfried Henssen, ed., *Volk erzählt: Münsterländische Sagen, Märchen, und Schwänke* (Münster: Aschendorff, 1935).
   6. Cf. *Lothringer erzählen*, I, 37–38; *Russische Volksmärchen*, p. vii.
   7. See *Gabe*, pp. 114–115, 142; cf. Friedrich Ranke, "Sage und Mär-

chen"; and Ranke, "Grundfragen der Volkssagenforschung," *NZfV,* 3 (1925), 20. Heinrich Burkhardt discusses the problems of the formation and the function of legends in his dissertation "Zur Psychologie der Erlebnissage," Zürich 1951. See also Chapter 7, note 32.

8. Like the legend, the saint's legend recounts a single event. Various saints' legends may form a cluster of stories devoted to the life of a single saint, but the saint's legend is not intrinsically multi-episodic, as is the folktale.

9. For Jacob Grimm, "spontaneous creation" (*Sichvonselbstmachen*) and "deliberate composition" (*Zubereitung*) are essential characteristics of folk poetry (*Naturpoesie*) and art poetry (*Kunstpoesie*), respectively; see his correspondence with Achim von Arnim in *Achim von Arnim und die ihm nahe standen,* ed. Reinhold Steig and Herman Grimm, III (Stuttgart: Cotta, 1913), p. 118. Cf. Jolles, pp. 183 ff.

10. For example, *Plattdeutsche Volksmärchen,* pp. 244–245; KHM No. 54; Bolte-Polívka, I, 474–475.

11. Werner Spanner, "Das Märchen als Gattung," Diss. Giessen, 1939, p. 32; for excerpts from the dissertation see *Wege der Märchenforschung* (note 1 above), pp. 155–176.

12. Mackensen, p. 316; Berendsohn, p. 36.

13. The term is coined by Jolles, p. 202.

14. Cf. also the appropriate remarks by Robert Petsch, *Wesen und Formen der Erzählkunst,* 2nd ed. (Halle: Niemeyer, 1942), p. 52.

15. When Petsch, *ibid.,* p. 54, states that "torn out of the context of the folktale, Little Red Riding Hood's grandmother and Snow White's evil stepmother would leave us completely indifferent," he forgets that exactly the same must be said of Snow White and Little Red Riding Hood as well.

16. It is understandable that precisely because it satisfies such high demands, a folktale can easily turn into a farcical tale (*Schwank*). See further p. 96 above.

17. Petsch, "Die Kunstform des Volksmärchens," p. 6; cf. p. 30.

18. Cf. Lessing's definition of what constitutes a work of art in piece 70 of his *Hamburgische Dramaturgie.*

19. Cf. Helmut de Boor, "Märchenforschung," *ZfdU,* 42 (1928), 561 ff., rpt. in *Wege der Märchenforschung* (note 1 above), pp. 128–154.

20. Petsch, *Wesen und Formen der Erzählkunst,* pp. 53, 47.

21. Regarding the characteristic features of the epic style, see Emil Staiger, *Grundbegriffe der Poetik,* 4th ed. (Zürich: Atlantis, 1959).

22. Cf. Hermann Pongs, "Über die Bedeutung des Symbols in der Novelle," in *Das Bild in der Dichtung,* 2nd ed., II, 286.

23. Petsch, "Die Kunstform des Volksmärchens," p. 29, defines it as "the archetype of high or 'symbolic' narrative." According to him, all the

highly developed forms of the art of narration still in some measure point back to the folktale and to its stages of development (p. 3). "As long as mankind knows and values folktales, poets and readers will again and again absorb from them a great belief in ultimate systems of order and in the general value of setting goals. Every work of high literary art that somehow operates in this belief ultimately derives its power of life and persuasion from the sacred ground that the folktale has prepared" (p. 30).

24. Cf. Jung's critique of Freud's interpretation of dream symbols, "General Aspects of Dream Psychology," in *The Collected Works of Carl G. Jung*, trans. R. F. C. Hull, Bollingen Series 20, Vol. VIII, 2nd ed. (Princeton: Princeton Univ. Press, 1969), pp. 237-280.

25. Cf. Jung in Jung and Kerényi, *Essays on a Science of Mythology*, pp. 224-225: "Because of its unconscious component the self is so far removed from the conscious mind that it can only be *partially expressed through human figures*; the other part of it has to be expressed through *objective, abstract symbols*. The human figures are father and son, mother and daughter, king and queen, god and goddess. Theriomorphic symbols are the dragon, the snake, elephant, lion, bear, and other powerful animals, or again the spider, crab, butterfly, beetle, worm, etc. Plant symbols are generally flowers (lotus and rose). These lead on to geometrical figures like the circle, the sphere, the square, the quaternity, the clock, the firmament, and so on. The indefinite extent of the unconscious component makes a comprehensive description of the human personality impossible. Accordingly, the unconscious supplements the picture with living figures ranging from the animal to the divine, as the two extremes outside man, and rounds out the animal extreme, through the addition of vegetable and inorganic abstractions, into a microcosm."

26. "The symbol anticipates a nascent state of consciousness" (Jung and Kerényi, p. 121).

27. See p. 1 above and Chapter 4, note 21. Lüthi here refers to Christoph Martin Wieland (1733-1813), who in his *Musarion* (published in 1769) retold certain Greek folktales in light, urbane verse, and to Johann Karl August Musäus (1735-1787), whose polished collection *Volksmärchen der Deutschen* (first published in 1782-1787) prepared the way for the more serious and scholarly collection of the Grimms.—*Trans.*

28. See Bühler, *Das Märchen und die Phantasie des Kindes*, pp. 10, 19-24, 71.

29. C. W. von Sydow, "Das Volksmärchen als indogermanische Tradition," German abstract in *NZfV*, 4 (1926), 207 ff. (cf. Friedrich Ranke, "Märchenforschung," *DVfL*, 14 [1936], 237 ff.); Peuckert, *Deutsches Volkstum in Märchen und Sage, Schwank und Rätsel.*

30. See, respectively, Otto Rank, *Psychoanalytische Beiträge zur*

Mythenforschung, especially essay 13, "Mythus und Märchen," and Reinhard Nolte, *Analyse der freien Märchenproduktion* (Langensalza: H. Beyer and Sons, 1931), p. 19.

31. Cf. in addition Fritz Moritz Heichelheim, *Wirtschaftsgeschichte des Altertums* (Leiden: Sijthoff, 1938), I, 46, 67.

32. Peuckert, pp. 14–15, 25; cf. Chapter 1, note 8 above.

33. Bausinger, "Lebendiges Erzählen," Diss. Tübingen, 1952, p. 105.

34. Huth, "Wesen und Herkunft des Märchens," *Universitas*, 4 (1949), 651–654, and "Märchen und Megalithreligion," *Paideuma*, 5 (1950), 12–22.

35. De Vries, *Betrachtungen zum Märchen, besonders in seinem Verhältnis zu Heldensage und Mythos*, FFC No. 150 (Helsinki, 1954), pp. 171–179. Cf. pp. 114–117 above.

36. Such as, for example, the explanation Hans Vordemfelde believes he has to give for supernatural elements having lost their force. He sees this loss as stemming from our folktales' descent into children's tales ("Die Hexe im deutschen Volksmärchen," in *Festschrift Eugen Mogk* [Halle: Niemeyer, 1924], pp. 558–574).

37. Peuckert, whose sagacious observations and conclusions are extremely instructive as to the history of culture and ideas, tends to attribute the characteristic traits of the different narrative forms somewhat too one-sidedly to different times of origin (pp. 15–18). His folkloristic methods must be supplemented by stylistic analysis.

38. As L. F. Weber, "Märchen und Schwank," Diss. Kiel 1904, pp. 64–65, and Berendsohn, *Grundformen*, p. 38, supported by certain aspects of the content of tales, would have the genre to be. For an opposing point of view see Mackensen, p. 316.

39. Only in this sense may the folktale be described as "the novel of primitive people," as Mackensen and Spanner would have it. Cf. the judgment of C. W. von Sydow: "The logical, quite deliberate structure of the folktale is not particularly primitive and reflects its culture, which is considerably higher than that of the bushmen and the Australian aborigines. But its conceptual sphere is primitive and mirrors a level of culture that is long since past" ("Das Märchen als indogermanische Tradition," p. 214). Friedrich Ranke writes of the position of the folktale narrator among the folk: "The legend is . . . the most genuinely communal product, whereas the folktale seems to separate the individual narrator much more distinctly from his audience" ("Aufgaben volkskundlicher Märchenforschung," p. 208). Cf. Merkelbach-Pinck, *Lothringer erzählen*, I, 38–39: "The folktale narrators are as well known in the village as are the singers. They are also aware of their special position. . . . The narrators specifically emphasize that they have heard their stories at an early date, in the spinning room (*Spinnstube*) or braiding room," from their grandfather, grandmother, un-

cle, or some very old man. [The *Spinnstube* was a room where "spinsters" (in the original sense) worked at spinning and held a party the rest of the evening, joined by their boyfriends. Singing and tale-telling were often featured. See the *Wörterbuch der deutschen Volkskunde,* s.v. *Spinnstube.*]

40. Cf. Friedrich Ranke, "Märchen," in *Die deutsche Volkskunde*, ed. Adolf Spamer (Leipzig: Bibliographisches Institut, 1934), p. 258. Albert Wesselski, *Versuch einer Theorie des Märchens,* pp. 35–36, takes a different point of view and criticizes Friedrich von der Leyen's dream theory (*Das Märchen,* pp. 51 ff.) with insufficient arguments and with barely understandable severity.

41. "The dream is generally not as emotion-filled as the psychological materials out of which it has evolved." Sigmund Freud, *Traumdeutung,* 5th ed. (Vienna: Deuticke, 1919), p. 317.

42. Freud mentions "the lack of fantasy in almost all dreams" (p. 93 n.).

43. Freud calls daydreams "dreams without dream distortion" (p. 365); cf. also Otto Rank, *Psychoanalytische Beiträge zur Mythenforschung,* pp. 2, 4, 13–14, and Friedrich Ranke, "Märchen," p. 249. Concerning the origin of the folktale, Ranke writes (pp. 257–258): "The once dominant idea that individual folktales came into being by themselves in unconscious natural growth and from motifs joined together spontaneously, as it were, cannot hold up in the face of the excellence and artfulness that their composition sometimes shows. At the origin of every individual tale there must stand a narrator, an 'artist' who has 'created' it as a work of artful narration. The raw materials with which such a narrator works can be of the most diverse types and origins."

44. Against the view that the folktale evolved as a wish-fulfilling fantasy of the oppressed (as *"Armeleutedichtung"*), see pp. 87 and 90–91 above and *Gabe,* pp. 142–143. Wesselski does not even want to grant the role of the folk as cultivators of folktales, but his arguments (based on his experiments with schoolchildren) are not convincing.

45. Hypotheses concerning the prototypes of the folktale may be found in Petsch, "Die Kunstform des Märchens," and in Peuckert.

46. Thus, for example, Mackensen in "Das deutsche Volksmärchen."

47. To demonstrate the different stylistic character of the folktale and the legend was the aim of my thesis on the motif of the gift in these two forms (*Gabe*). In *Proverbial Comparisons and Similes from California* (Berkeley: Univ. of California Press, 1954), Archer Taylor establishes that folk ballads, folktales, and folk riddles all have characteristic stylistic tendencies that cannot be explained by the necessities of their technique of transmission or their meter. Each genre goes its own way, even up to its smallest formulas (p. 7): " 'As white as milk,' which is . . . almost never

found in tales, is the most popular of all color similes in ballads. In riddles, 'As black as a raven' almost never occurs, and 'As black as pitch,' which Whiting found only once in more than two thousand ballads, is very popular. . . . Ballad singers and riddlers use freely 'As green as grass,' which could not be easily introduced into a tale." Concerning color words in the folktale, see pp. 27–28 above.

48. The national character of German, Russian, and French folktales has been analyzed in two special comparative studies: A. von Löwis of Menar, "Der Held im deutschen und im russischen Märchen," Diss. Jena 1912, and Elisabeth Koechlin, *Wesenszüge des deutschen und des französischen Volksmärchens: Eine vergleichende Studie zum Märchentypus von "Amor und Psyche" und vom "Tierbräutigam"* (Basel: Schwabe and Co., 1945).

49. *Lettisch-litauische Volksmärchen,* p. 215.

50. *Nordische Volksmärchen,* II, No. 24.

51. *Balkanmärchen,* Nos. 23 and 27 (cf. No. 28).

52. For example, Wilhelm Schoof, *Zur Entstehungsgeschichte der Grimmschen Märchen* (Hamburg: Hauswedel, 1959), p. 175. Concerning the Grimms' editing of their materials and documents, see also Hermann Hamann, *Die literarischen Vorlagen der Kinder- und Hausmärchen und ihre Bearbeitung durch die Brüder Grimm* (Berlin: Mayer and Müller, 1906); Ernest Tonnelat, *Les contes des frères Grimm: Étude sur la composition et le style* (Paris: Colin, 1912); Elisabeth Freitag, "Die Kinder- und Hausmärchen der Brüder Grimm im ersten Stadium ihrer stilgeschichtlichen Entwicklung," Diss. Frankfurt 1929; Karl Schulte-Kemminghausen, *Die niederdeutschen Märchen der Brüder Grimm* (Münster: Aschendorff, 1929); Kurt Schmidt, "Die Entwicklung der Grimmschen Kinder- und Hausmärchen seit der Urhandschrift," Diss. Halle 1932; Friedrich Panzer, Introduction to *Die Kinder- und Hausmärchen der Brüder Grimm: In ihrer Urgestalt herausgegeben* (Hamburg: Strom, 1948); Rolf Hagen, "Der Einfluss der Perraultschen Contes auf das volkstümliche deutsche Erzählgut und besonders auf die Kinder- und Hausmärchen der Brüder Grimm," Diss. Göttingen 1954; and Hagen, "Perraults Märchen und die Brüder Grimm," *Zeitschrift für deutsche Philologie,* 74 (1955), 392–410.

53. See also M. Lüthi, *Rapunzel* (Zürich: Schweizerischer Lehrerverein, 1958); Lüthi, "Die Herkunft des Grimmschen Rapunzelmärchens," *Fabula,* 3 (1959), 95–118; and cf. pp. 111–112 above. [Lüthi has discussed the same tale, incorporating parts of the foregoing publications, in *Volksmärchen und Volkssage,* pp. 62–96, and in *Once Upon a Time: On the Nature of Fairy Tales,* pp. 109–119.]

54. See Hesse's work cited in note 56 below.—*Trans.*

55. Thomas Mann, *Der junge Joseph* (Berlin: Fischer, 1934), pp. 314 and 316.

56. Hermann Hesse, *Das Glasperlenspiel* (Zürich: Fretz and Wasmuth, 1943), I, 55 [English trans. by Richard and Clara Winston, *Magister Ludi (The Glass Bead Game)* (New York: Holt, 1969), p. 27].

CHAPTER SEVEN

1. Melchior Sooder, *Zelleni us em Haslital* (Basel: Helbing and Lichtenhahn, 1943). See also Lutz Röhrich, "Die Märchenforschung seit dem Jahre 1945," *DJfV*, I (1955), 292.

2. P. I. Milliopoulos, "Die Bedeutung der Volksdichtung und die Art des Sammelns von Märchen," an essay written for the 1959 Congress of the International Society for Folk-Narrative Research held in Kiel and Copenhagen.

3. Cf. Jürgen Bieringer-Eyssen, "Das romantische Kunstmärchen in seinem Verhältnis zum Volksmärchen," Diss. Tübingen, 1953.

4. See Chapter 2, note 3. The folktale of *The Little Earth Cow* was printed c. 1560, Giambattista Basile's collection in 1634–36, and Charles Perrault's collection in 1696–97.

5. See Gottfried Henssen, *Überlieferung und Persönlichkeit: Die Erzählungen und Lieder des Egbert Gerrits* (Münster: Aschendorff, 1951). According to the evidence of the verses and other details, Gerrits seems to be dependent on the later editions of the Grimms' folktale anthology, as is to be expected. If one could accept this conclusion, then in another area as well the true folktale manner has prevailed against the Grimms. In the Grimms' version the stepmother casts first just one, then two bowls of lentils into the ashes prior to her departure. With Gerrits, the folktale technique of trebling appears in conjunction with a clear variation in form: the stepmother scatters peas prior to her first departure, beans prior to her second, and lentils prior to her third. Even *Achtergewicht* ("the weight of the stern") is present, as the small lentils are the most difficult to pick out of the ashes. In a rather poor Swabian version from Hungary, the corresponding feature is missing completely: see Irma Györgypál-Eckert, "Die deutsche Volkserzählung in Hajós," Diss. Berlin 1941, p. 80. In another German version from Hungary the stepmother scatters first beans, then wheat, then other cereals, and in a third version, first wheat, then beans, then hemp seeds: see Elli Zenker-Starzacher, *Eine deutsche Märchenerzählerin aus Ungarn* (Munich: Hoheneichen, 1941), pp. 50–54; I have received this work, which has now become rare, by the kindness of Dr. Karl Haiding of

Stainach, to whom I am indebted for other information and help as well. The last-mentioned variant was graciously put at my disposal in manuscript form by Dr. Zenker-Starzacher of Vienna. These three variants from Hungary do not seem to depend unequivocally on Grimm, as a visit to church has replaced the prince's ball. Still, the clear division of the narrative into three episodes in the narratives of Henssen and Zenker-Starzacher is a sign that what we have described as the true folktale style is more readily evident in genuine folk narratives than in Grimm (which all the same, in the first edition, has the sequence lentils/tares/peas).

It is noteworthy that in Györgypál-Eckert's version, Cinderella receives her beautiful shoes and red silk dress in a nutshell, while in Zenker-Starzacher she receives each of the three dresses in a box (from a bird!). Thus the folktale's tendencies toward concentrated expression, sharply defined outlines, and a geometrical mode of perception all find simultaneous expression, as does the effortless linking of disparate things: a bird bestows a box of dresses. If people often speak of the tendency of many folktale narrators to engage in affectionate and intricate "word-painting," then generally this does not at all have to do with the description of landscapes, houses, cities, and so on, but with the division of the plot into separate episodes or with the inclusion of short passages of action. This can be observed very nicely, for example, in Karl Haiding, "Burgenländische Spielformen zur Heimkehr des Helden in erbärmlichem Aufzuge," *RJfV*, 10 (1960), 51–78. On the whole question see Friedrich Ranke, "Kunstmärchen im Volksmund," *ZfV*, N.S. 8 (1938), 123–133, and Kurt Ranke, "Der Einfluss der Grimmschen Kinder- und Hausmärchen auf das volkstümliche deutsche Erzählgut," in *Papers of the International Congress of European and Western Ethnology* (Stockholm, 1956), pp. 126–133, as well as Kurt Ranke's remarks in *Fabula*, 3 (1959), 188.

6. Cf. the pertinent observations by Verena Bänninger on pp. 108–109 of her 1957 Zürich dissertation on Goethe's *Natürliche Tochter*. Bänninger identifies features of the style of Goethe's drama that are closely related to those of the folktale (abstraction, sublimation, objectification, externalization, and others) without, however, noticing this similarity. See also M. Lüthi, "Volkskunde und Literaturwissenschaft," *RJfV*, 9 (1958), 270–271 [rpt. in his *Volksmärchen und Volkssage*, 2nd ed., pp. 160–184].

7. For the communication of the version from Danzig (Zentralarchiv der deutschen Volkserzählung, Marburg, No. 130,322, I must thank Professor Gottfried Henssen and Dr. J. Schwebe, both of Marburg. The German-Hungarian variant is from Györgypál-Eckert, p. 75. Cf. pp. 103–104 above.

8. On the history of the folktale of *Rapunzel* see Lüthi's publications cited in Chapter 6, note 53.—*Trans.*

9. Walter Anderson, *Kaiser und Abt*, FFC No. 42 (Helsinki, 1923), pp. 399 ff.; *Ein volkskundliches Experiment*, FFC No. 141 (Helsinki, 1951); and *Eine neue Arbeit zur experimentellen Volkskunde*, FFC No. 168 (Helsinki, 1956). See in addition Kurt Schier, "Praktische Untersuchung zur mündlichen Wiedergabe von Volkserzählungen," Diss. Munich 1955.

10. See Erich Seemann and Walter Wiora, "Volkslied," in *Deutsche Philologie im Aufriss*, ed. Wolfgang Stammler, II (Berlin: Schmidt, 1952), 1–42, and Seemann, "Volkslied und Literaturwissenschaft," in *Actes du congrès international d'ethnologie régionale* (Arnhem, 1956), pp. 121–124. Cf. M. Lüthi, "Das Volksmärchen als Dichtung und als Aussage," *Der Deutschunterricht*, 8:6 (1956), 5–17.

11. Cf. M. Lüthi, "Zum Stil des Volksmärchens," *Neue Zürcher Zeitung*, 20 March 1960 (No. 929).

12. Von der Leyen, "Mythos und Märchen," *DVfL*, 33 (1959), 358.

13. *Das Märchen: Dichtung und Deutung*, p. 51.

14. De Vries, *Betrachtungen zum Märchen*, particularly pp. 171–179; "Les contes populaires," *Diogène*, 22 (1958), 3–20; and "Märchen, Mythos und Mythenmärchen," in *Internationaler Kongress der Volkserzählungsforscher in Kiel und Kopenhagen, 1959: Vorträge und Referate*, ed. Kurt Ranke (Berlin: de Gruyter, 1961), pp. 464–469.

15. Leo Frobenius, *Kulturgeschichte Afrikas* (Zürich: Phaidon, 1933), p. 307; Karl Meuli, "Scythia," *Hermes*, 70 (1935), 121–176. Cf. also M. Lüthi, "Volkskunde und Literaturwissenschaft" (note 6 above), pp. 266–267.

16. Eliade, "Les savants et les contes de fées," *Nouvelle Revue Française*, 4 (1956), 884–891; von der Leyen, "Mythos und Märchen"; and Resatz, "Das Märchen als Ausdruck elementarer Wirklichkeit," in *Die Freundesgabe: Jahrbuch der Gesellschaft zur Pflege des Märchengutes der europäischen Völker* (Münster, 1959), II, 35–41.

17. See Chapter 6, note 34.

18. See Richard Weiss, *Volkskunde der Schweiz: Grundriss* (Zürich: Rentsch, 1946), p. 10, for example.

19. Letter to Gustav Heckenast dated February 16, 1847, in *Adalbert Stifters Briefe*, ed. Moriz Enzinger (Innsbruck: Wagner'sche Univ.-Buchdruckerei, 1947), p. 80.

20. Von Beit, *Symbolik des Märchens: Versuch einer Deutung*, 3 vols. (Bern: Francke, 1952–1957). See further my thorough review in *Fabula*, 2 (1958), 182–189. This work, of more than 1700 pages, is based on the psychological theories of C. G. Jung, whose own discussions of the folktale "The Phenomenology of the Spirit in Fairytales" and "The Spirit Mercurius" are included in his *Collected Works*, trans. R. F. C. Hull, Vol. IX, Part 1, 2nd ed. (1968), 207–272, and Vol. XIII (1967), 191–250 (esp.

193–199), respectively. A short survey of folktale motifs from the point of view of depth psychology is offered by Gabriele Leber in *Praxis der Kinderpsychologie*, 4 (1955), 274–285.

21. Kurt Ranke, *Schleswig-Holsteinische Volksmärchen*, 3 vols. (Kiel: F. Hirt, 1955–1962). Vol. I includes AT 300–402; Vol. II, AT 403–665; Vol. III, AT 670–960. The work contains an exceptionally large number of variants of many tales, occasionally including different versions told by the same narrator.

22. Wossidlo, *Mecklenburger erzählen: Märchen, Schwänke und Schnurren*, ed. Henssen (Berlin: Akademie-Verlag, 1957).

23. *Märchen der europäischen Völker: Unveröffentlichte Quellen*, 10 vols. to date (Münster: Aschendorff, 1961–1976).

24. Liungman, *Sveriges samtliga Folksagor i Ord och Bild*, 3 vols. (Stockholm: Lindfors Bokförlag, 1949–1952). The third volume offers a scholarly commentary, indexes of variants, and a nearly comprehensive general index of recorded Swedish folktales.

25. Delarue, *Le conte populaire français: Catalogue raisonné des versions de France et des pays de langue française d'outre-mer* (Paris: Éditions Érasme, 1957). In 1964 a second volume appeared and in 1976 a third, both published by Maisonneuve et Larose and coedited by Marie-Louise Tenèze, who also has custody of Delarue's other projects.

26. Haiding, *Österreichs Märchenschatz: Ein Hausbuch für Jung und Alt* (Vienna: Pro Domo, 1953)—note that the book contains a number of dialect pieces—and Italo Calvino, *Fiabe italiane* (Turin: Einaudi, 1956) [available in English as *Italian Fables*, trans. Louis Brigante (New York: Orion Press, 1959)]. Naturally, representative editions have also appeared in other countries of Western and Eastern Europe side by side with important regional collections. As everywhere, only examples can be mentioned here. Worthy of note is G. A. Megas, *Hellenika Paramythia*, 2nd ed. (Athens: Kollarou, 1956), including modern Greek animal tales, ordinary folktales, and jocular tales; the English folklorist R. M. Dawson's collections *Modern Greek Folktales* and *More Greek Folktales* (Oxford: Clarendon, 1953 and 1955); and Gyula Ortutay, *Ungarische Volksmärchen*, 4th ed. (Budapest: Corvina, 1967), a collection of Hungarian tales in German translation [also trans. into English as *Hungarian Folk Tales* (Budapest: Corvina, 1962)].

27. *Eine sibirische Märchenerzählerin* has now been translated into English: Mark Azadovskii, *A Siberian Tale Teller*, trans. James R. Dow, Monograph Series No. 2 (Austin: Univ. of Texas Center for Intercultural Studies in Folklore and Ethnomusicology, 1974).—*Trans.*

28. See Aarne, *Verzeichnis der Märchentypen*, FFC No. 3 (Helsinki, 1910), and Aarne and Thompson, *The Types of the Folktale*, 2nd revision,

FFC No. 184 (Helsinki, 1973). Thompson also includes the categories of "formula tales" (for example, cumulative tales, rounds, and never-ending tales) and "unclassified tales." In regard to the formula tales, see the important article by Archer Taylor in Mackensen's *Handwörterbuch des deutschen Märchens*, II, 165-191.

29. Thompson, *Motif-Index of Folk-Literature: A Classification of Narrative Elements in Folktales, Ballads, Myths, Fables, Mediaeval Romances, Exempla, Fabliaux, Jest-Books, and Local Legends*, 6 vols. (Bloomington: Indiana Univ. Press, 1955-1958).

30. Peuckert's reviews are available in Will-Erich Peuckert and Otto Lauffer, *Volkskunde: Quellen und Forschungen seit 1930* (Bern: Francke, 1951), pp. 123-176, and in his important article "Märchen" in *Deutsche Philologie im Aufriss*, ed. Wolfgang Stammler, III, 2nd ed. (Berlin: Schmidt, 1957), cols. 2677-2726.

31. Röhrich, "Die Märchenforschung seit dem Jahre 1945," *DJfV*, 1 (1955), 279-296; 2 (1956), 274-319; and 3 (1957), 213-224 and 494-514; and "Neue Wege der Märchenforschung," *Der Deutschunterricht*, 8:6 (1956), 92-116.

32. Ranke, "Betrachtungen zum Wesen und zur Funktion des Märchens," *Studium Generale*, 11 (1958), 647-664. The same volume contains equally fundamental discussions of the folk legend (by Lutz Röhrich), of the saint's legend (by S. Sudhof), and of the farcical tale and joke (by Hermann Bausinger). A short research report taking as example a single folktale is presented by Bausinger, "Aschenputtel: Zum Problem der Märchensymbolik," *ZfV*, 52 (1955), 144-155. F. von der Leyen and K. Schier, *Das Märchen: Ein Versuch* (Chapter 5, note 4 above), pp. 23-26, make a similar attempt with *Sleeping Beauty* as an example. The book by J.-Ö. Swahn (see note 37 below) contains a fifty-page index of sources and literature that, while not comprehensive, is nevertheless very welcome as an extensive bibliography of essential works.

33. Mackensen's *Handwörterbuch* was abandoned after the publication of two volumes. As of 1981, three volumes of the great *Enzyklopädie* have appeared (Berlin and New York: de Gruyter, 1977-1981), including items from *A* to *Erasmus.—Trans.*

34. Röhrich, *Märchen und Wirklichkeit: Eine volkskundliche Untersuchung* (Wiesbaden: Steiner, 1956).

35. Cf. my definition of the folktale on p. 82 above, and see Chapter 6, note 47, and Chapter 5, note 32.

36. See Walter Anderson's summary of the historic-geographic ("Finnish") method in Mackensen's *Handwörterbuch des deutschen Märchens*, II, 508-522, as well as the remarks by J.-Ö. Swahn on pp. 415-418 of his study of Cupid and Psyche (next note). [The standard work on the subject

is Kaarle Krohn, *Die folkloristische Arbeitsmethode* (1926), trans. by Roger Welsch as *Folklore Methodology* (Austin: Univ. of Texas Press, 1971). See further Stith Thompson, *The Folktale* (notes 38 and 39 below), pp. 428–448.]
    37. Rooth, *The Cinderella Cycle* (Lund: Gleerup, 1951); Swahn, *The Tale of Cupid and Psyche* (Lund: Gleerup, 1955), reviewed by W. Anderson in *Hessische Blätter für Volkskunde*, 46 (1955), 118–130 (with reply and rejoinder in vol. 47 [1956], 111–118) and by Kurt Ranke in *Arv*, 12 (1956), 158–167; Roberts, *The Tale of the Kind and the Unkind Girls* (Berlin: de Gruyter, 1958).
    38. Ranke, *Die zwei Brüder: Eine Studie zur vergleichenden Märchenforschung*, FFC No. 114 (Helsinki, 1934), extensively reviewed by Stith Thompson, *The Folktale*, 2nd ed. (New York: Holt, 1951), pp. 24–32.
    39. Thompson's study is now readily available in a paperback reprint published in 1977 by the Univ. of California Press.—*Trans.*

SUPPLEMENT

    1. Vladimir Jakovlevič Propp, *Morfológija skázki* (Leningrad, 1928; 2nd ed. Moscow, 1969, with an essay by E. M. Meletinskij).—*Morphology of the Folktale* (Bloomington, 1958; 2nd ed. Austin: Univ. of Texas Press, 1968).—*Morfologia della fabia* (Turin: Einaudi, 1966), with an essay by Claude Lévi-Strauss, "La struttura e la forma," and a reply by Propp, "Struttura e storia nello studio della favola."—*Morphologie du conte* (Paris, 1970), in two different translations, the edition by Gallimard from the first Russian edition, the edition by du Seuil from the second.—*Morfología del cuento* (Madrid: Editorial fundamentos, 1971).—*Morphologie des Märchens* (Munich: Hanser, 1972), after the second Russian edition. This includes the essay by Meletinskij, "Zur strukturell-typologischen Erforschung des Volksmärchens" (translated also in the Spanish edition and in the French edition by du Seuil), as well as an essay by Propp already published in 1928, "Transformationen von Zaubermärchen." For the German edition see my reviews in *ZfV*, 69 (1973), 291–293, and in *Neue Zürcher Zeitung*, October 21, 1973 (No. 488), p. 50. The title that Propp originally considered using, *Morphology of the Russian Folktale*, had already been generalized to its present form in the first Russian edition. [Unless otherwise indicated, page references to Propp's *Morphology* will be to the 1968 English translation.]
    2. J. L. Fischer in *Current Anthropology*, 4 (1963), 289; cf. B. N. Colby, *ibid.*, p. 275, and Claude Bremond, "Le Message narratif," *Communications*, 4 (1964), 15.

3. *Morfologia della fiaba*, p. 219.

4. "Transformationen von Zaubermärchen," in *Morphologie des Märchens*, p. 167.

5. *Ibid.*, p. 163.

6. V. J. Propp, *Istoricheskie korni volshebnoi skázki* (Leningrad, 1946), translated into Italian as *Le radici storiche dei racconti di fate* (Turin: Boringhieri, 1972).

7. "Transformationen," in *Morphologie des Märchens*, p. 166.

8. *Ibid.*, p. 170.

9. Propp (Eng. trans.), pp. 22–23, 89, 106, and 114; "Transformationen," p. 163; and cf. Meletinskij, p. 193.

10. "Transformationen," p. 170 (cf. p. 192 of the du Seuil French translation).

11. "[By] function is understood . . . an act of a character, defined from the point of view of its significance for the course of the action" (p. 21).

12. Dundes, "From Etic to Emic Units in the Structural Study of Folktales," *JAF*, 75 (1962), 101.

13. E.g. Heda Jason, "The Narrative Structure of Swindler Tales," *Arv*, 27 (1971), 143: "The following terms are proposed: *function-slot* for Propp's concept of 'function' (Dundes' 'motifeme'); *function-filler* for the concrete action in a specific text (Dundes' 'allomotif')."

14. See Meletinskij in *Morphologie des Märchens*, p. 181.

15. See *Goethes morphologische Schriften*, ed. Wilhelm Troll (Jena: Diederichs, 1932). A translation of Goethe's 1790 essay "Versuch die Metamorphose der Pflanzen zu erklären" is included in his *Botanical Writings*, trans. Bertha Mueller (Honolulu: Univ. of Hawaii Press, 1952). Propp uses quotations from Goethe as epigraphs five times (on pp. 9, 11, 25, 87, and 91 of the German translation). These are omitted in the English translation.—*Trans.*

16. "Leggi formali . . . cosi ferree" (*Morfologia della fabia*, p. 222).

17. *Morfologia della fabia*, p. 206.

18. See Meletinskij on A. J. Greimas' *Sémantique structurale* (Paris, 1966), in *Morphologie des Märchens*, p. 195.

19. Here the translation is based on Lüthi's paraphrase of the German text, *Morphologie des Märchens* (p. 91), rather than duplicating the wording of the 1968 English edition (p. 92).—*Trans.*

20. See Marie-Louise Tenèze, "Du conte merveilleux comme genre," in *Approches de nos traditions orales* (Paris: Maisonneuve et Larose, 1970), pp. 16, 22; and Dundes, p. 103.

21. Goethe, *Wilhelm Meisters Lehrjahre*, the next-to-last sentence (cf. Petsch, *Wesen und Formen der Erzählkunst*, p. 67).

22. Helwig, *Dramaturgie des menschlichen Lebens* (Stuttgart: Klett, 1958), p. 52.

23. Propp, p. 100 (cf. p. 90: "The fairy tale in its morphological bases represents a *myth*," and p. 99: "Quite a large number of legends, individual tales about animals, and isolated novellas display the same structure").

24. *Morphologie des Märchens*, pp. 201, 206.

25. *Ibid.*, p. 206; cf. Meletinskij, "The Structural-Typological Study of Folklore," *Social Sciences* [Moscow], 3 (1971), 76–77, and "Problème de la morphologie historique du conte populaire,' *Semiotica*, 2 (1970), 131–132.

26. Meletinskij, "The Structural-Typological Study of Folklore," p. 77.

27. See *Gabe*, pp. 112–113.

28. See Bremond (note 2 above), pp. 11–19.

29. Propp, pp. 13–14; cf. Meletinskij in *Morphologie des Märchens*, p. 181 (where the word *folgen* "follow" should be replaced by *vorausgehen* "precede") and p. 186: "According to Propp's belief, synchronic studies should precede diachronic."

30. See Walter Anderson, "Geographisch-historische Methode," in Mackensen's *Handwörterbuch des deutschen Märchens*, II, 509.

31. See Dundes' introduction to the second edition of *Morphology of the Folktale* (pp. xi–xvii) and Breymayer's essay "Vladimir Jakovlevič Propp (1895–1970): Leben, Wirken und Bedeutsamkeit," *Linguistica Biblica*, 15/16 (1972), 36–77.

32. See the bibliographies in Lüthi, *Märchen*, 7th ed. (Stuttgart: Metzler, 1979), pp. 129–133, and in Breymayer, pp. 72–77. Also consulted should be Archer Taylor, "The Biographical Pattern in Traditional Narrative," *Journal of the Folklore Institute*, 1 (1964), 114–129; Vilmus Voigt, "Some Problems of Narrative Structure Universals in Folklore," *Linguistica Biblica*, 15/16 (1972), 78–90; Isidor Levin, "Vladimir Propp: An Evaluation on his Seventieth Birthday," *Journal of the Folklore Institute*, 4 (1967), 32–49 (with a remark on the "ubiquity of similar scientific ideas under diverse social and political conditions": "Propp's train of thought here sounds like a Marxist version of Helmut de Boor's hypotheses" [p. 44]; see De Boor's essay "Märchenforschung," *Zeitschrift für Deutschkunde*, 42 [1928], 561–581, rpt. in *Wege der Märchenforschung* [Chapter 6, note 1 above], pp. 129–154); and Heda Jason, "Übersetzung und Kommentierung von A. I. Nikiforovs 1927 russisch erschienenem Aufsatz 'On the Morphological Study of Folklore,' " *Linguistica Biblica*, 27/28 (1973), 25–35. Jason considers the concepts of Nikiforov to be not only prior to those of Propp, but superior to them, for she views Propp's model as merely taxonomic, whereas Nikiforov offers a generative model and moreover distinguishes

between different kinds of "functions" and roles instead of reducing all "functions" to the same narrative line. See also Jason, "A Model for Narrative Structure," in *Patterns in Oral Literature*, ed. Jason and Dmitri Segal (The Hague: Mouton, 1977), pp. 99–137, as well as five essays by Alan Dundes: "The Binary Structure of 'Unsuccessful Repetition' in Lithuanian Folk Tales," *Western Folklore*, 21 (1962), 165–174; "Structural Typology in North American Indian Folktales," *Southwestern Journal of Anthropology*, 19 (1963), 121–130; "Toward a Structural Definition of the Riddle," *JAF*, 76 (1963), 111–118 (with Robert A. Georges); "On Game Morphology: A Study of the Structure of Non-Verbal Folklore," *New York Folklore Quarterly*, 20 (1964), 276–288; and "From Emic to Etic Units in the Structural Study of Folktales" (note 12 above).

Index of Tale Types

I. International tale types (from Antti Aarne and Stith Thompson, *The Types of the Folktale*, 2nd revision, FFC No. 184 [Helsinki: Suomalainen Tiedeakatemia, 1973]). The following list is by no means exhaustive of all the tales mentioned in the text, most of which are not identified by type number. The Aarne-Thompson number is given unless the Grimm version seems to be uppermost in the author's mind. — *Trans.*

General Index

Twentieth-century authors are cited if they are discussed in the main body of Lüthi's text or are featured (not merely mentioned) in the notes.